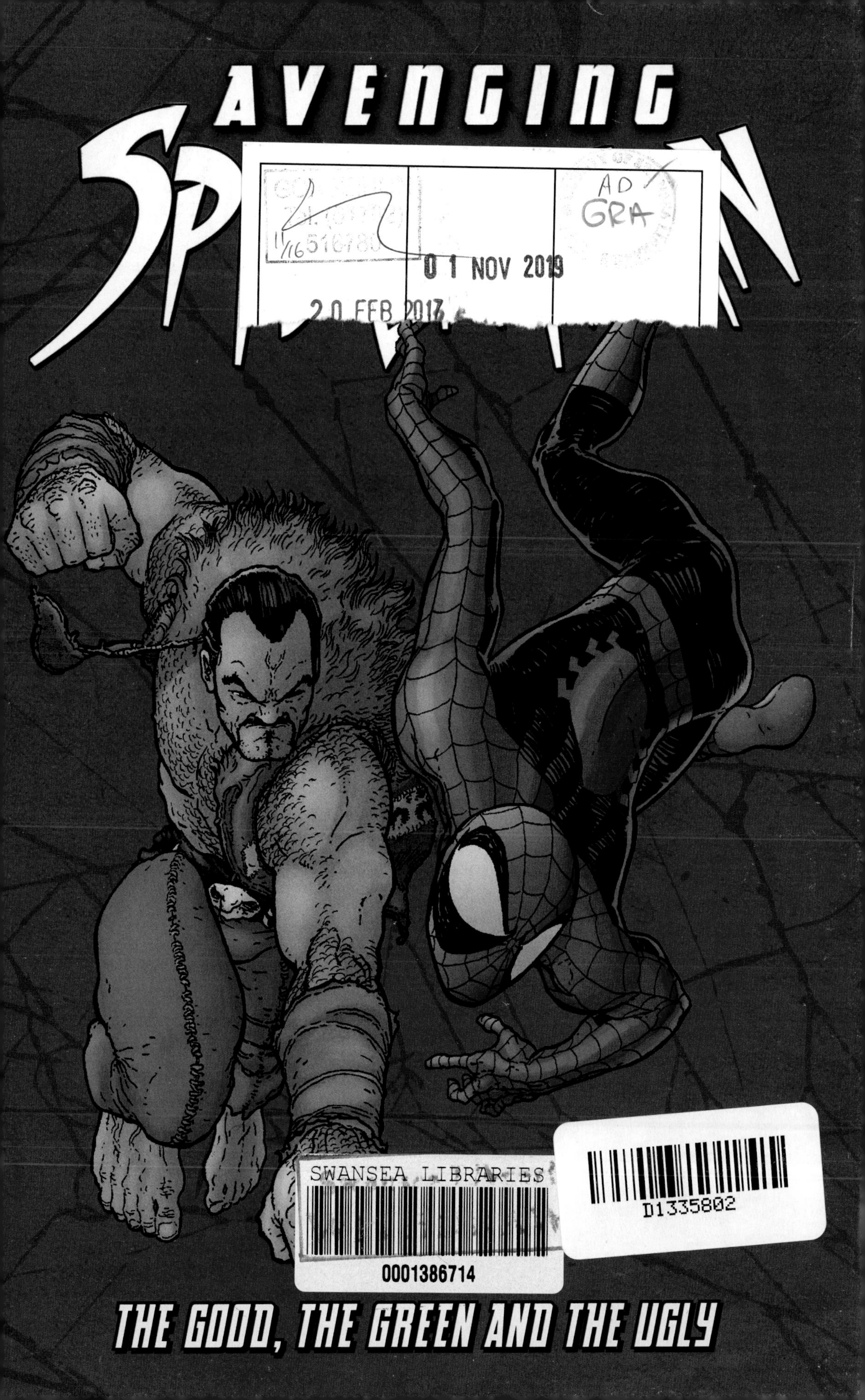
AVENGING
SP
THE GOOD, THE GREEN AND THE UGLY

AVENGING SPIDER-MAN

THE GOOD, THE GREEN AND THE UGLY

#7

WRITER
KATHRYN IMMONEN

PENCILER
STUART IMMONEN

INKER
WADE VON GRAWBADGER

COLORIST
MATT HOLLINGSWORTH

COVER ART
STUART IMMONEN, WADE VON GRAWBADGER & MATT HOLLINGSWORTH

#9-10

WRITER
KELLY SUE DeCONNICK

PENCILER
TERRY DODSON

INKER
RACHEL DODSON

COLORIST
EDGAR DELGADO

COVER ART
TERRY DODSON & RACHEL DODSON

#12-13

WRITER
KEVIN SHINICK

PENCILER
AARON KUDER

COLOR ARTIST
MATT HOLLINGSWORTH

COVER ART
SHANE DAVIS, MARK MORALES & MATT HOLLINGSWORTH

LETTERER: VC'S JOE CARAMAGNA ASSISTANT EDITOR: ELLIE PYLE

ASSOCIATE EDITOR: SANA AMANAT EDITOR: STEPHEN WACKER WITH ELLIE PYLE (ISSUE #10)

EXECUTIVE EDITOR: TOM BREVOORT

Collection Editor: Cory Levine • Assistant Editors: Alex Starbuck & Nelson Ribeiro • Editors, Special Projects: Jennifer Grünwald & Mark D. Beazley
Senior Editor, Special Projects: Jeff Youngquist • SVP of Digital & Print Publishing: David Gabriel • Book Design: Jeff Powell
Editor in Chief: Axel Alonso • Chief Creative Officer: Joe Quesada • Publisher: Dan Buckley • Executive Producer: Alan Fine

AVENGING SPIDER-MAN: THE GOOD, THE GREEN AND THE UGLY. Contains material originally published in magazine form as AVENGING SPIDER-MAN #7, #9-10 and #12-13. First printing 2013. ISBN# 978-0-7851-5780-9. Published by MARVEL WORLDWIDE, INC., a subsidiary of MARVEL ENTERTAINMENT, LLC. OFFICE OF PUBLICATION: 135 West 50th Street, New York, NY 10020. **Printed in the U.S.A.** ALAN FINE, EVP - Office of the President, Marvel Worldwide, Inc. and EVP & CMO Marvel Characters B.V.; DAN BUCKLEY, Publisher & President - Print, Animation & Digital Divisions; JOE QUESADA, Chief Creative Officer; TOM BREVOORT, SVP of Publishing; DAVID BOGART, SVP of Operations & Procurement, Publishing; RUWAN JAYATILLEKE, SVP & Associate Publisher, Publishing; C.B. CEBULSKI, SVP of Creator & Content Development; DAVID GABRIEL, SVP of Print & Digital Publishing Sales; JIM O'KEEFE, VP of Operations & Logistics; DAN CARR, Executive Director of Publishing Technology; SUSAN CRESPI, Editorial Operations Manager; ALEX MORALES, Publishing Operations Manager; STAN LEE, Chairman Emeritus. For information regarding advertising in Marvel Comics or on Marvel.com, please contact Niza Disla, Director of Marvel Partnerships, at ndisla@marvel.com. For Marvel subscription inquiries, please call 800-217-9158. **Manufactured between 1/3/2013 and 2/5/2013 by QUAD/GRAPHICS, DUBUQUE, IA, USA.**

10 9 8 7 6 5 4 3 2 1

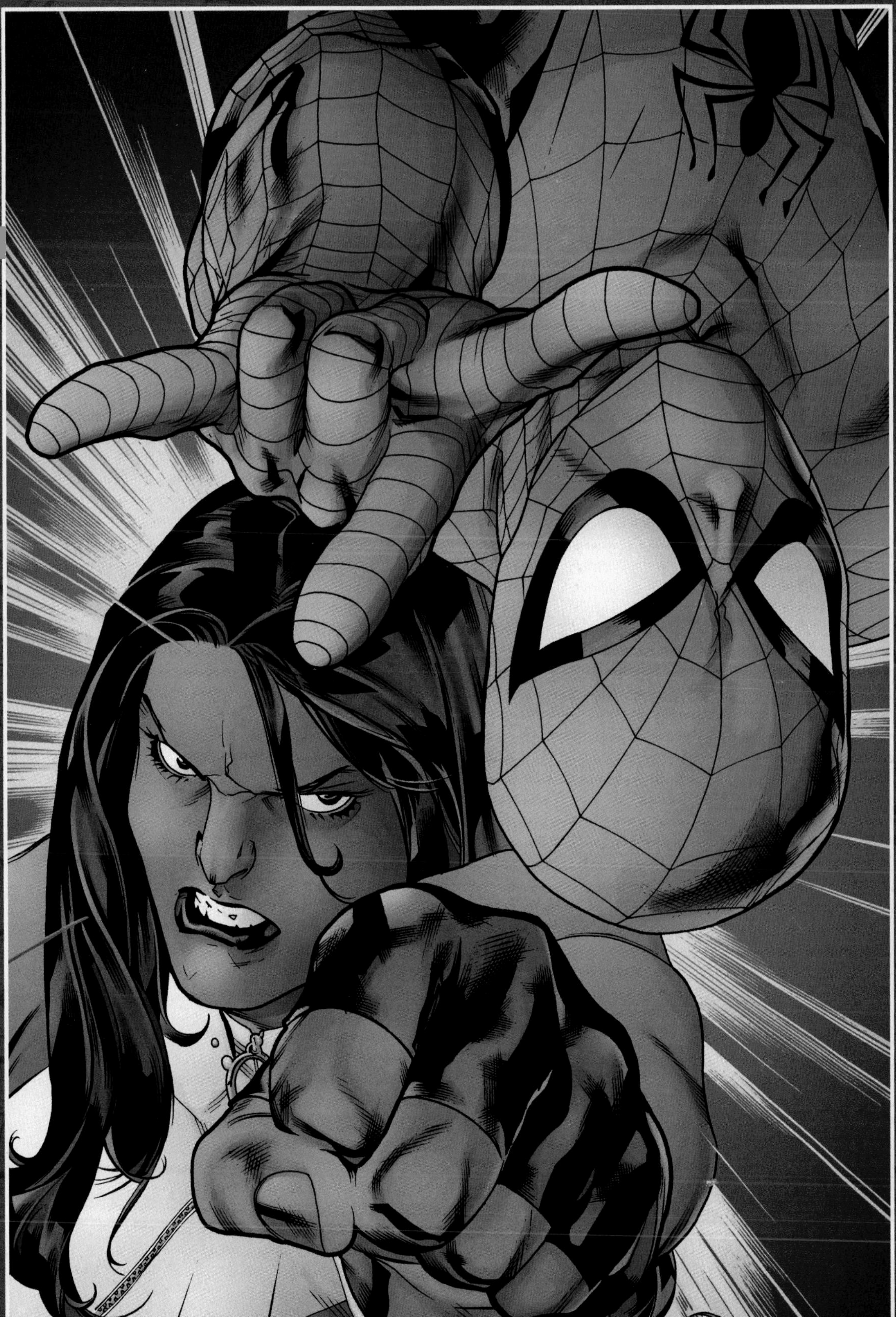

7

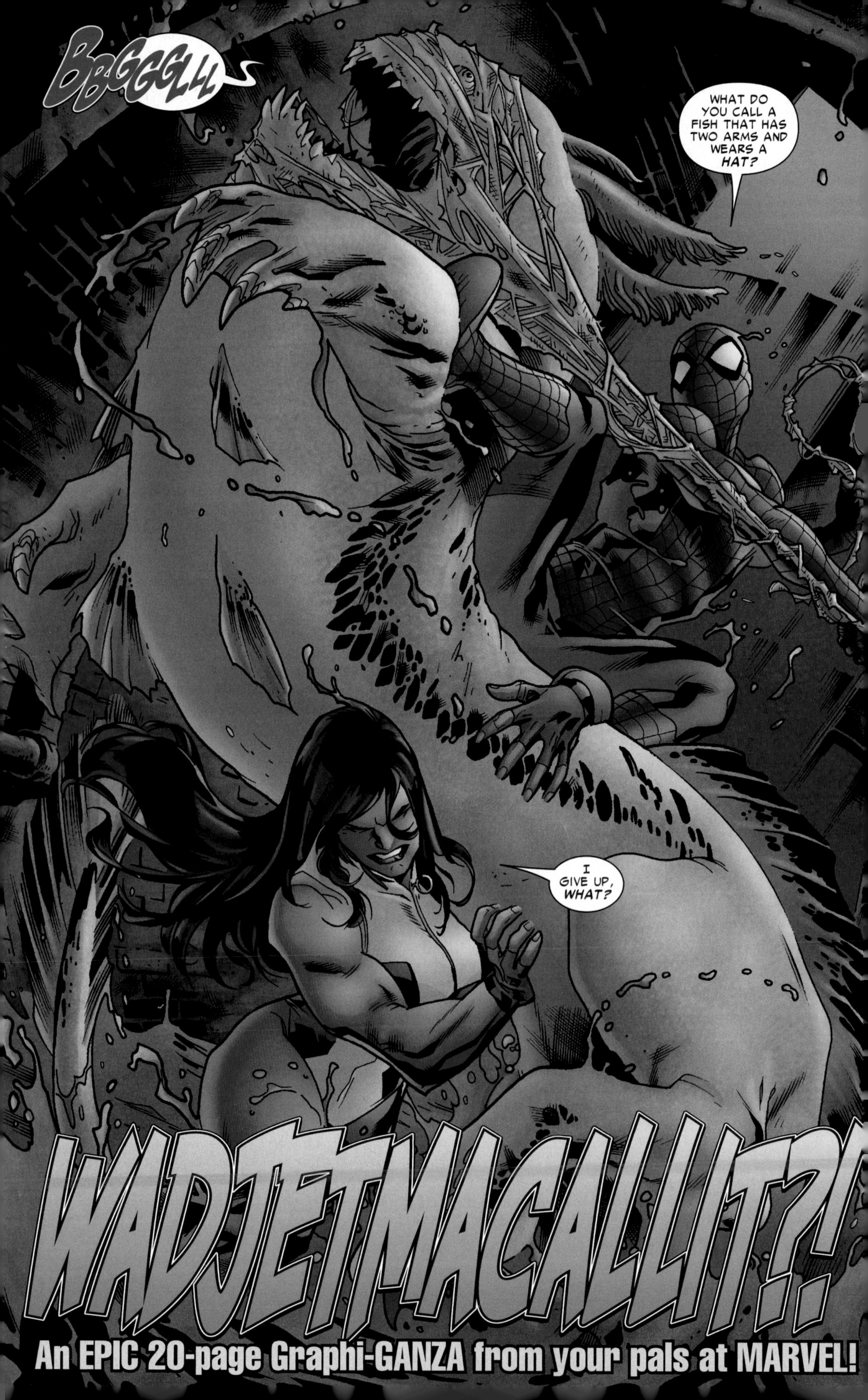
BBGGGLLL
WHAT DO YOU CALL A FISH THAT HAS TWO ARMS AND WEARS A HAT?
I GIVE UP, WHAT?
WADJETMACALLIT?!
An EPIC 20-page Graphi-GANZA from your pals at MARVEL!

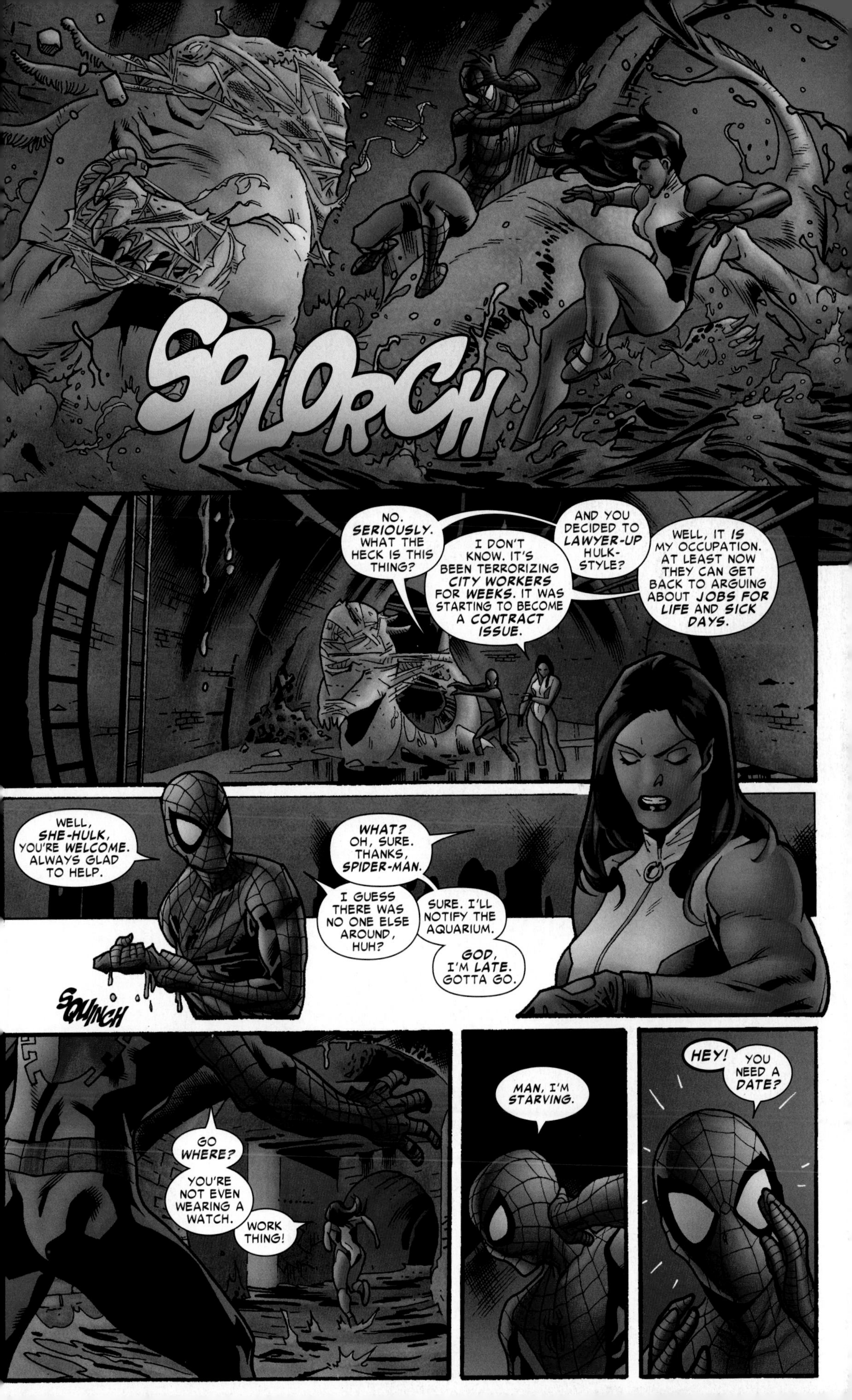
SPLORCH
NO. SERIOUSLY. WHAT THE HECK IS THIS THING?
I DON'T KNOW. IT'S BEEN TERRORIZING CITY WORKERS FOR WEEKS. IT WAS STARTING TO BECOME A CONTRACT ISSUE.
AND YOU DECIDED TO LAWYER-UP HULK-STYLE?
WELL, IT IS MY OCCUPATION. AT LEAST NOW THEY CAN GET BACK TO ARGUING ABOUT JOBS FOR LIFE AND SICK DAYS.
WELL, SHE-HULK, YOU'RE WELCOME. ALWAYS GLAD TO HELP.
WHAT? OH, SURE. THANKS, SPIDER-MAN.
I GUESS THERE WAS NO ONE ELSE AROUND, HUH?
SURE. I'LL NOTIFY THE AQUARIUM.
GOD, I'M LATE. GOTTA GO.
SQUINCH
GO WHERE?
YOU'RE NOT EVEN WEARING A WATCH.
WORK THING!
MAN, I'M STARVING.
HEY!
YOU NEED A DATE?

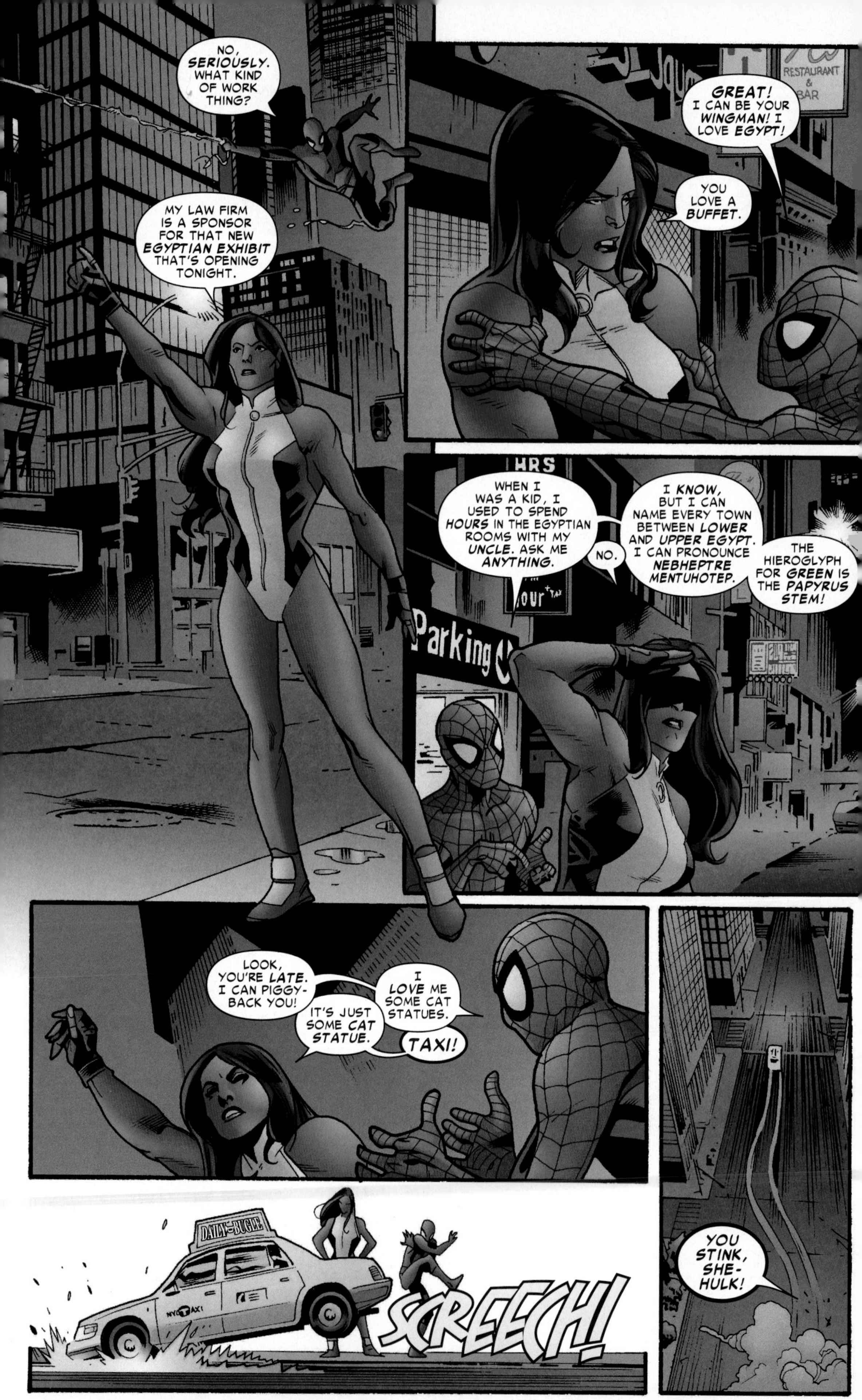
NO, SERIOUSLY. WHAT KIND OF WORK THING?
MY LAW FIRM IS A SPONSOR FOR THAT NEW EGYPTIAN EXHIBIT THAT'S OPENING TONIGHT.
GREAT! I CAN BE YOUR WINGMAN! I LOVE EGYPT!
YOU LOVE A BUFFET.
WHEN I WAS A KID, I USED TO SPEND HOURS IN THE EGYPTIAN ROOMS WITH MY UNCLE. ASK ME ANYTHING.
NO.
I KNOW, BUT I CAN NAME EVERY TOWN BETWEEN LOWER AND UPPER EGYPT. I CAN PRONOUNCE NEBHEPTRE MENTUHOTEP.
THE HIEROGLYPH FOR GREEN IS THE PAPYRUS STEM!
LOOK, YOU'RE LATE. I CAN PIGGY-BACK YOU!
IT'S JUST SOME CAT STATUE.
I LOVE ME SOME CAT STATUES.
TAXI!
SCREECH!
YOU STINK, SHE-HULK!

While attending a demonstration in radiology, high school student Peter Parker was bitten by a spider which had accidentally been exposed to radioactive rays. Through a miracle of science, Peter soon found that he had gained the spider's powers…and had, in effect, become a human spider! Later he joined the Avengers (who have a movie out now). And now he is the...

AVENGING SPIDER-MAN

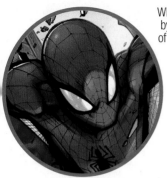

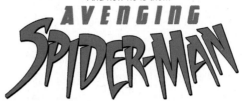

Jennifer Walters was the small, shy daughter of a Los Angeles County Sheriff until the day she was shot by one of her father's enemies. She received a blood transfusion from her cousin, Bruce Banner (aka: the Hulk) and the combination of his radioactive blood and her rage transformed her into a villain-smashing jade giantess! From that day forward to today, she fights for justice as a lawyer and as...

THE SENSATIONAL SHE-HULK

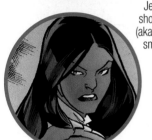

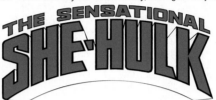

Little is known about the history of cats other than that they were first domesticated in Ancient Egypt and might have prevented the Bubonic Plague if Medieval European cultures hadn't killed so many of them for being in league with the devil. They achieved great theatrical success in the 1980s that inexplicably continued until the year 2000. But their greatest achievement came when they were the first to master all the star-making potential of "new media" and now they rule the internet as…

KITTY CATS

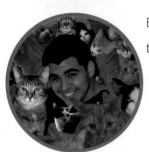

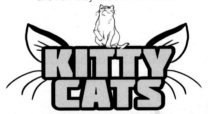

PREVIOUSLY...

hings completely unrelated to this issue occurred in Avenging Spider-Man 6, Punisher 10 and Daredevil 11. But they were incredibly awesome and beautifully drawn things that it would really be a shame if you missed out on. So while you're still here, in the store (where no doubt you had to read this recap page immediately for the vital information it contains), you should see if they still have copies. Which they won't. Because it was awesome and you missed it. NEVER LET THAT HAPPEN AGAIN!

WRITER: KATHRYN IMMONEN PENCILS: STUART IMMONEN

INKER: WADE VON GRAWBADGER (NO RELATION) COLORS: MATT HOLLINGSWORTH

LETTERER: VC's JOE CARAMAGNA COVER: IMMONEN, VON GRAWBADGER, HOLLINGSWORTH

PRODUCTION: MANNY MEDEROS ASSISTANT EDITOR: ELLIE PYLE DOG LOVER: STEPHEN WACKER

EXECUTIVE EDITOR: TOM BREVOORT EDITOR IN CHIEF: AXEL ALONSO

CHIEF CREATIVE OFFICER: JOE QUESADA PUBLISHER: DAN BUCKLEY EXECUTIVE PRODUCER: ALAN FINE

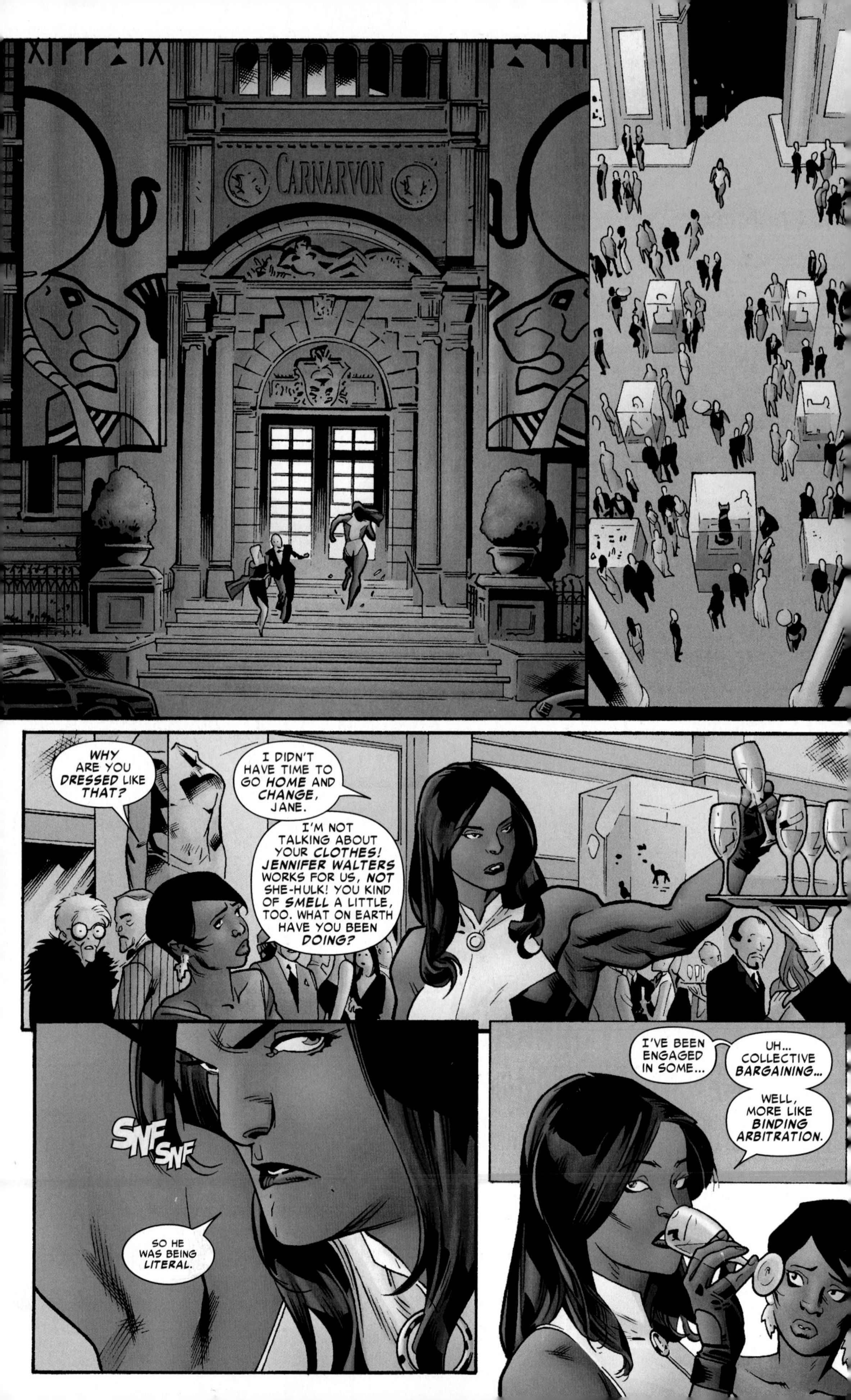
CARNARVON
WHY ARE YOU DRESSED LIKE THAT?
I DIDN'T HAVE TIME TO GO HOME AND CHANGE, JANE.
I'M NOT TALKING ABOUT YOUR CLOTHES! JENNIFER WALTERS WORKS FOR US, NOT SHE-HULK! YOU KIND OF SMELL A LITTLE, TOO. WHAT ON EARTH HAVE YOU BEEN DOING?
SNF SNF
SO HE WAS BEING LITERAL.
I'VE BEEN ENGAGED IN SOME...
UH... COLLECTIVE BARGAINING...
WELL, MORE LIKE BINDING ARBITRATION.

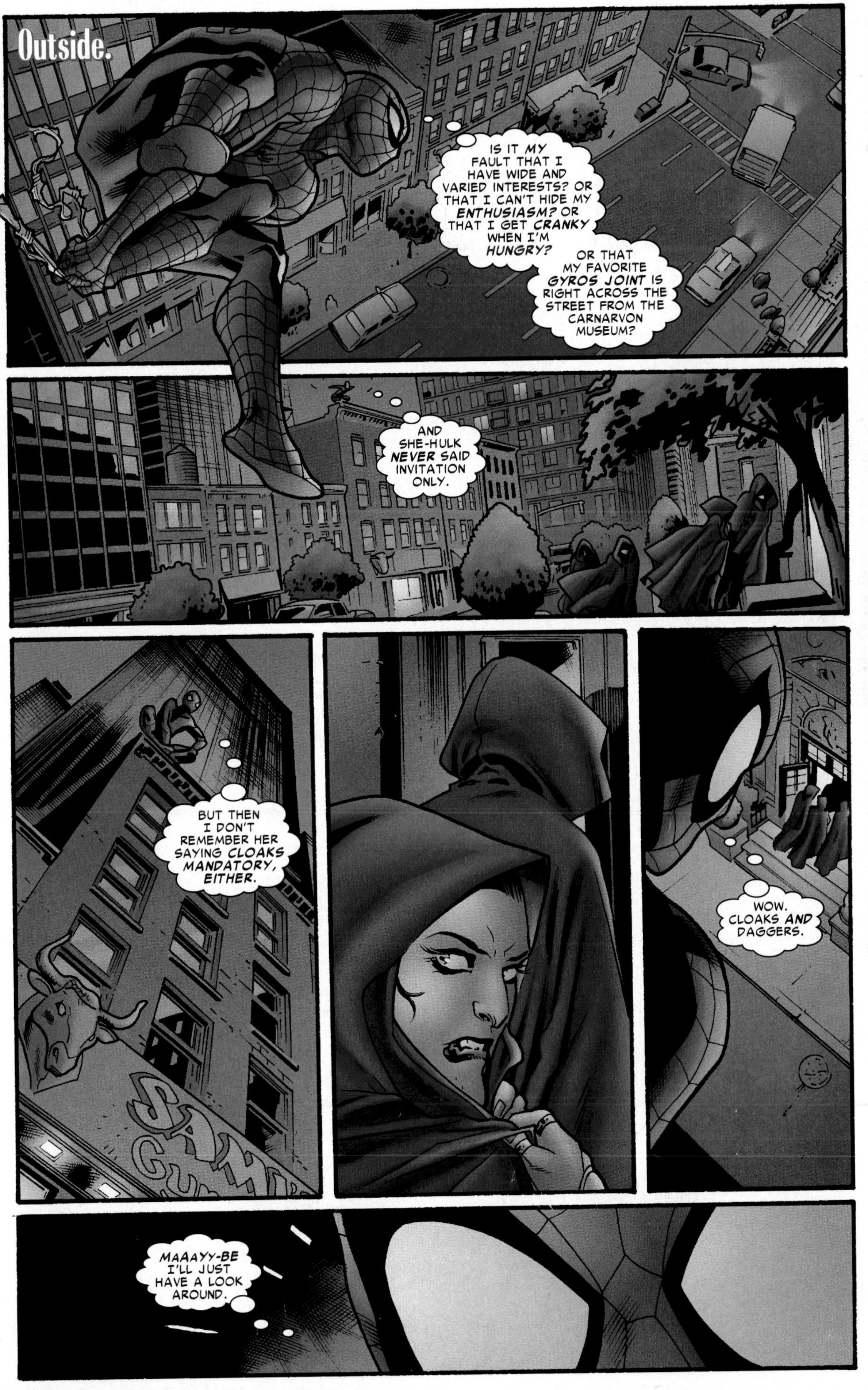
Outside.
IS IT MY FAULT THAT I HAVE WIDE AND VARIED INTERESTS? OR THAT I CAN'T HIDE MY ENTHUSIASM? OR THAT I GET CRANKY WHEN I'M HUNGRY?
OR THAT MY FAVORITE GYROS JOINT IS RIGHT ACROSS THE STREET FROM THE CARNARVON MUSEUM?
AND SHE-HULK NEVER SAID INVITATION ONLY.
BUT THEN I DON'T REMEMBER HER SAYING CLOAKS MANDATORY, EITHER.
WOW. CLOAKS AND DAGGERS.
MAAAYY-BE I'LL JUST HAVE A LOOK AROUND.

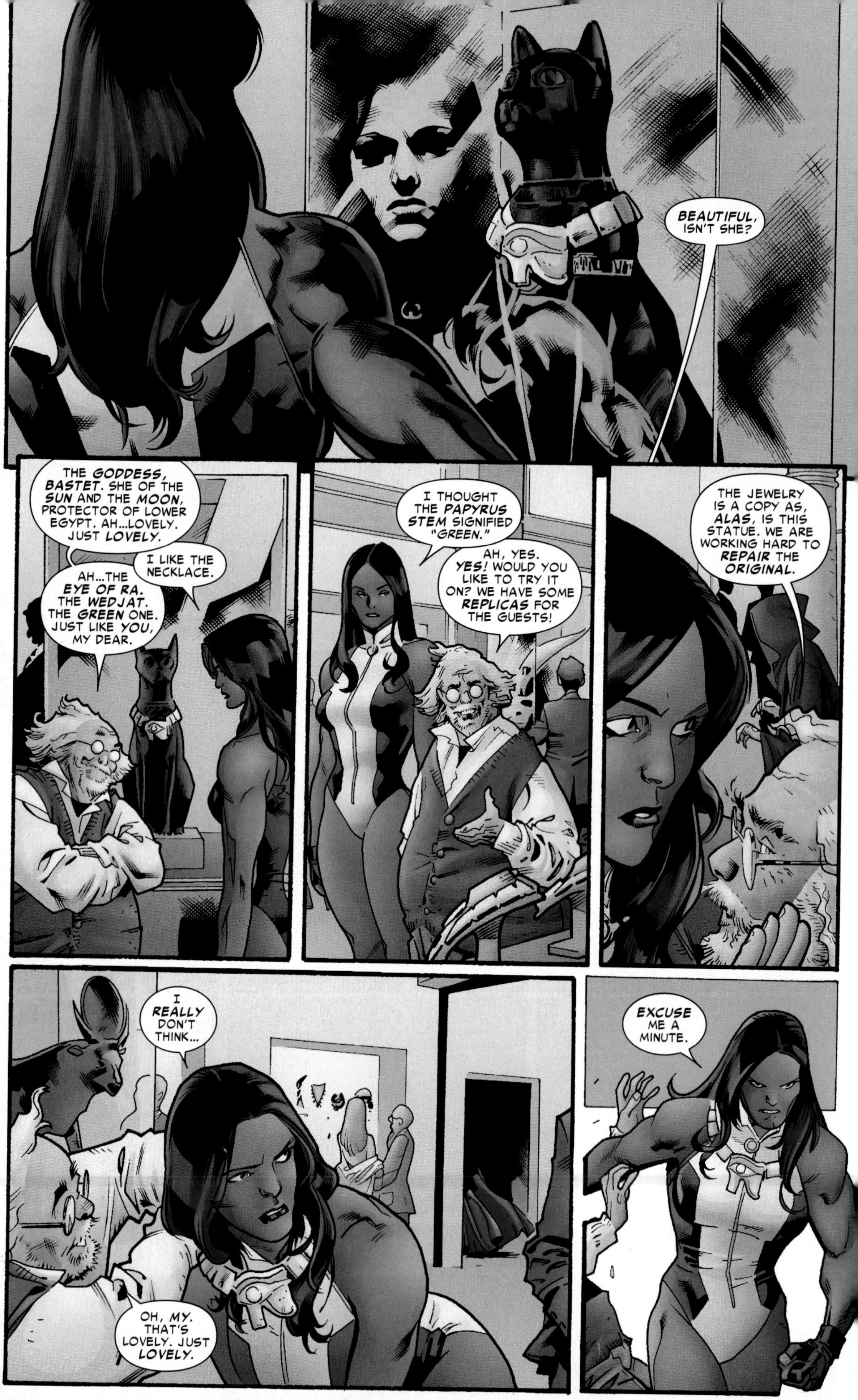
BEAUTIFUL, ISN'T SHE?
THE GODDESS, BASTET. SHE OF THE SUN AND THE MOON, PROTECTOR OF LOWER EGYPT. AH...LOVELY. JUST LOVELY.
I LIKE THE NECKLACE.
AH...THE EYE OF RA. THE WEDJAT. THE GREEN ONE. JUST LIKE YOU, MY DEAR.
I THOUGHT THE PAPYRUS STEM SIGNIFIED "GREEN."
AH, YES. YES! WOULD YOU LIKE TO TRY IT ON? WE HAVE SOME REPLICAS FOR THE GUESTS!
THE JEWELRY IS A COPY AS, ALAS, IS THIS STATUE. WE ARE WORKING HARD TO REPAIR THE ORIGINAL.
I REALLY DON'T THINK...
OH, MY. THAT'S LOVELY. JUST LOVELY.
EXCUSE ME A MINUTE.

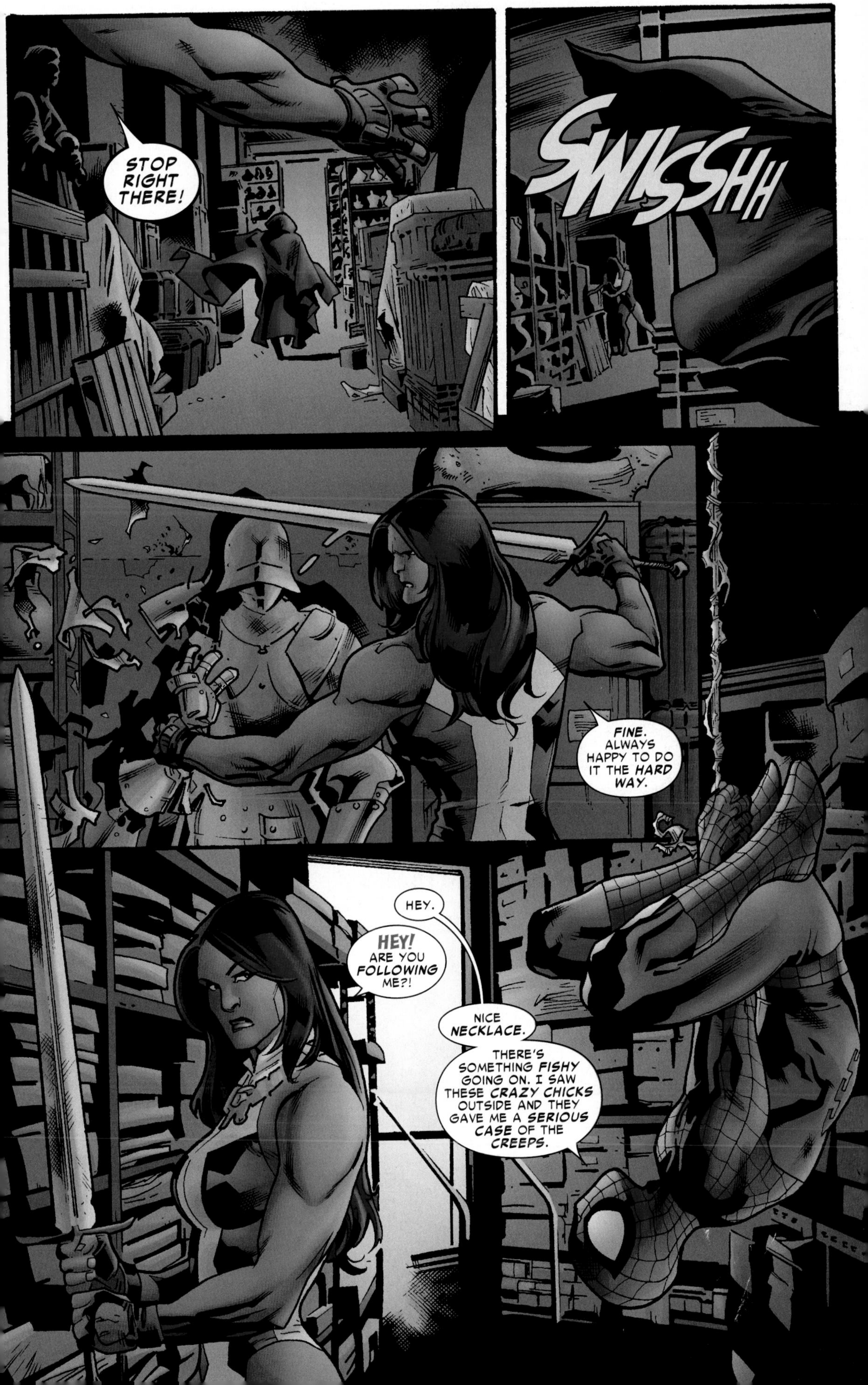

STOP RIGHT THERE!
SWISSHH
FINE. ALWAYS HAPPY TO DO IT THE HARD WAY.
HEY.
HEY! ARE YOU FOLLOWING ME?!
NICE NECKLACE.
THERE'S SOMETHING FISHY GOING ON. I SAW THESE CRAZY CHICKS OUTSIDE AND THEY GAVE ME A SERIOUS CASE OF THE CREEPS.

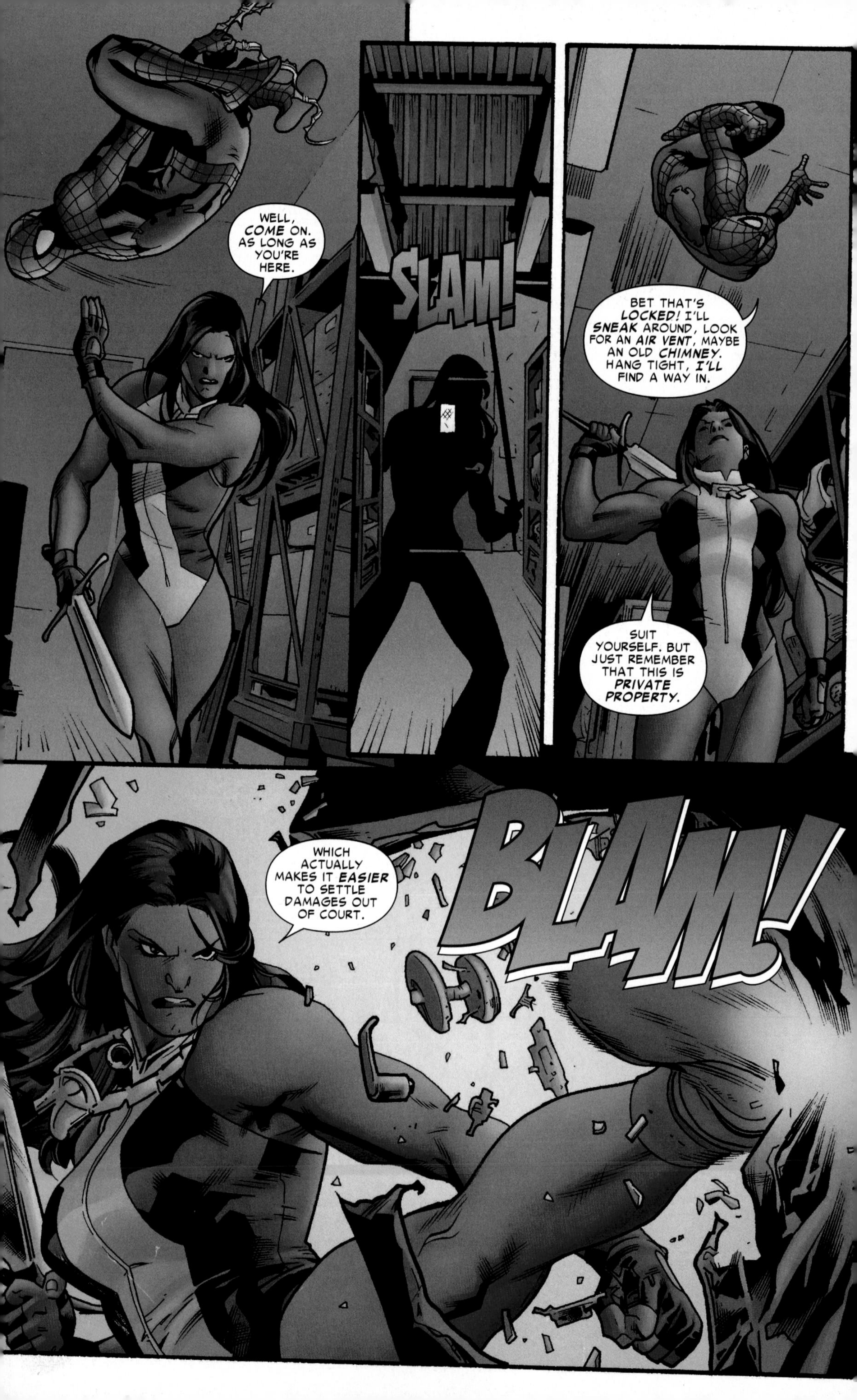

WELL, COME ON. AS LONG AS YOU'RE HERE.
SLAM!
BET THAT'S LOCKED! I'LL SNEAK AROUND, LOOK FOR AN AIR VENT, MAYBE AN OLD CHIMNEY. HANG TIGHT, I'LL FIND A WAY IN.
SUIT YOURSELF. BUT JUST REMEMBER THAT THIS IS PRIVATE PROPERTY.
WHICH ACTUALLY MAKES IT EASIER TO SETTLE DAMAGES OUT OF COURT.
BLAM!

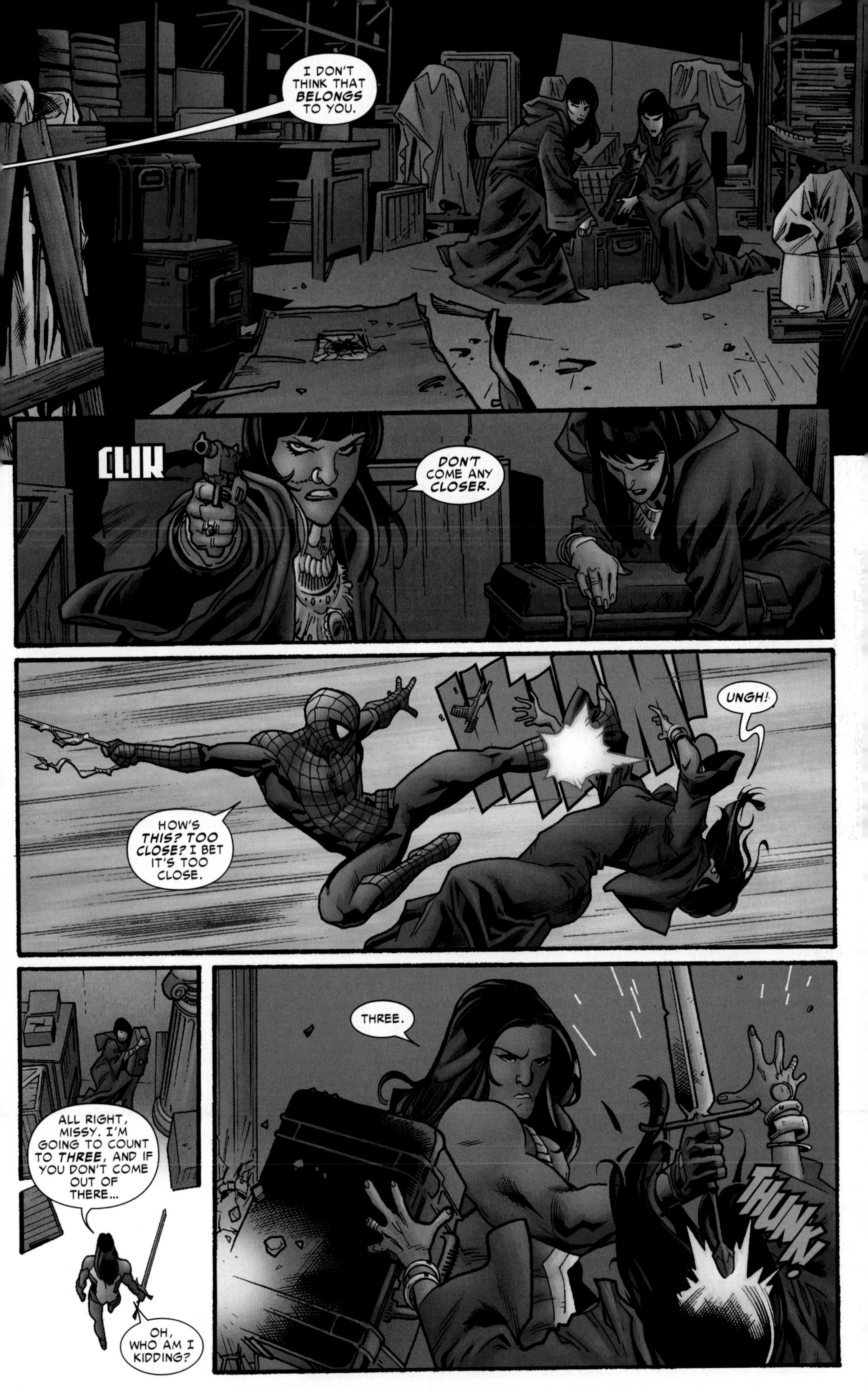
I DON'T THINK THAT BELONGS TO YOU.
CLIK
DON'T COME ANY CLOSER.
HOW'S THIS? TOO CLOSE? I BET IT'S TOO CLOSE.
UNGH!
ALL RIGHT, MISSY. I'M GOING TO COUNT TO THREE, AND IF YOU DON'T COME OUT OF THERE...
OH, WHO AM I KIDDING?
THREE.
THUNK!

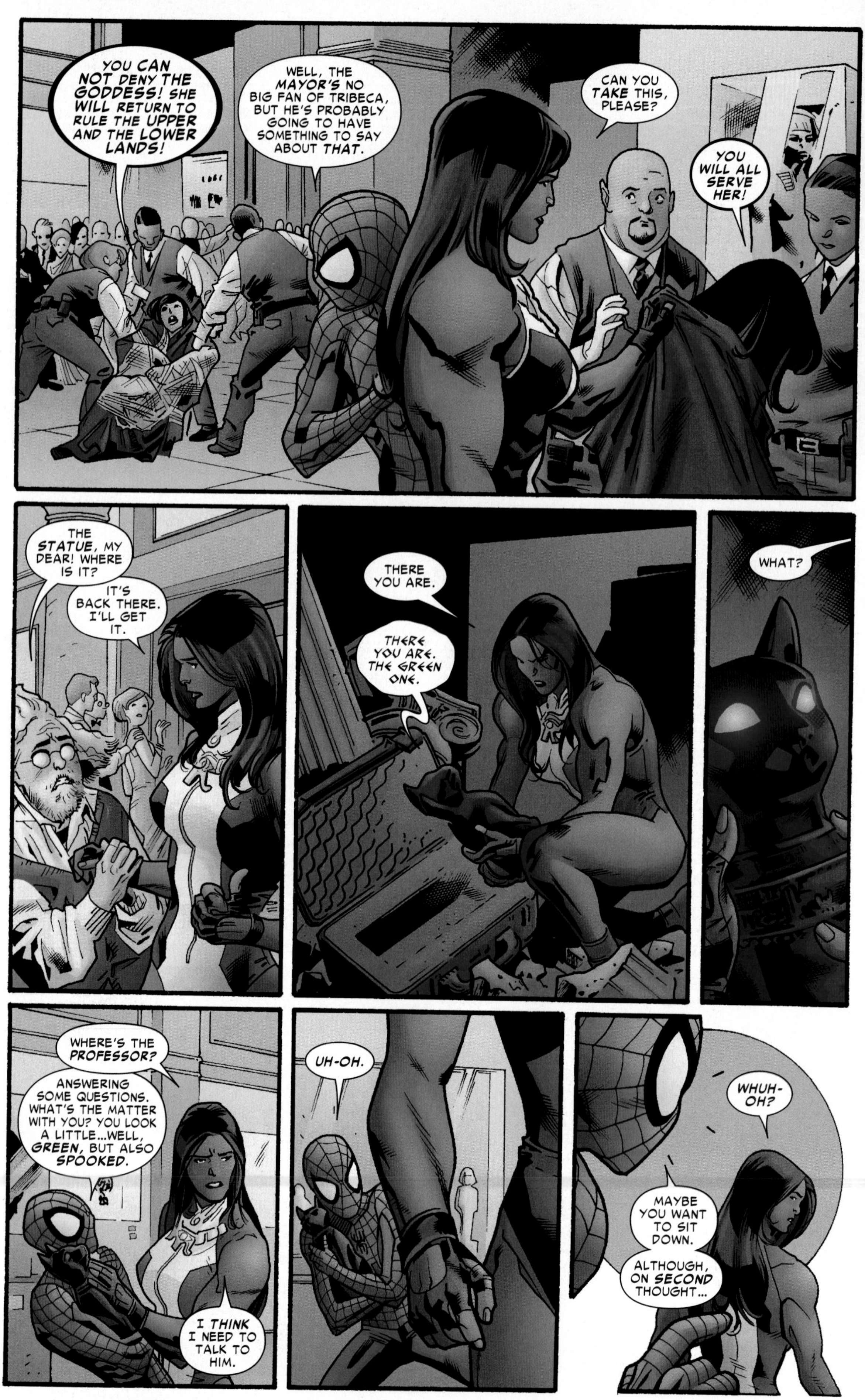
YOU CAN NOT DENY THE GODDESS! SHE WILL RETURN TO RULE THE UPPER AND THE LOWER LANDS!
WELL, THE MAYOR'S NO BIG FAN OF TRIBECA, BUT HE'S PROBABLY GOING TO HAVE SOMETHING TO SAY ABOUT THAT.
CAN YOU TAKE THIS, PLEASE?
YOU WILL ALL SERVE HER!
THE STATUE, MY DEAR! WHERE IS IT?
IT'S BACK THERE. I'LL GET IT.
THERE YOU ARE.
THERE YOU ARE. THE GREEN ONE.
WHAT?
WHERE'S THE PROFESSOR?
ANSWERING SOME QUESTIONS. WHAT'S THE MATTER WITH YOU? YOU LOOK A LITTLE...WELL, GREEN, BUT ALSO SPOOKED.
I THINK I NEED TO TALK TO HIM.
UH-OH.
WHUH-OH?
MAYBE YOU WANT TO SIT DOWN.
ALTHOUGH, ON SECOND THOUGHT...

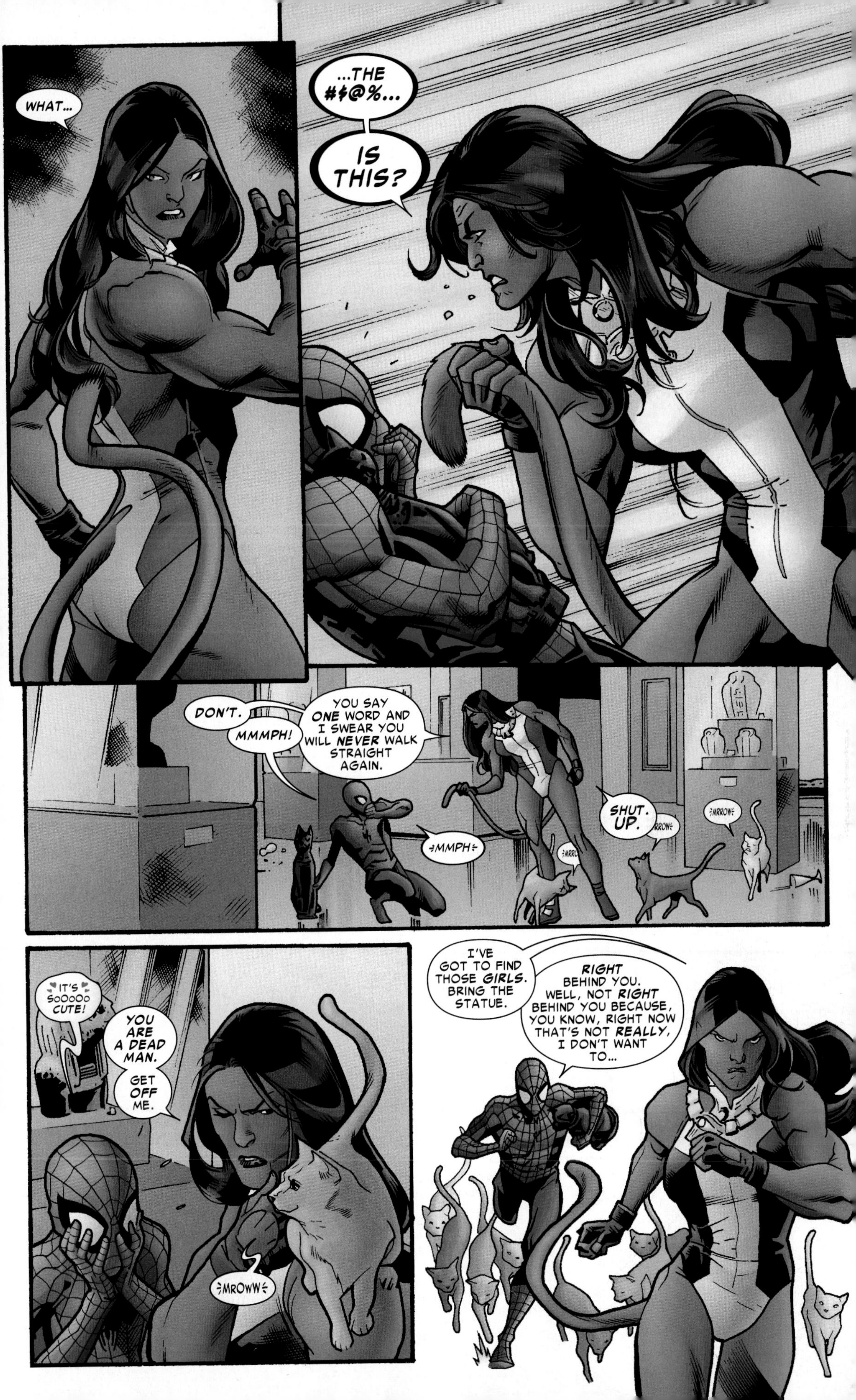
WHAT...
...THE #$@%...
IS THIS?
DON'T.
MMMPH!
YOU SAY ONE WORD AND I SWEAR YOU WILL NEVER WALK STRAIGHT AGAIN.
MMPH
SHUT. UP.
MRROW
MRROW
MRROW
IT'S SOOOOO CUTE!
YOU ARE A DEAD MAN.
GET OFF ME.
MROWW
I'VE GOT TO FIND THOSE GIRLS. BRING THE STATUE.
RIGHT BEHIND YOU. WELL, NOT RIGHT BEHIND YOU BECAUSE, YOU KNOW, RIGHT NOW THAT'S NOT REALLY, I DON'T WANT TO...

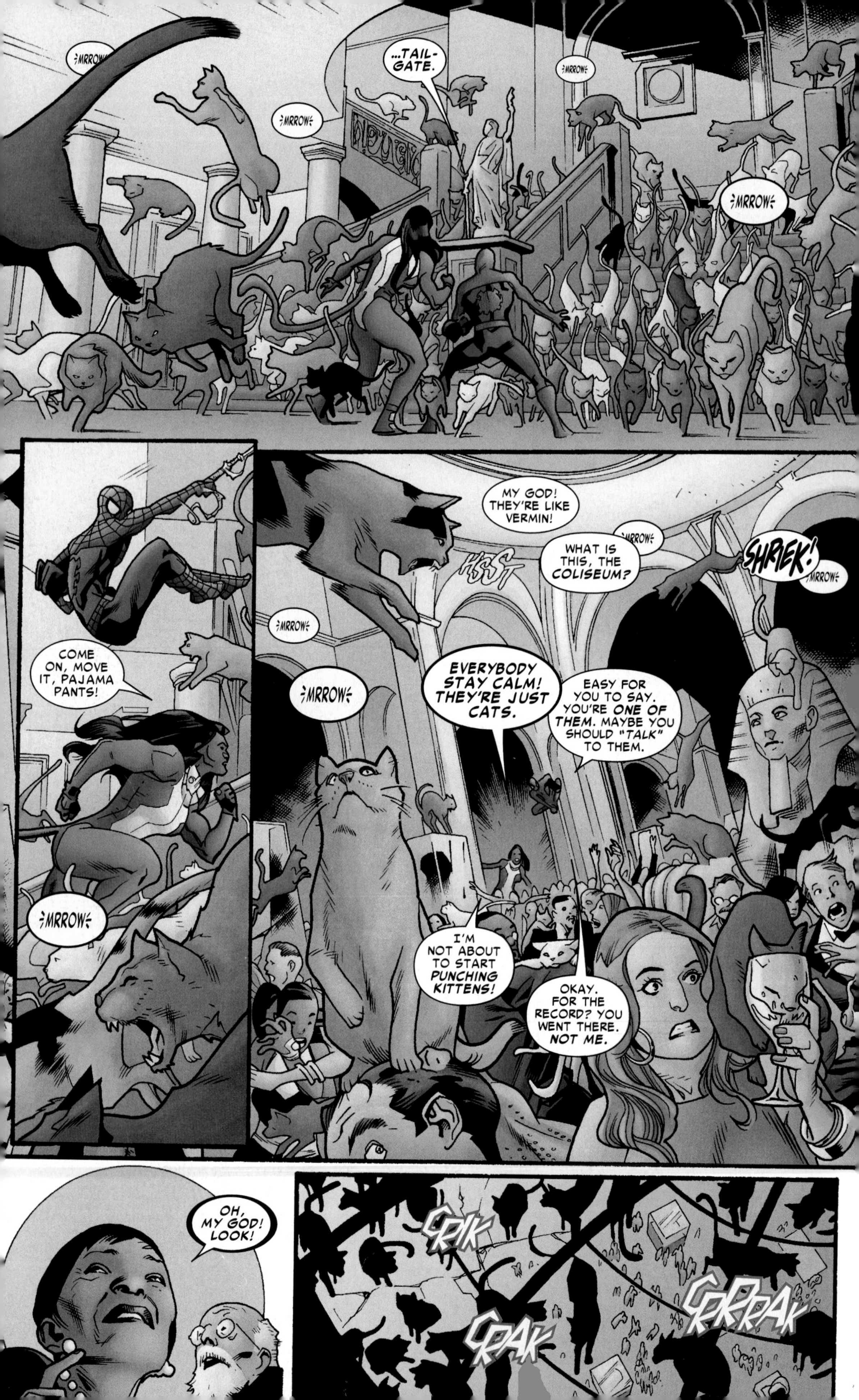

MRROW
...TAIL-GATE.
MRROW
MRROW
MRROW
COME ON, MOVE IT, PAJAMA PANTS!
MRROW
MY GOD! THEY'RE LIKE VERMIN!
MRROW
WHAT IS THIS, THE COLISEUM?
SHRIEK!
MRROW
HSST
MRROW
MRROW
EVERYBODY STAY CALM! THEY'RE JUST CATS.
EASY FOR YOU TO SAY. YOU'RE ONE OF THEM. MAYBE YOU SHOULD "TALK" TO THEM.
I'M NOT ABOUT TO START PUNCHING KITTENS!
OKAY. FOR THE RECORD? YOU WENT THERE. NOT ME.
OH, MY GOD! LOOK!
CRIK
CRAK
CRRRAK

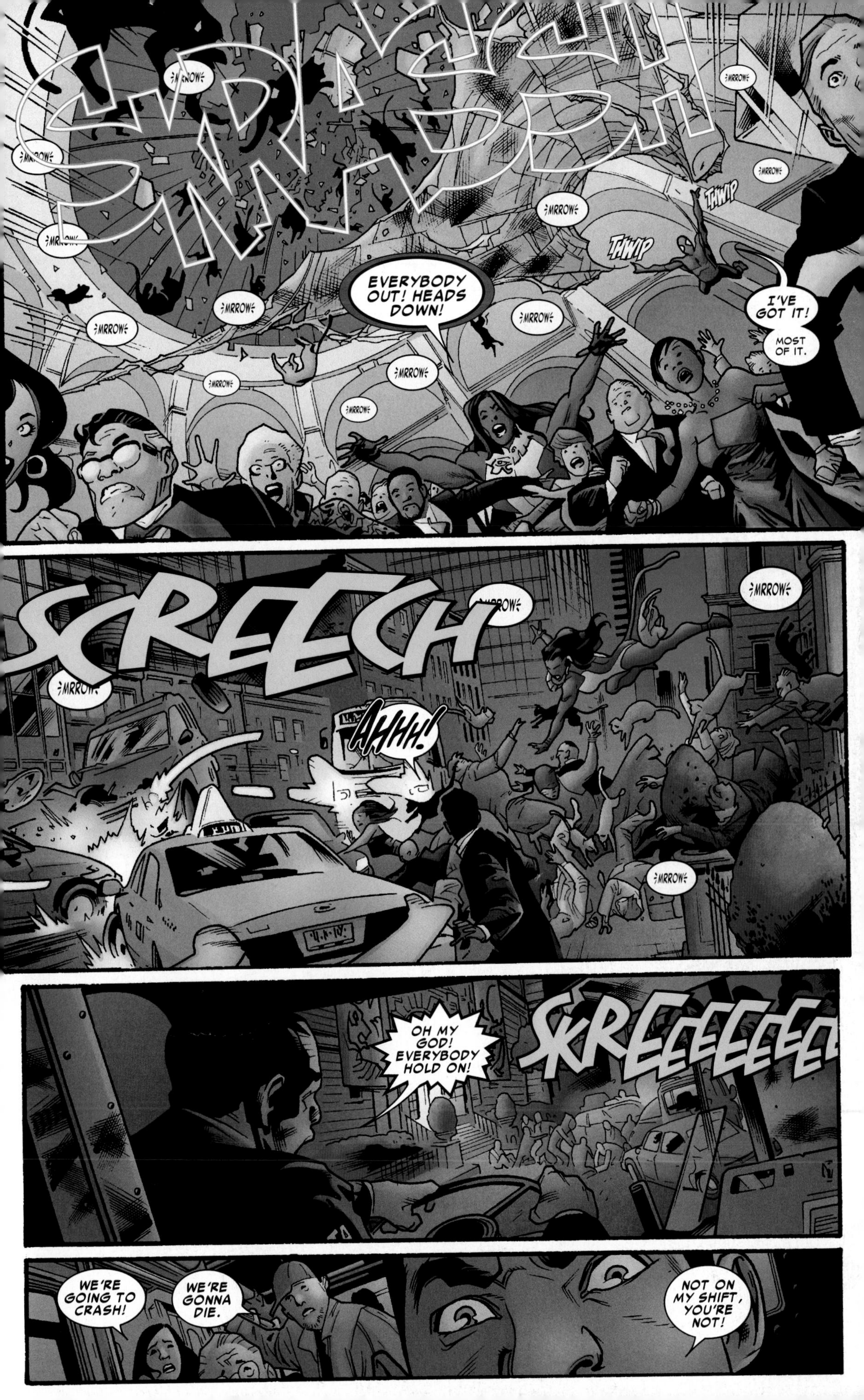
MRROW
MRROW
MRROW
MRROW
THWIP
THWIP
EVERYBODY OUT! HEADS DOWN!
MRROW
MRROW
MRROW
I'VE GOT IT!
MOST OF IT.
MRROW
MRROW
MRROW
SCREECH
MRROW
AHHH!
MRROW
OH MY GOD! EVERYBODY HOLD ON!
WE'RE GOING TO CRASH!
WE'RE GONNA DIE.
NOT ON MY SHIFT, YOU'RE NOT!

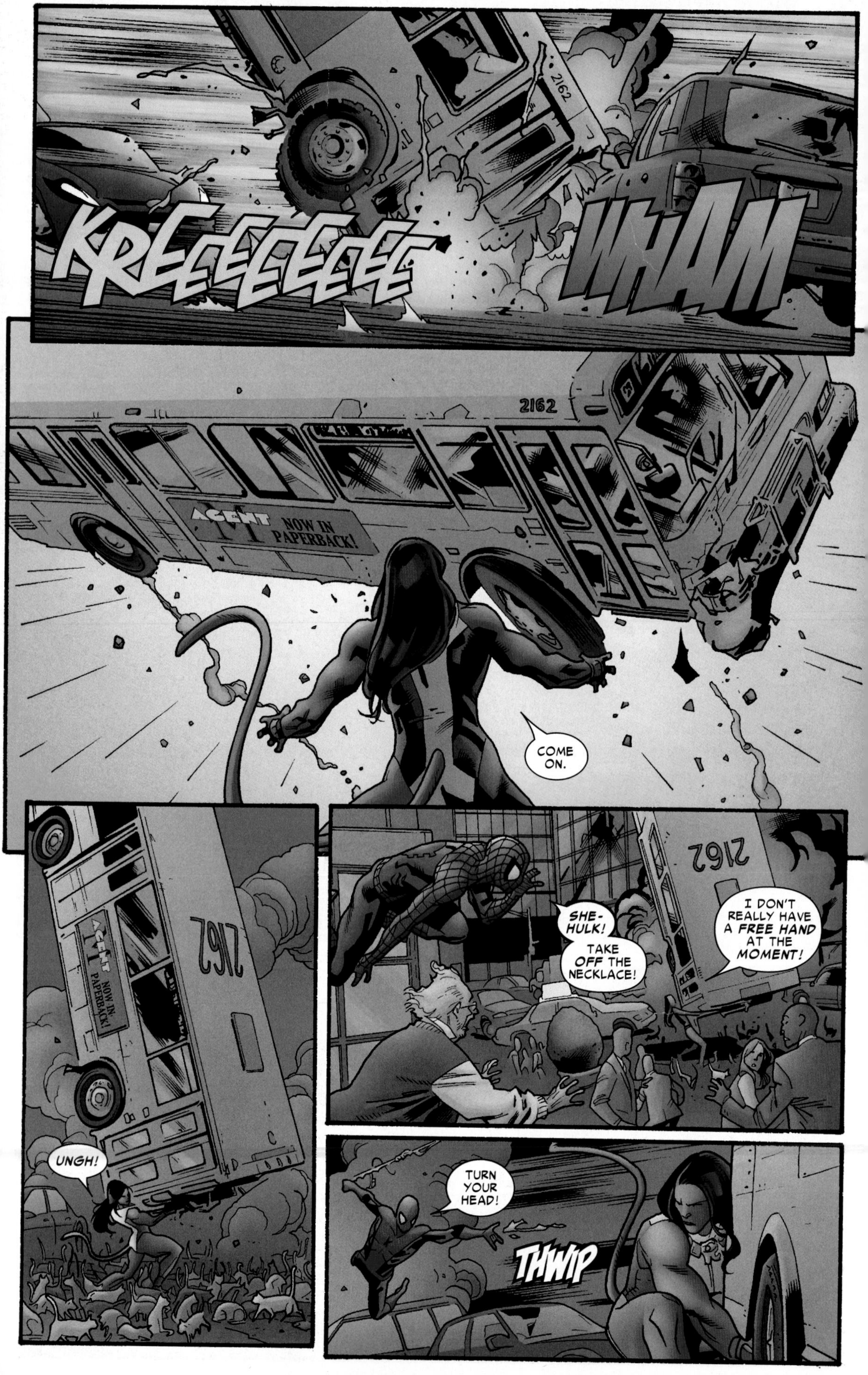
KREEEEEEEEE
WHAM
2162
AGENT M NOW IN PAPERBACK!
COME ON.
UNGH!
SHE-HULK!
TAKE OFF THE NECKLACE!
I DON'T REALLY HAVE A FREE HAND AT THE MOMENT!
TURN YOUR HEAD!
THWIP

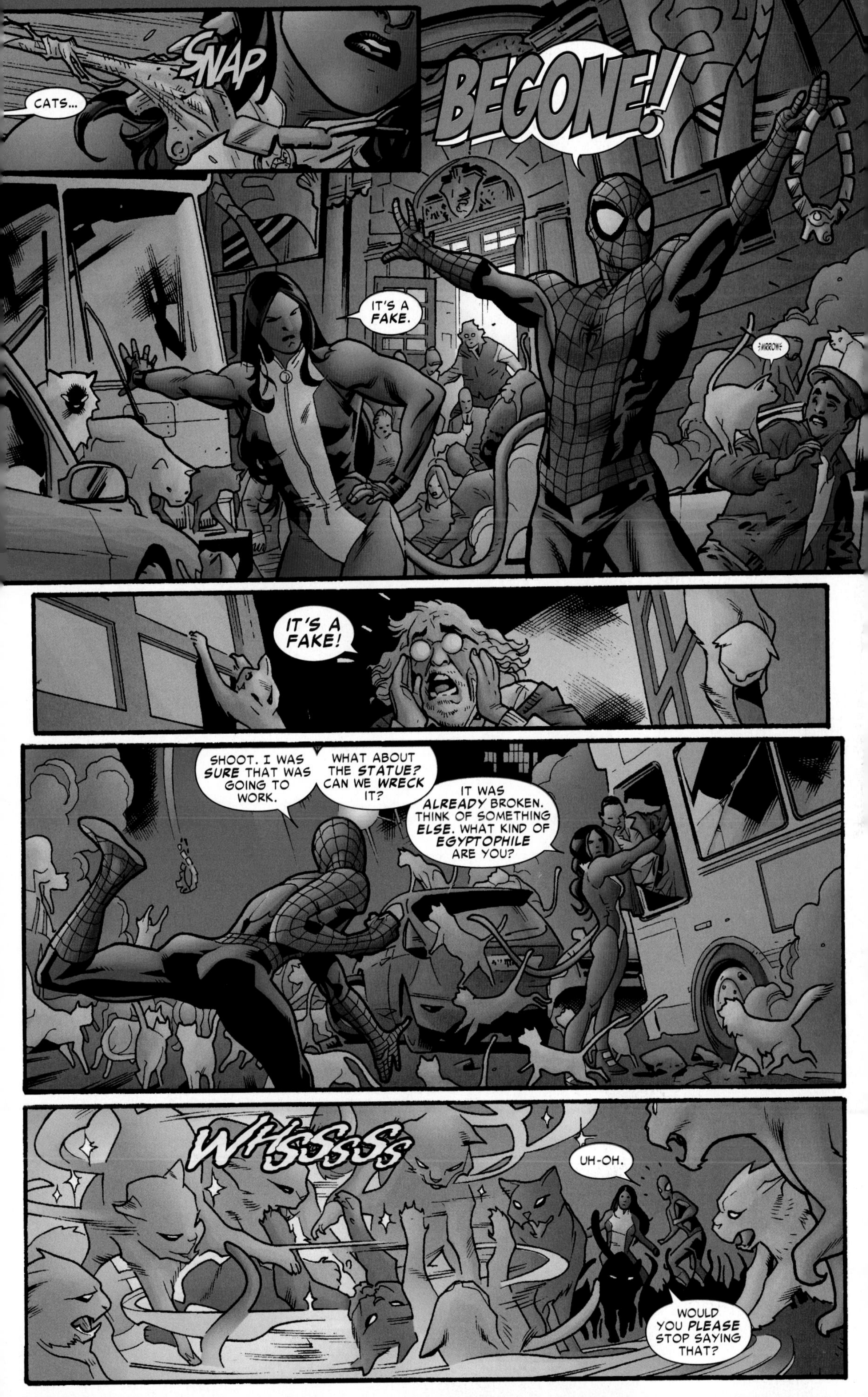
SNAP
CATS...
BEGONE!
IT'S A FAKE.
MRROW
IT'S A FAKE!
SHOOT. I WAS SURE THAT WAS GOING TO WORK.
WHAT ABOUT THE STATUE? CAN WE WRECK IT?
IT WAS ALREADY BROKEN. THINK OF SOMETHING ELSE. WHAT KIND OF EGYPTOPHILE ARE YOU?
WHSSSSS
UH-OH.
WOULD YOU PLEASE STOP SAYING THAT?

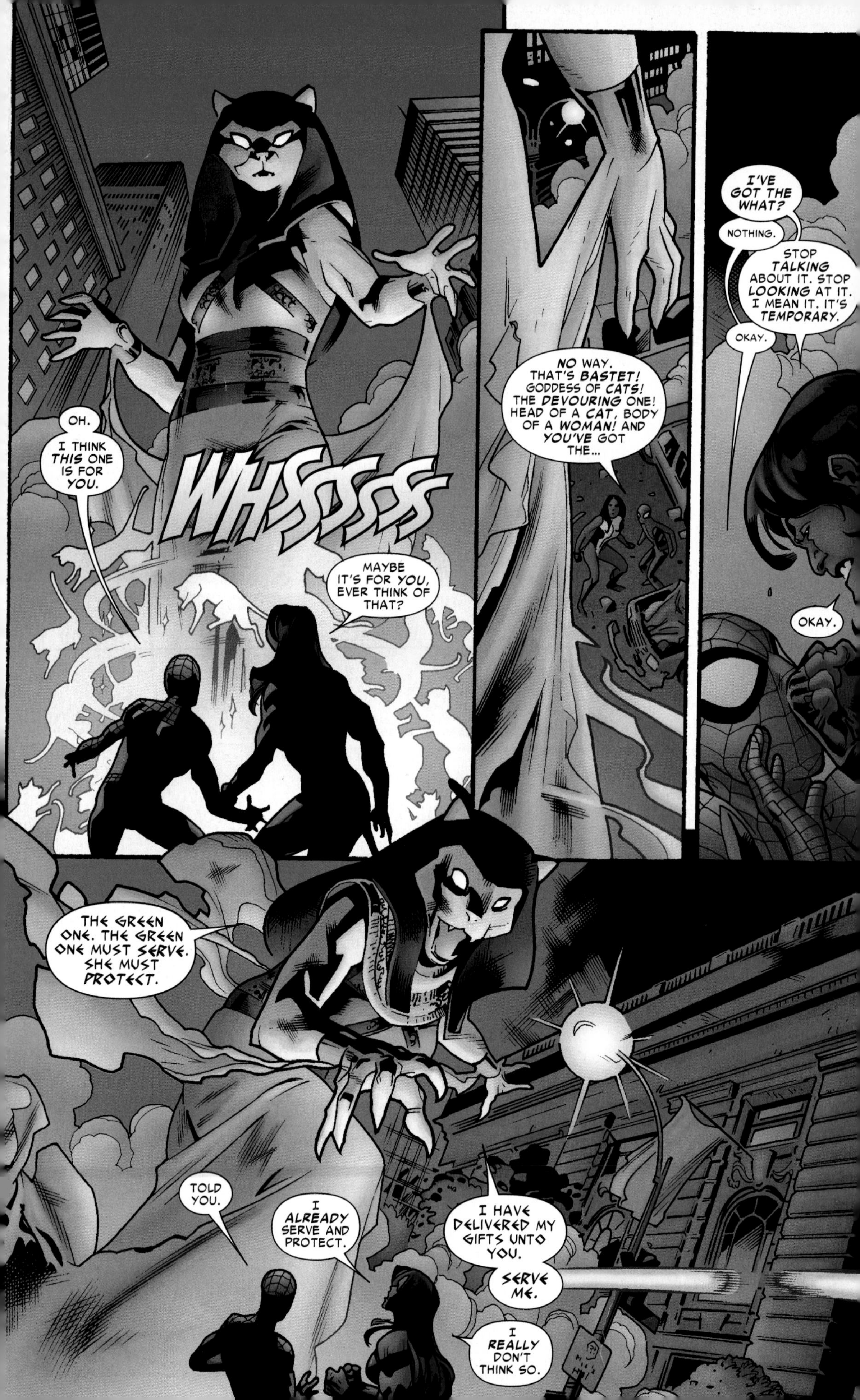

OH.
I THINK THIS ONE IS FOR YOU.
WHSSSSS
MAYBE IT'S FOR YOU, EVER THINK OF THAT?
NO WAY. THAT'S BASTET! GODDESS OF CATS! THE DEVOURING ONE! HEAD OF A CAT, BODY OF A WOMAN! AND YOU'VE GOT THE...
I'VE GOT THE WHAT?
NOTHING.
STOP TALKING ABOUT IT. STOP LOOKING AT IT. I MEAN IT. IT'S TEMPORARY.
OKAY.
OKAY.
THE GREEN ONE. THE GREEN ONE MUST SERVE. SHE MUST PROTECT.
TOLD YOU.
I ALREADY SERVE AND PROTECT.
I HAVE DELIVERED MY GIFTS UNTO YOU.
SERVE ME.
I REALLY DON'T THINK SO.

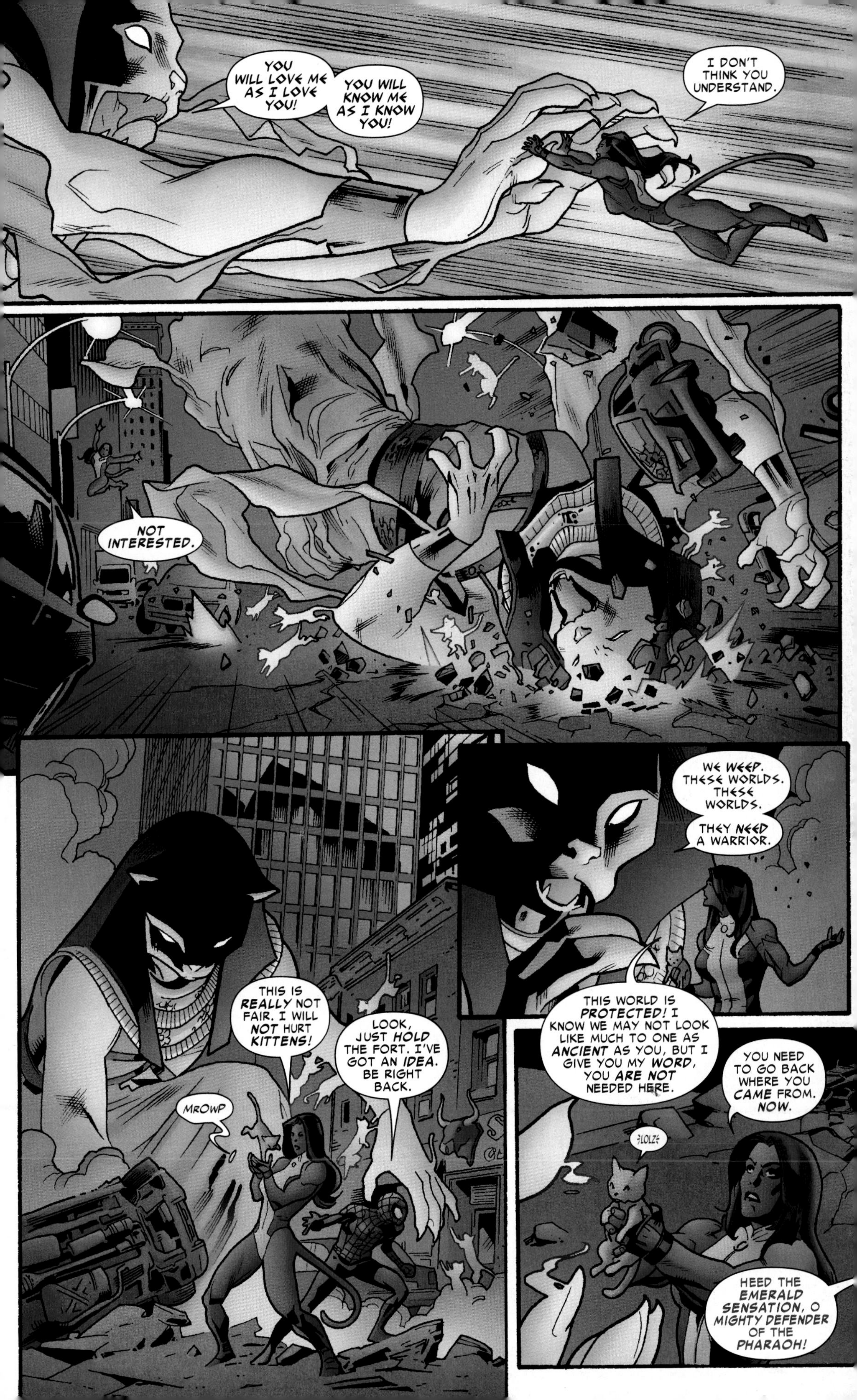
YOU WILL LOVE ME AS I LOVE YOU!
YOU WILL KNOW ME AS I KNOW YOU!
I DON'T THINK YOU UNDERSTAND.
NOT INTERESTED.
THIS IS REALLY NOT FAIR. I WILL NOT HURT KITTENS!
LOOK, JUST HOLD THE FORT. I'VE GOT AN IDEA. BE RIGHT BACK.
MROWP
WE WEEP. THESE WORLDS. THESE WORLDS.
THEY NEED A WARRIOR.
THIS WORLD IS PROTECTED! I KNOW WE MAY NOT LOOK LIKE MUCH TO ONE AS ANCIENT AS YOU, BUT I GIVE YOU MY WORD, YOU ARE NOT NEEDED HERE.
YOU NEED TO GO BACK WHERE YOU CAME FROM. NOW.
LOLZ
HEED THE EMERALD SENSATION, O MIGHTY DEFENDER OF THE PHARAOH!

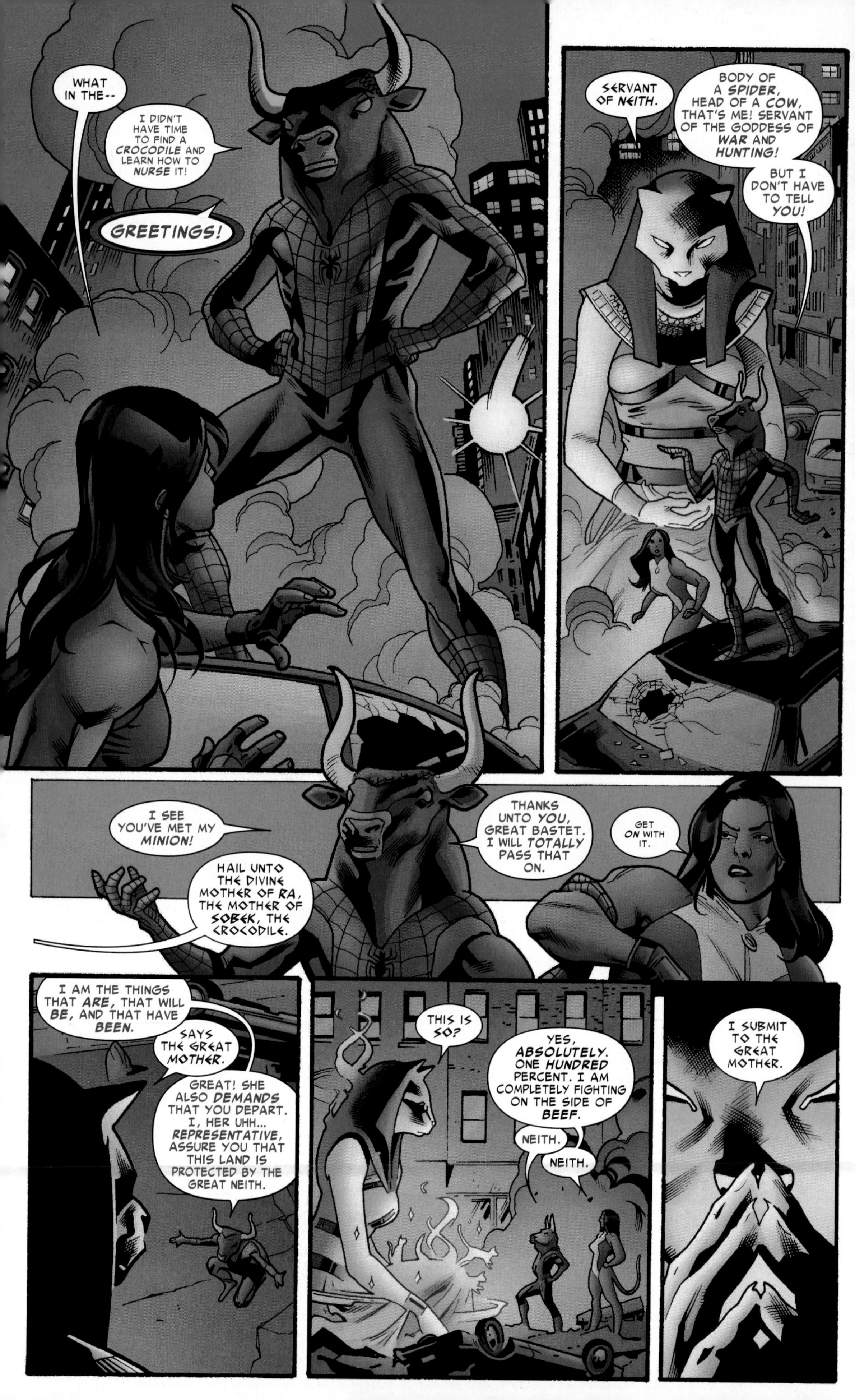
WHAT IN THE--
I DIDN'T HAVE TIME TO FIND A CROCODILE AND LEARN HOW TO NURSE IT!
GREETINGS!
SERVANT OF NEITH.
BODY OF A SPIDER, HEAD OF A COW, THAT'S ME! SERVANT OF THE GODDESS OF WAR AND HUNTING!
BUT I DON'T HAVE TO TELL YOU!
I SEE YOU'VE MET MY MINION!
HAIL UNTO THE DIVINE MOTHER OF RA, THE MOTHER OF SOBEK, THE CROCODILE.
THANKS UNTO YOU, GREAT BASTET. I WILL TOTALLY PASS THAT ON.
GET ON WITH IT.
I AM THE THINGS THAT ARE, THAT WILL BE, AND THAT HAVE BEEN.
SAYS THE GREAT MOTHER.
GREAT! SHE ALSO DEMANDS THAT YOU DEPART. I, HER UHH... REPRESENTATIVE, ASSURE YOU THAT THIS LAND IS PROTECTED BY THE GREAT NEITH.
THIS IS SO?
YES, ABSOLUTELY. ONE HUNDRED PERCENT. I AM COMPLETELY FIGHTING ON THE SIDE OF BEEF.
NEITH.
NEITH.
I SUBMIT TO THE GREAT MOTHER.

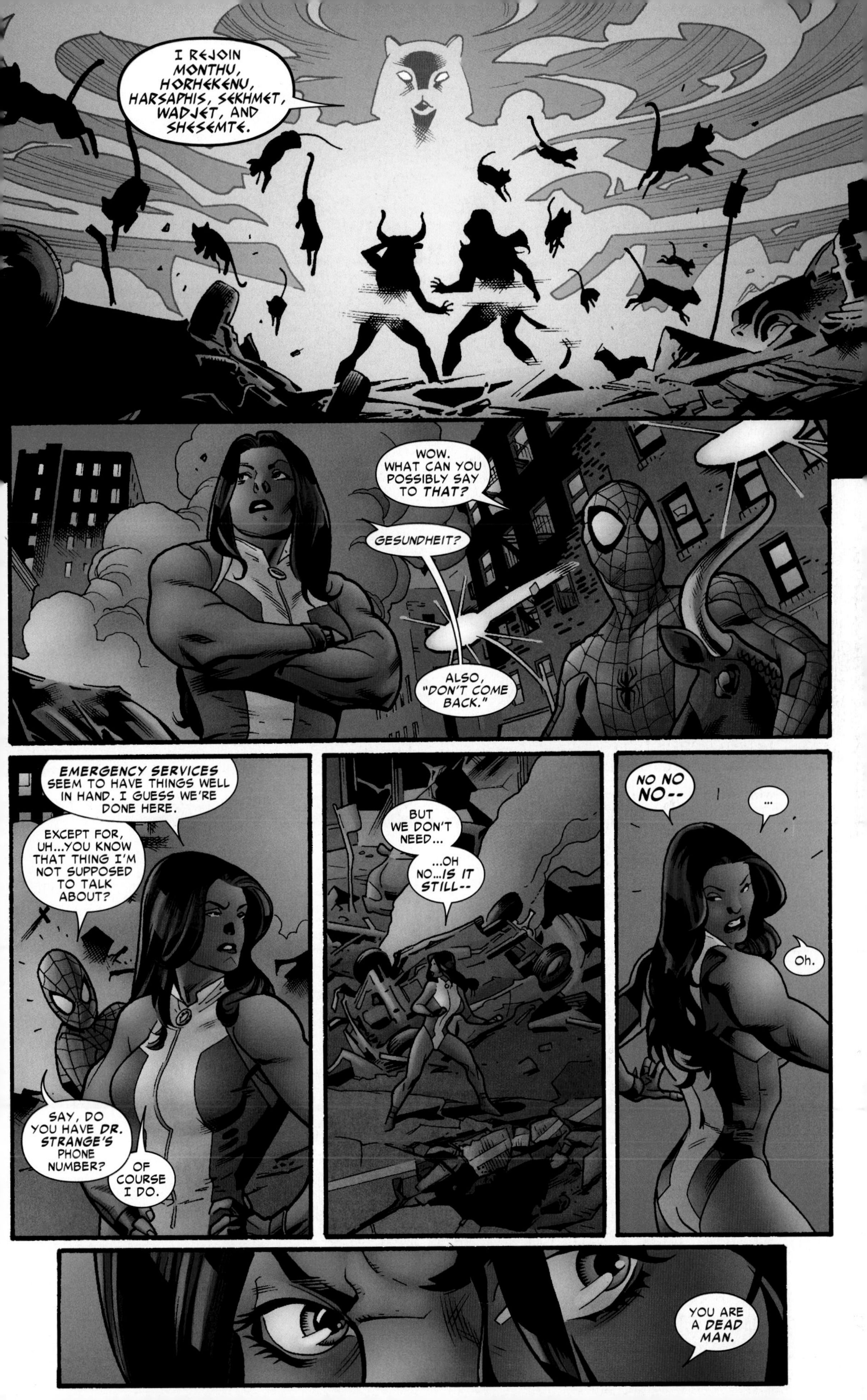
I REJOIN MONTHU, HORHEKENU, HARSAPHIS, SEKHMET, WADJET, AND SHESEMTE.
WOW. WHAT CAN YOU POSSIBLY SAY TO THAT?
GESUNDHEIT?
ALSO, "DON'T COME BACK."
EMERGENCY SERVICES SEEM TO HAVE THINGS WELL IN HAND. I GUESS WE'RE DONE HERE.
EXCEPT FOR, UH...YOU KNOW THAT THING I'M NOT SUPPOSED TO TALK ABOUT?
SAY, DO YOU HAVE DR. STRANGE'S PHONE NUMBER?
OF COURSE I DO.
BUT WE DON'T NEED...
...OH NO...IS IT STILL--
NO NO NO--
...
Oh.
YOU ARE A DEAD MAN.

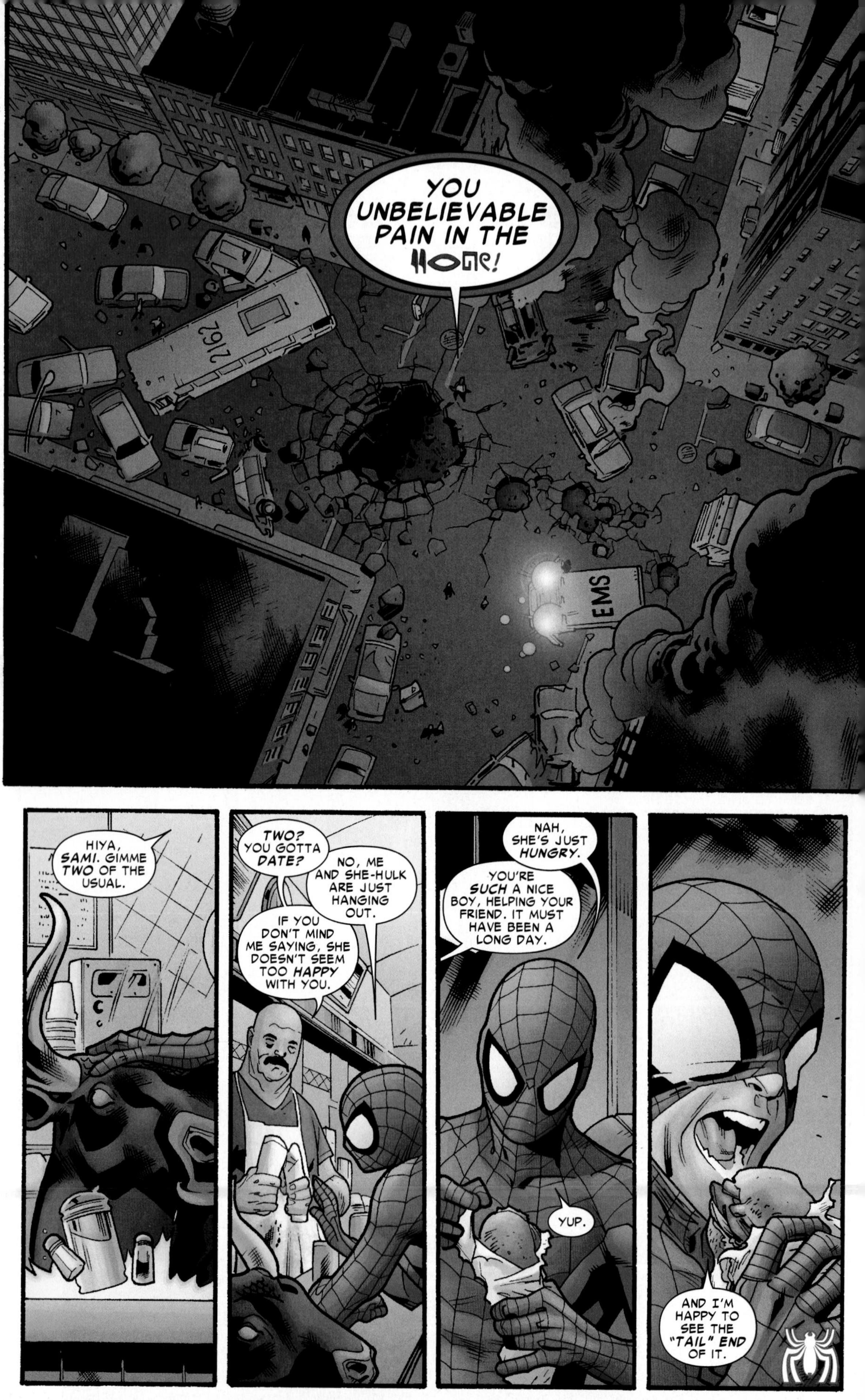
YOU UNBELIEVABLE PAIN IN THE
HIYA, SAMI. GIMME TWO OF THE USUAL.
TWO? YOU GOTTA DATE?
NO, ME AND SHE-HULK ARE JUST HANGING OUT.
IF YOU DON'T MIND ME SAYING, SHE DOESN'T SEEM TOO HAPPY WITH YOU.
NAH, SHE'S JUST HUNGRY.
YOU'RE SUCH A NICE BOY, HELPING YOUR FRIEND. IT MUST HAVE BEEN A LONG DAY.
YUP.
AND I'M HAPPY TO SEE THE "TAIL" END OF IT.

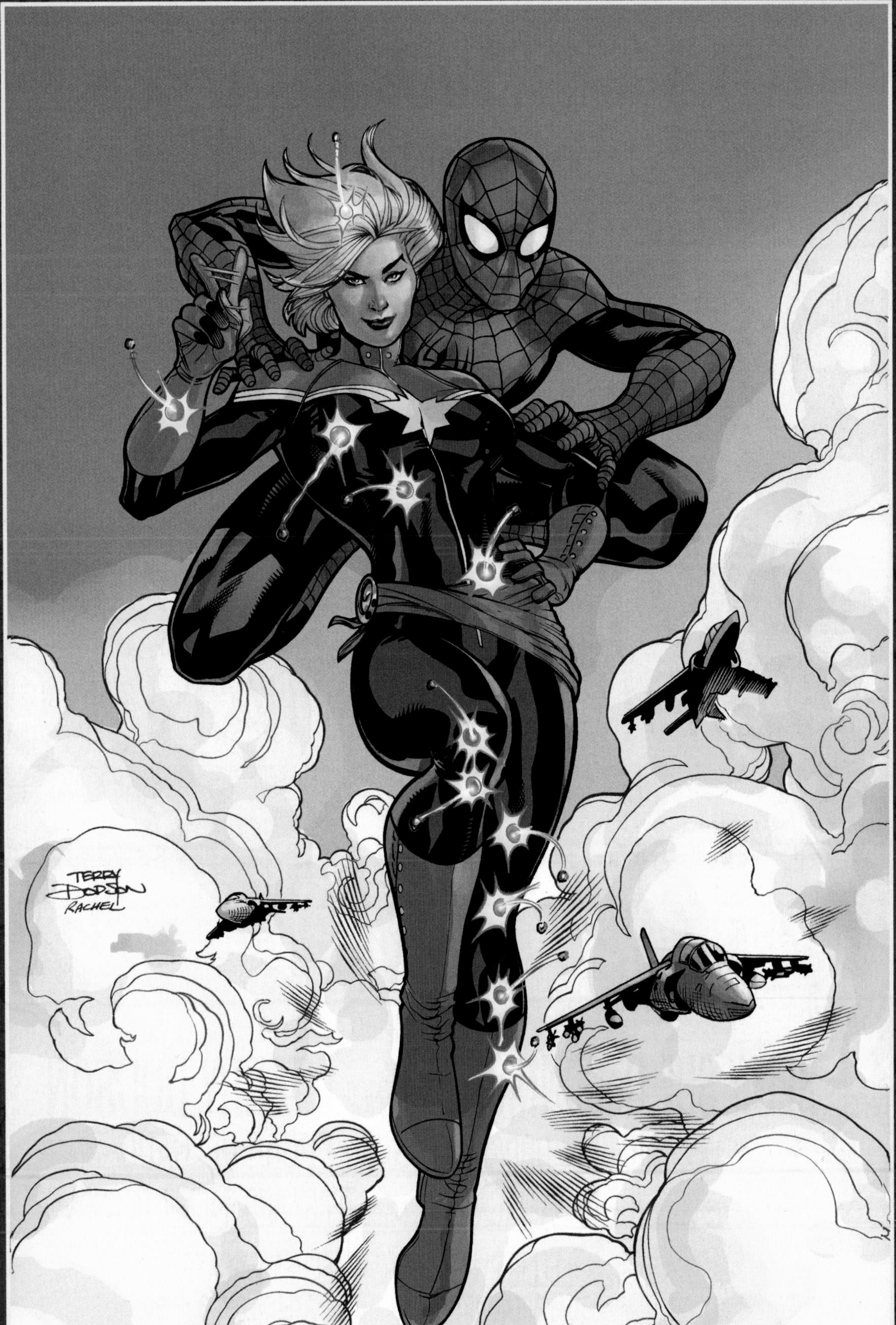
TERRY
DODSON
RACHEL

9

While attending a demonstration in radiology, high school student Peter Parker was bitten by a spider which had accidentally been exposed to radioactive rays. Through a miracle of science, Peter soon found that he had gained the spider's powers...and had, in effect, become a human spider! Later he joined the Avengers. And now he is the...

AVENGING

SPIDER-MAN

When adorable U.S. Air Force officer Col. Carol Danvers was caught in the explosion of an alien device with the Kree warrior Captain Marvel, Carol's genetic code was irreversibly altered, granting her the power to fly, incredib strength, and an ability to harness and project energy. The two were allies for a time, until Captain Marvel lo his life. Now, Carol has chosen to take up the mantle in his honor. She's an intergalactic girl adventurer, a space faring super heroine, and an Avenger. She's Earth's Mightiest (and Cutest!) Hero, the all-new...

CAPTAIN

MARVEL

Wacker, I'm going to choke you it you don't take this crap out! — Danvers

AVENGING
SPIDER-MAN

PREVIOUSLY...

Some time ago, Peter Parker's Aunt May moved to Boston. Also...

CAROL DANVERS GOT AN AWESOME NEW COSTUME AND IS NOW CAPTAIN MARVEL!

(You can find out more about that in Captain Marvel #1 which will be on sale next week! But this story takes place AFTER Captain Marvel #1 so "previously" still applies in a story sense and really what this means is that you are holding the FUTURE OF COMICS right in your very hands!)

WRITER: **KELLY SUE DeCONNICK**   PENCILS: **TERRY DODSON**

INKER: **RACHEL DODSON**   COLORS: **EDGAR DELGADO**

LETTERER: **VC's JOE CARAMAGNA**   COVER: **TERRY AND RACHEL DODSON**

ASSISTANT EDITOR: **ELLIE PYLE**   *Dead-itor* EDITOR: **STEPHEN WACKER**

EXECUTIVE EDITOR: **TOM BREVOORT**   EDITOR IN CHIEF: **AXEL ALONSO**

CHIEF CREATIVE OFFICER: **JOE QUESADA**   PUBLISHER: **DAN BUCKLEY**   EXECUTIVE PRODUCER: **ALAN FINE**

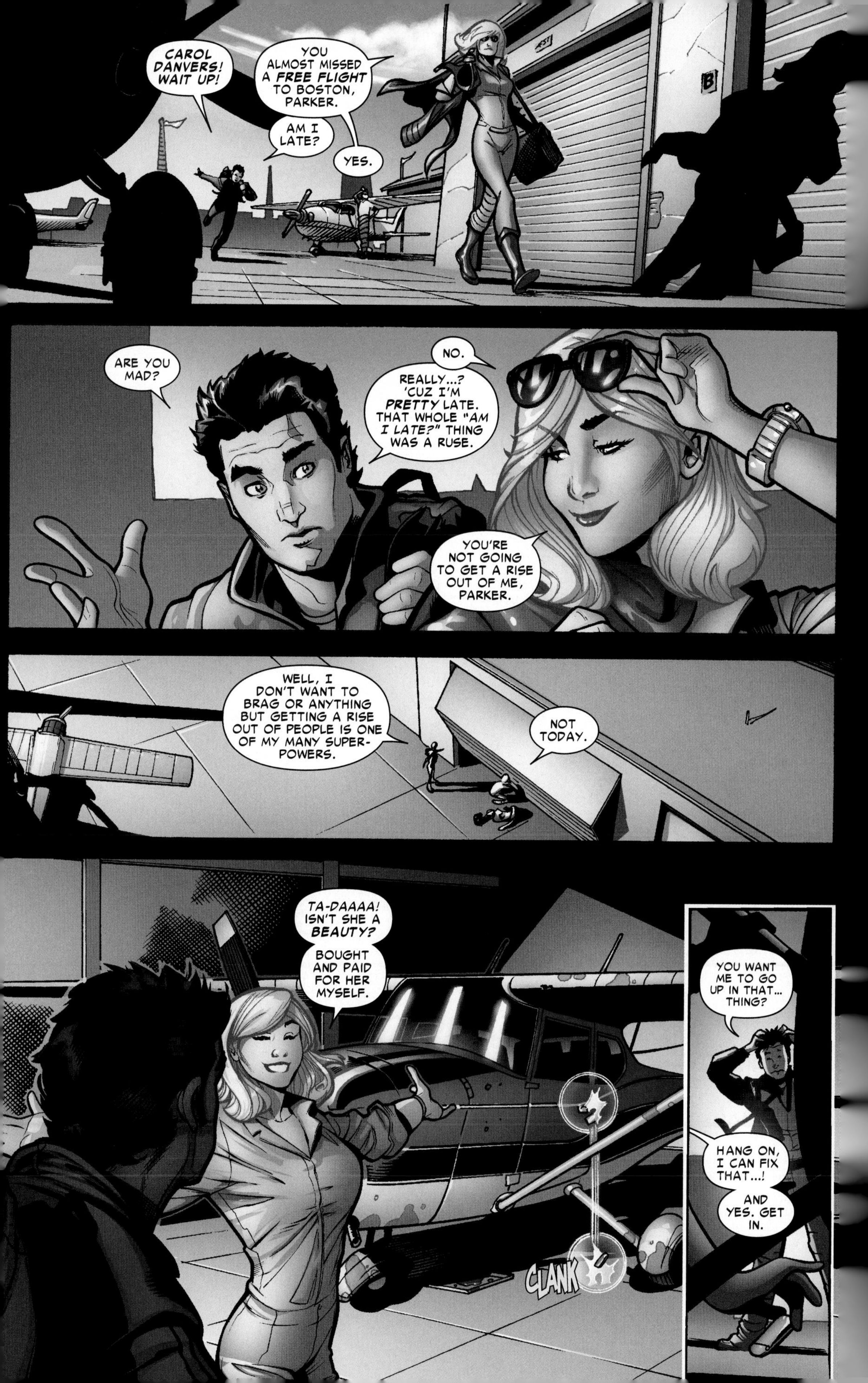

CAROL DANVERS! WAIT UP!
YOU ALMOST MISSED A FREE FLIGHT TO BOSTON, PARKER.
AM I LATE?
YES.
ARE YOU MAD?
NO.
REALLY...? 'CUZ I'M PRETTY LATE. THAT WHOLE "AM I LATE?" THING WAS A RUSE.
YOU'RE NOT GOING TO GET A RISE OUT OF ME, PARKER.
WELL, I DON'T WANT TO BRAG OR ANYTHING BUT GETTING A RISE OUT OF PEOPLE IS ONE OF MY MANY SUPER-POWERS.
NOT TODAY.
TA-DAAAA! ISN'T SHE A BEAUTY?
BOUGHT AND PAID FOR HER MYSELF.
CLANK
YOU WANT ME TO GO UP IN THAT... THING?
HANG ON, I CAN FIX THAT...!
AND YES. GET IN.

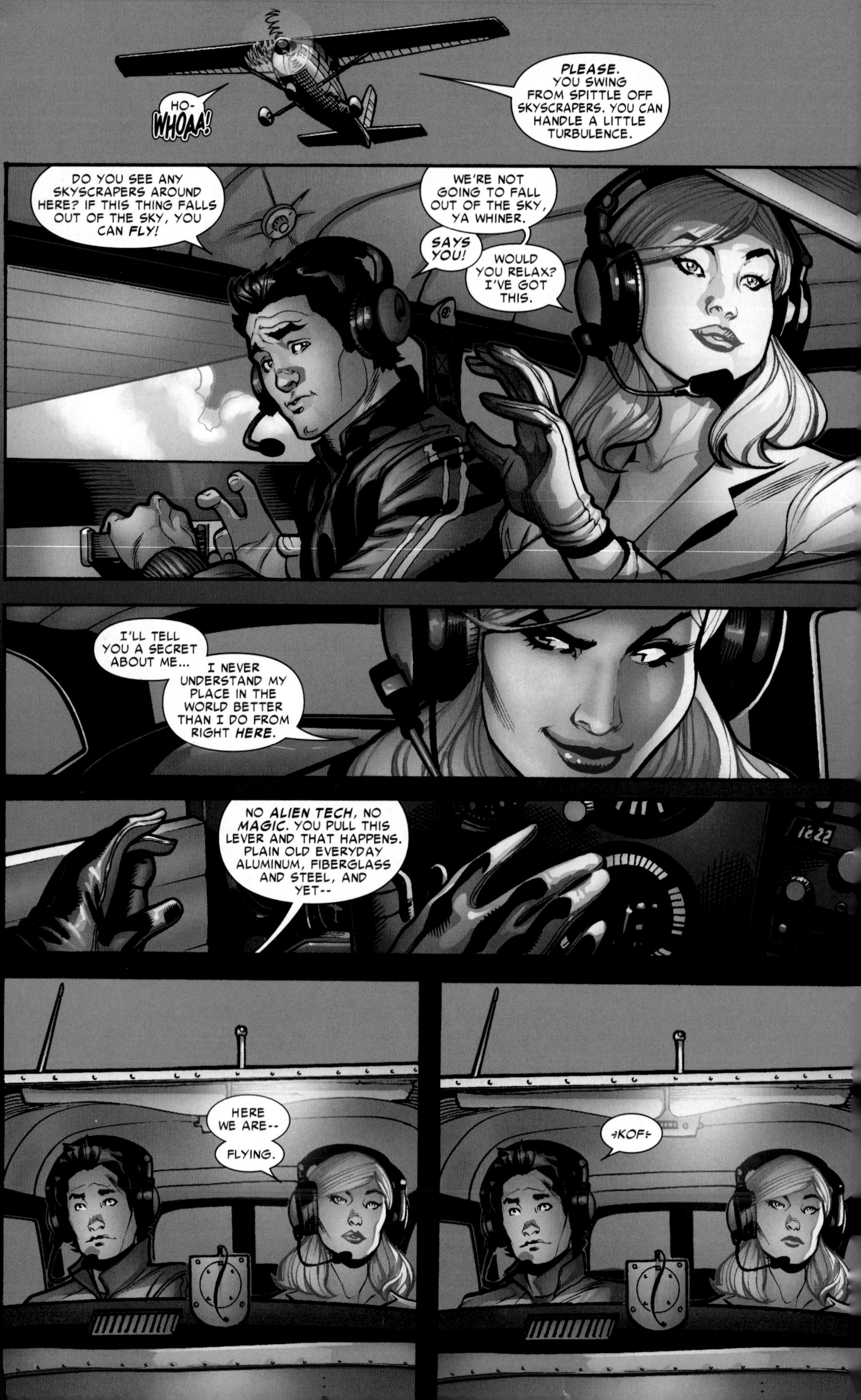
HO-WHOAA!
PLEASE. YOU SWING FROM SPITTLE OFF SKYSCRAPERS. YOU CAN HANDLE A LITTLE TURBULENCE.
DO YOU SEE ANY SKYSCRAPERS AROUND HERE? IF THIS THING FALLS OUT OF THE SKY, YOU CAN FLY!
WE'RE NOT GOING TO FALL OUT OF THE SKY, YA WHINER.
SAYS YOU!
WOULD YOU RELAX? I'VE GOT THIS.
I'LL TELL YOU A SECRET ABOUT ME...
I NEVER UNDERSTAND MY PLACE IN THE WORLD BETTER THAN I DO FROM RIGHT HERE.
NO ALIEN TECH, NO MAGIC. YOU PULL THIS LEVER AND THAT HAPPENS. PLAIN OLD EVERYDAY ALUMINUM, FIBERGLASS AND STEEL, AND YET--
12:22
HERE WE ARE--
FLYING.
≠KOF≠

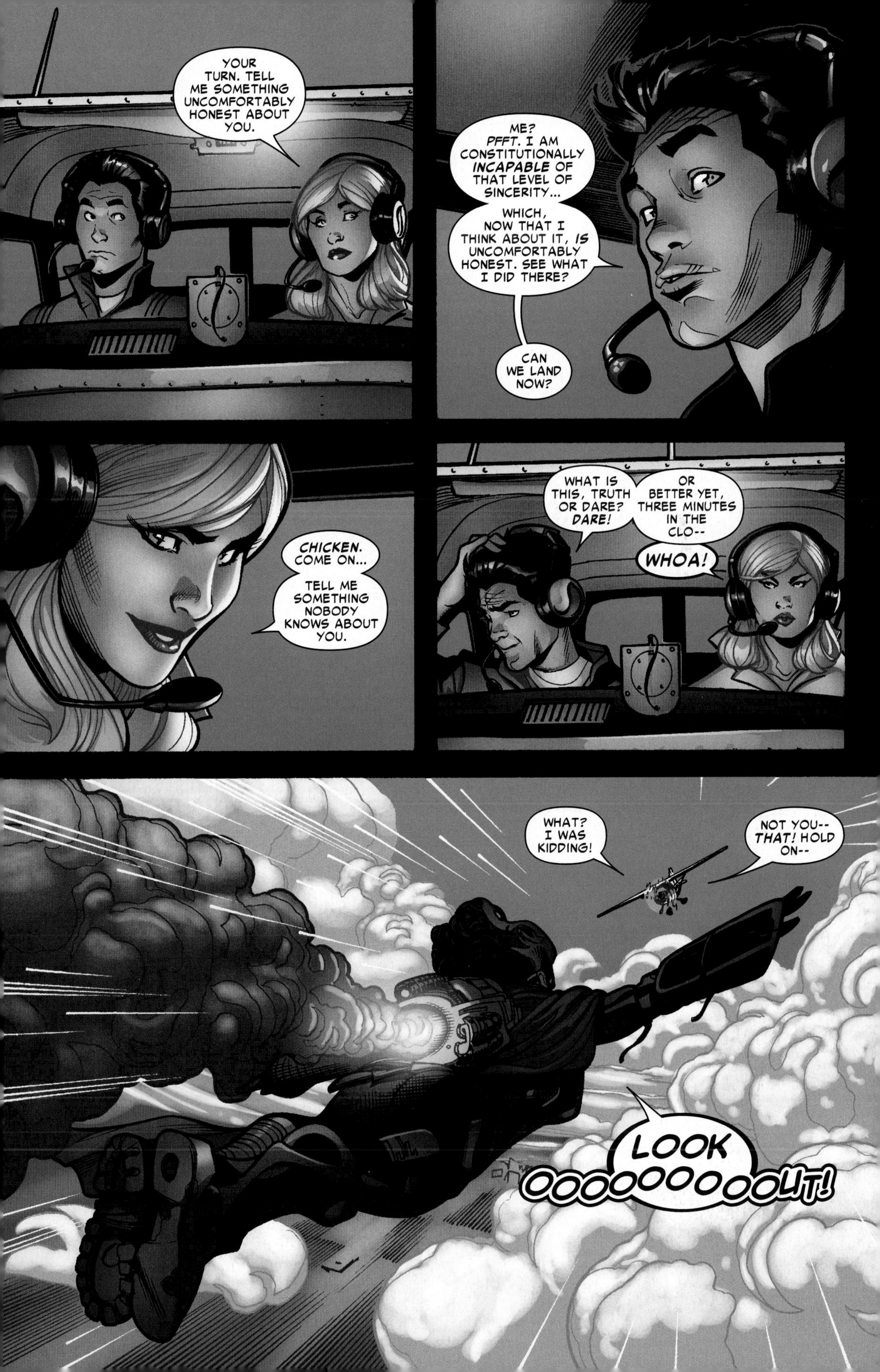
YOUR TURN. TELL ME SOMETHING UNCOMFORTABLY HONEST ABOUT YOU.
ME? PFFT. I AM CONSTITUTIONALLY INCAPABLE OF THAT LEVEL OF SINCERITY...
WHICH, NOW THAT I THINK ABOUT IT, IS UNCOMFORTABLY HONEST. SEE WHAT I DID THERE?
CAN WE LAND NOW?
CHICKEN. COME ON...
TELL ME SOMETHING NOBODY KNOWS ABOUT YOU.
WHAT IS THIS, TRUTH OR DARE? DARE!
OR BETTER YET, THREE MINUTES IN THE CLO--
WHOA!
WHAT? I WAS KIDDING!
NOT YOU-- THAT! HOLD ON--
LOOK OOOOOOOOOOUT!

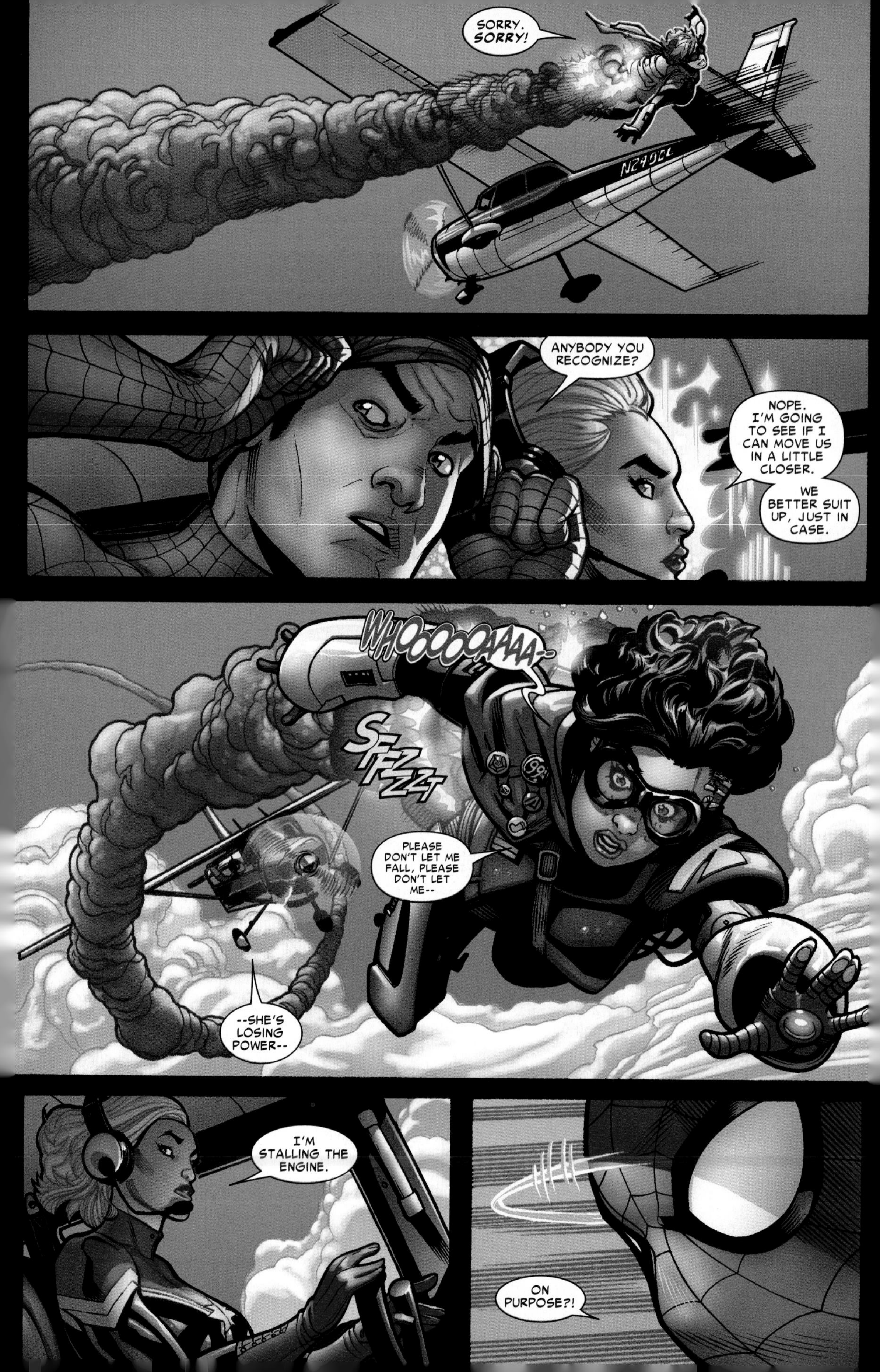
SORRY. SORRY!
N249CL
ANYBODY YOU RECOGNIZE?
NOPE. I'M GOING TO SEE IF I CAN MOVE US IN A LITTLE CLOSER.
WE BETTER SUIT UP, JUST IN CASE.
WHOOOOOAAAA--
SFFZZZT
PLEASE DON'T LET ME FALL, PLEASE DON'T LET ME--
--SHE'S LOSING POWER--
I'M STALLING THE ENGINE.
ON PURPOSE?!

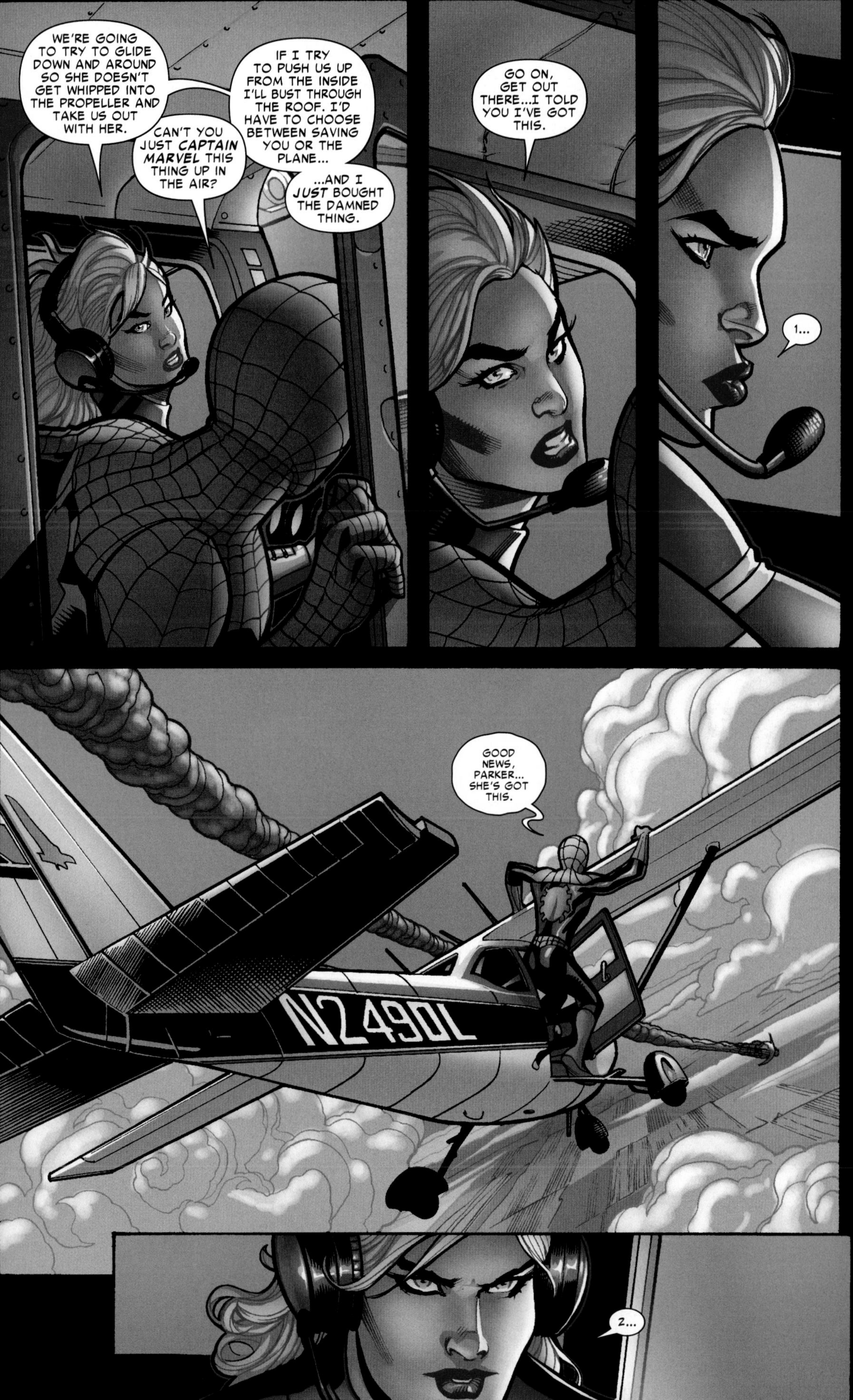
WE'RE GOING TO TRY TO GLIDE DOWN AND AROUND SO SHE DOESN'T GET WHIPPED INTO THE PROPELLER AND TAKE US OUT WITH HER.
CAN'T YOU JUST CAPTAIN MARVEL THIS THING UP IN THE AIR?
IF I TRY TO PUSH US UP FROM THE INSIDE I'LL BUST THROUGH THE ROOF. I'D HAVE TO CHOOSE BETWEEN SAVING YOU OR THE PLANE...
...AND I JUST BOUGHT THE DAMNED THING.
GO ON, GET OUT THERE...I TOLD YOU I'VE GOT THIS.
1...
GOOD NEWS, PARKER... SHE'S GOT THIS.
N2490L
2...

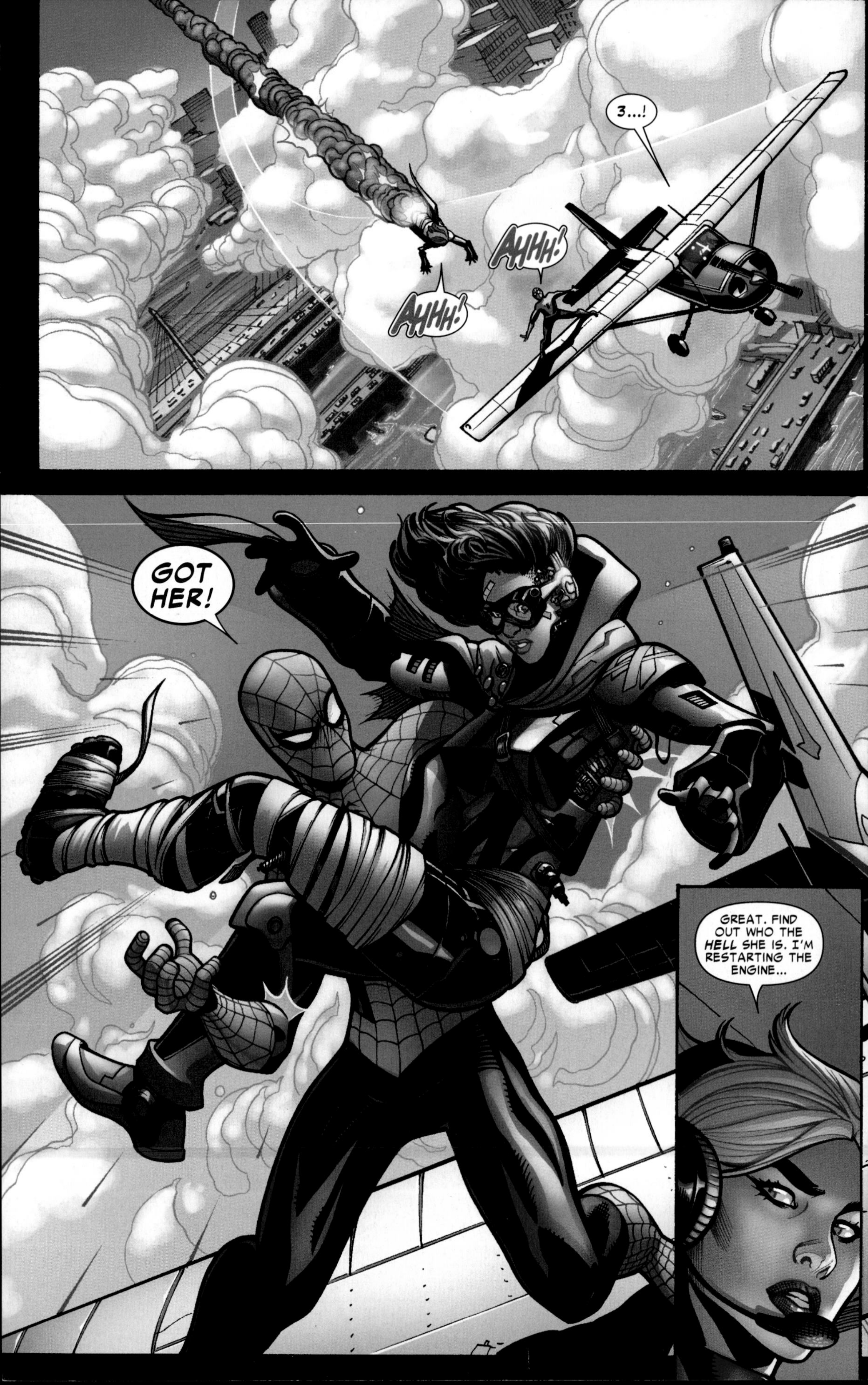
3...!
AHHH!
AHHH!
GOT HER!
GREAT. FIND OUT WHO THE HELL SHE IS. I'M RESTARTING THE ENGINE...

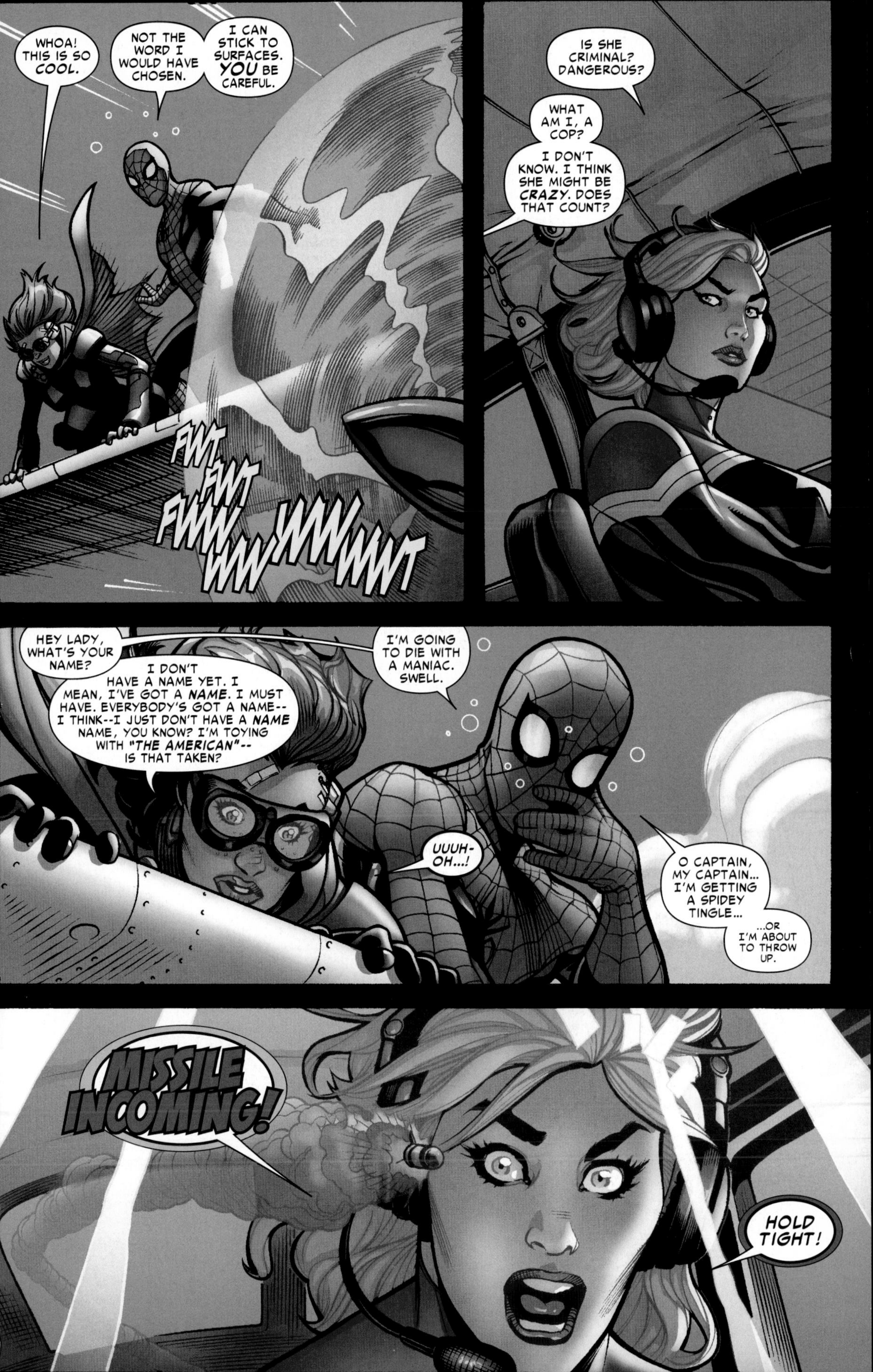
WHOA! THIS IS SO COOL.
NOT THE WORD I WOULD HAVE CHOSEN.
I CAN STICK TO SURFACES. YOU BE CAREFUL.
FWT FWT FWWWWWWWWWWWWT
IS SHE CRIMINAL? DANGEROUS?
WHAT AM I, A COP?
I DON'T KNOW. I THINK SHE MIGHT BE CRAZY. DOES THAT COUNT?
HEY LADY, WHAT'S YOUR NAME?
I DON'T HAVE A NAME YET. I MEAN, I'VE GOT A NAME. I MUST HAVE. EVERYBODY'S GOT A NAME-- I THINK--I JUST DON'T HAVE A NAME NAME, YOU KNOW? I'M TOYING WITH "THE AMERICAN"-- IS THAT TAKEN?
I'M GOING TO DIE WITH A MANIAC. SWELL.
UUUH-OH...!
O CAPTAIN, MY CAPTAIN... I'M GETTING A SPIDEY TINGLE...
...OR I'M ABOUT TO THROW UP.
MISSILE INCOMING!
HOLD TIGHT!

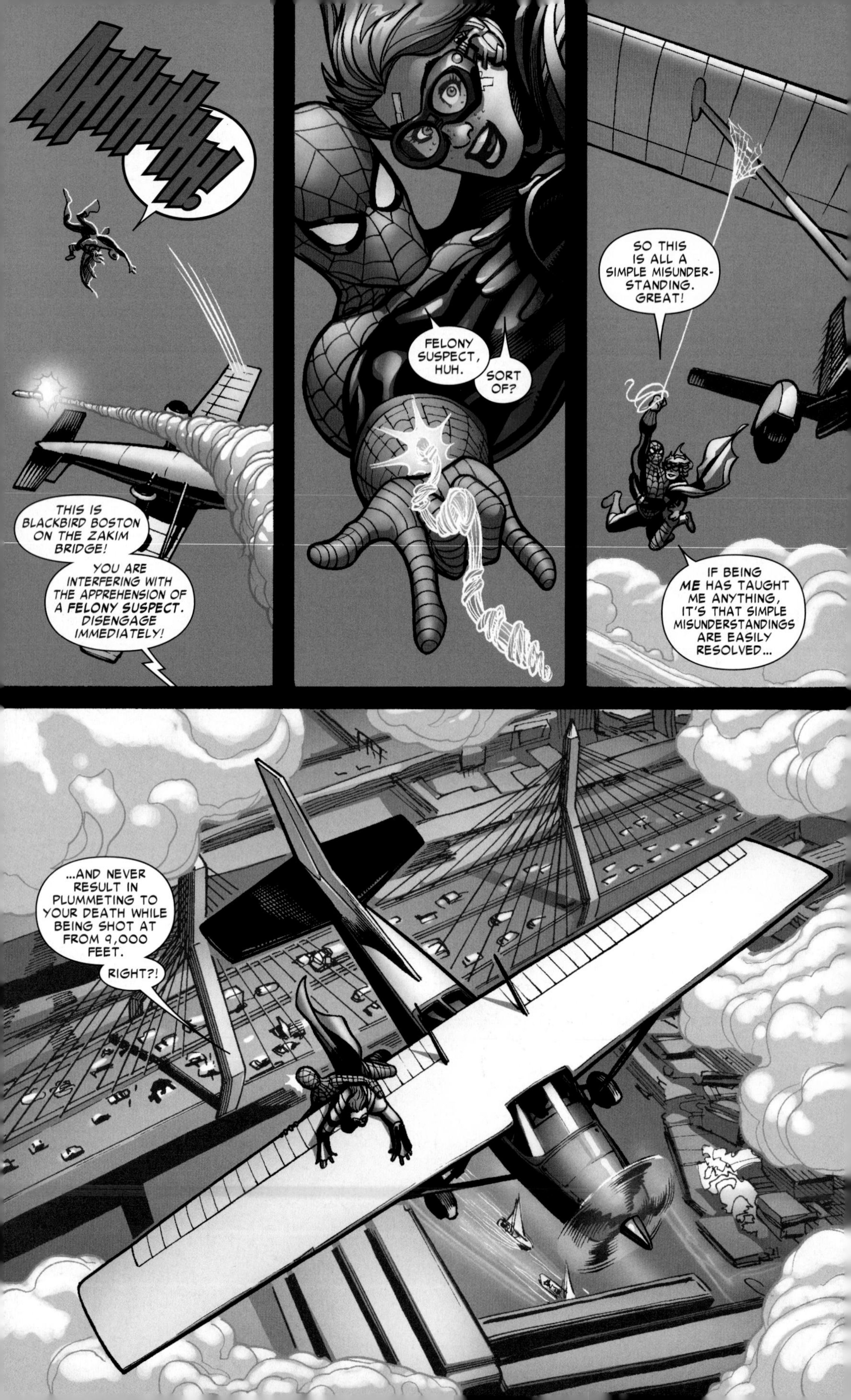
AHHHHHH!
THIS IS BLACKBIRD BOSTON ON THE ZAKIM BRIDGE!
YOU ARE INTERFERING WITH THE APPREHENSION OF A FELONY SUSPECT. DISENGAGE IMMEDIATELY!
FELONY SUSPECT, HUH.
SORT OF?
SO THIS IS ALL A SIMPLE MISUNDER-STANDING. GREAT!
IF BEING ME HAS TAUGHT ME ANYTHING, IT'S THAT SIMPLE MISUNDERSTANDINGS ARE EASILY RESOLVED...
...AND NEVER RESULT IN PLUMMETING TO YOUR DEATH WHILE BEING SHOT AT FROM 9,000 FEET.
RIGHT?!

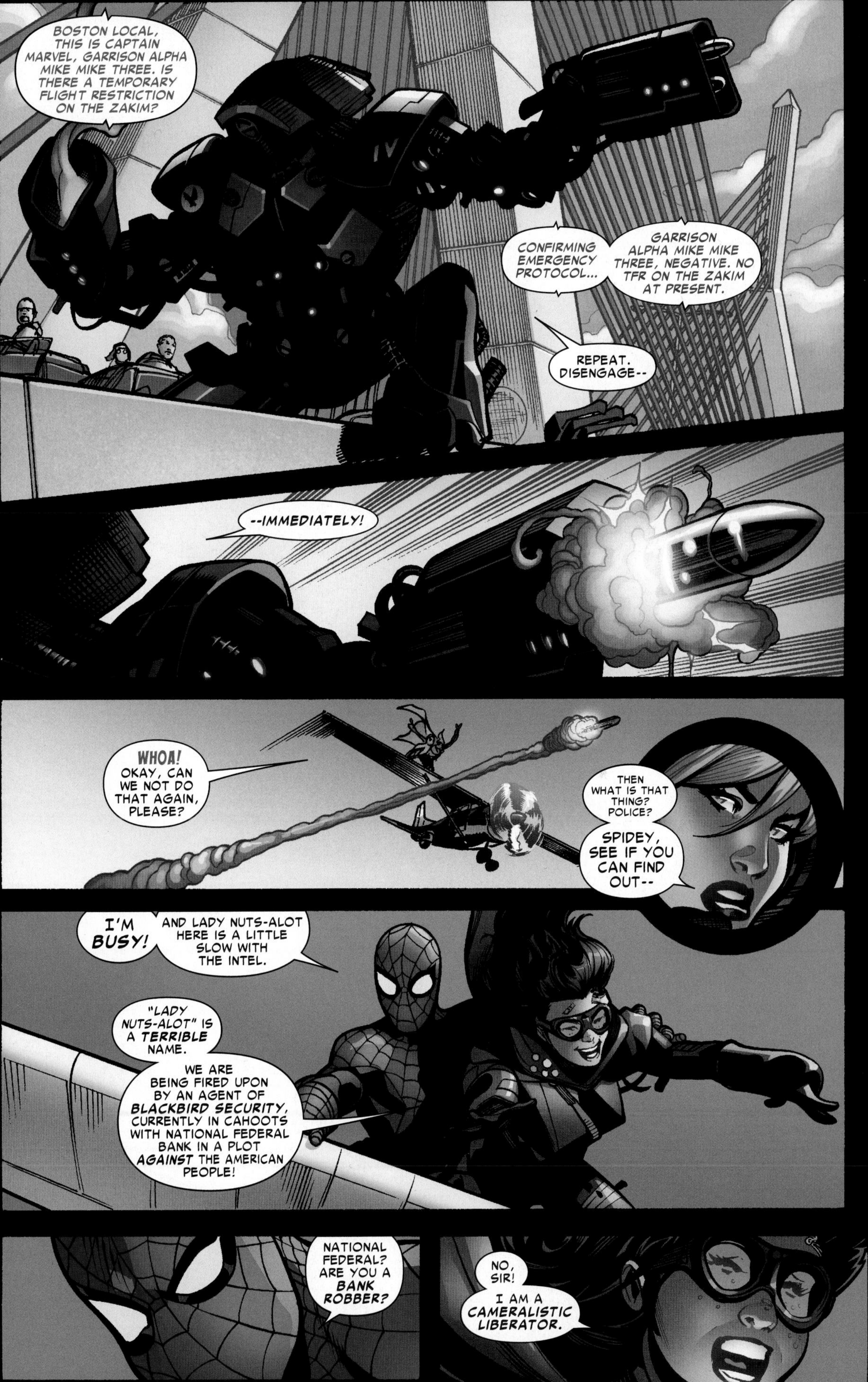
BOSTON LOCAL, THIS IS CAPTAIN MARVEL, GARRISON ALPHA MIKE MIKE THREE. IS THERE A TEMPORARY FLIGHT RESTRICTION ON THE ZAKIM?
CONFIRMING EMERGENCY PROTOCOL...
GARRISON ALPHA MIKE MIKE THREE, NEGATIVE. NO TFR ON THE ZAKIM AT PRESENT.
REPEAT. DISENGAGE--
--IMMEDIATELY!
WHOA! OKAY, CAN WE NOT DO THAT AGAIN, PLEASE?
THEN WHAT IS THAT THING? POLICE?
SPIDEY, SEE IF YOU CAN FIND OUT--
I'M BUSY!
AND LADY NUTS-ALOT HERE IS A LITTLE SLOW WITH THE INTEL.
"LADY NUTS-ALOT" IS A TERRIBLE NAME.
WE ARE BEING FIRED UPON BY AN AGENT OF BLACKBIRD SECURITY, CURRENTLY IN CAHOOTS WITH NATIONAL FEDERAL BANK IN A PLOT AGAINST THE AMERICAN PEOPLE!
NATIONAL FEDERAL? ARE YOU A BANK ROBBER?
NO, SIR!
I AM A CAMERALISTIC LIBERATOR.

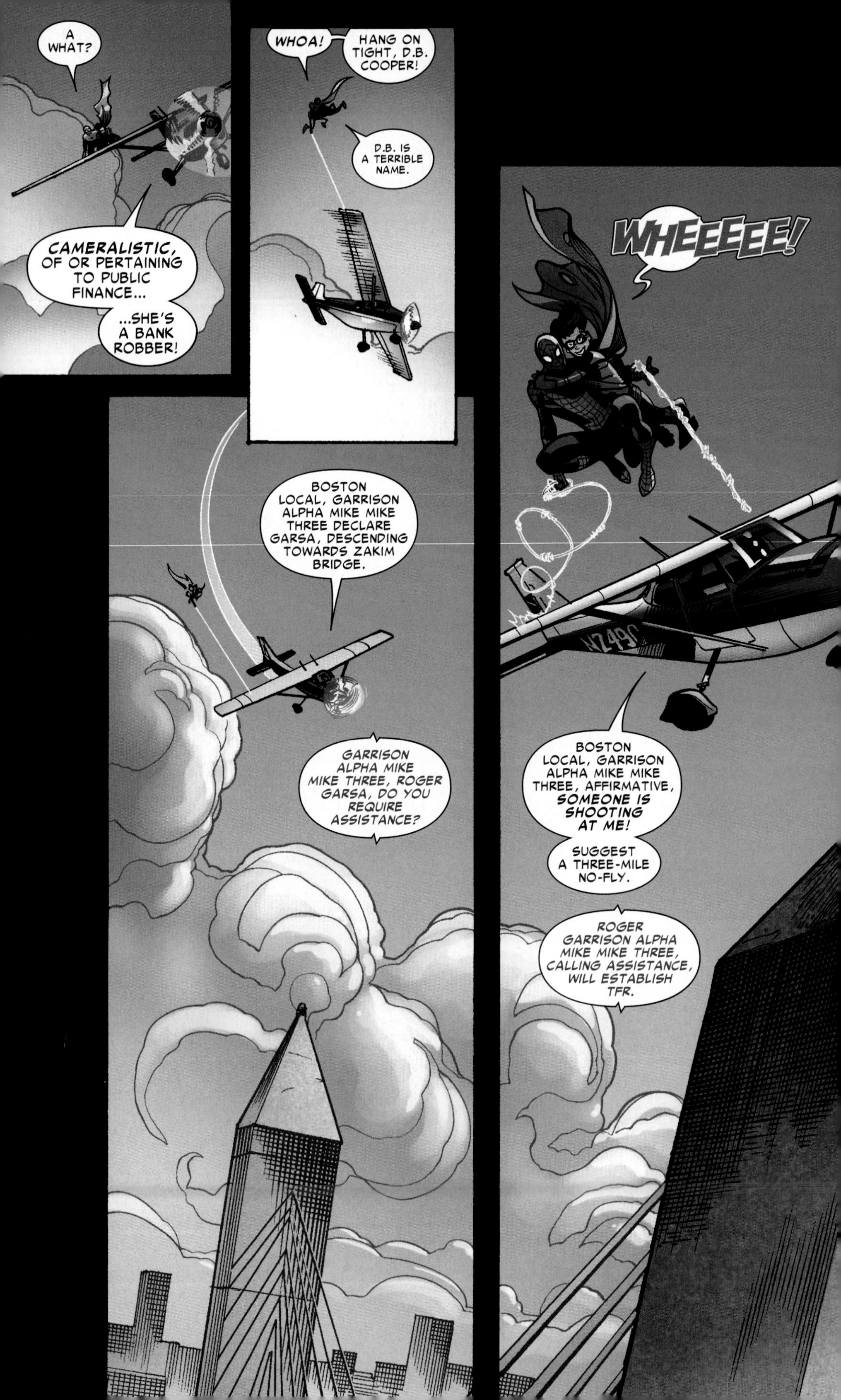

A WHAT?
CAMERALISTIC, OF OR PERTAINING TO PUBLIC FINANCE...
...SHE'S A BANK ROBBER!
WHOA!
HANG ON TIGHT, D.B. COOPER!
D.B. IS A TERRIBLE NAME.
WHEEEEE!
BOSTON LOCAL, GARRISON ALPHA MIKE MIKE THREE DECLARE GARSA, DESCENDING TOWARDS ZAKIM BRIDGE.
GARRISON ALPHA MIKE MIKE THREE, ROGER GARSA, DO YOU REQUIRE ASSISTANCE?
BOSTON LOCAL, GARRISON ALPHA MIKE MIKE THREE, AFFIRMATIVE, SOMEONE IS SHOOTING AT ME!
SUGGEST A THREE-MILE NO-FLY.
ROGER GARRISON ALPHA MIKE MIKE THREE, CALLING ASSISTANCE, WILL ESTABLISH TFR.

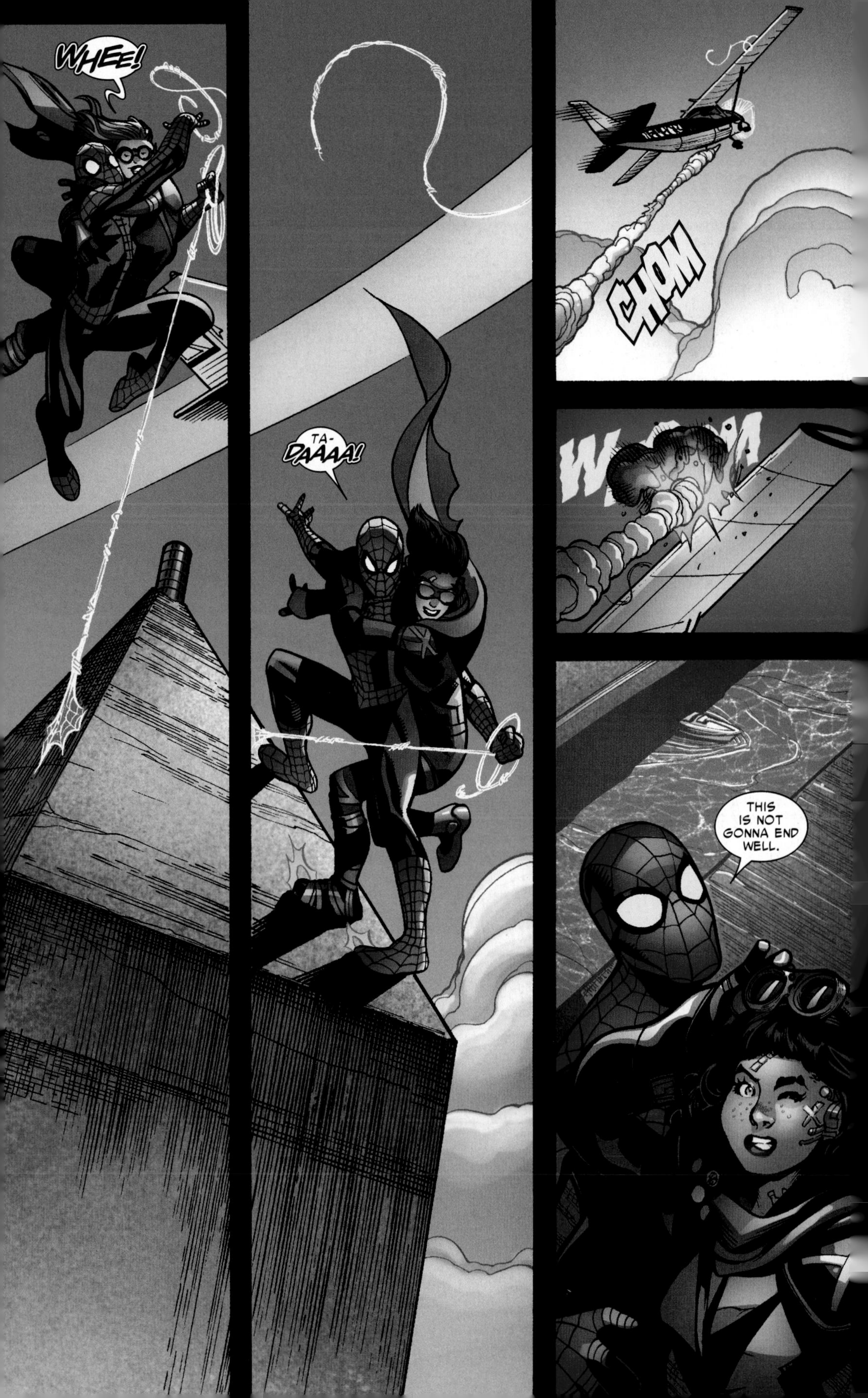
WHEE!
TA-DAAAA!
CHOM
THIS IS NOT GONNA END WELL.

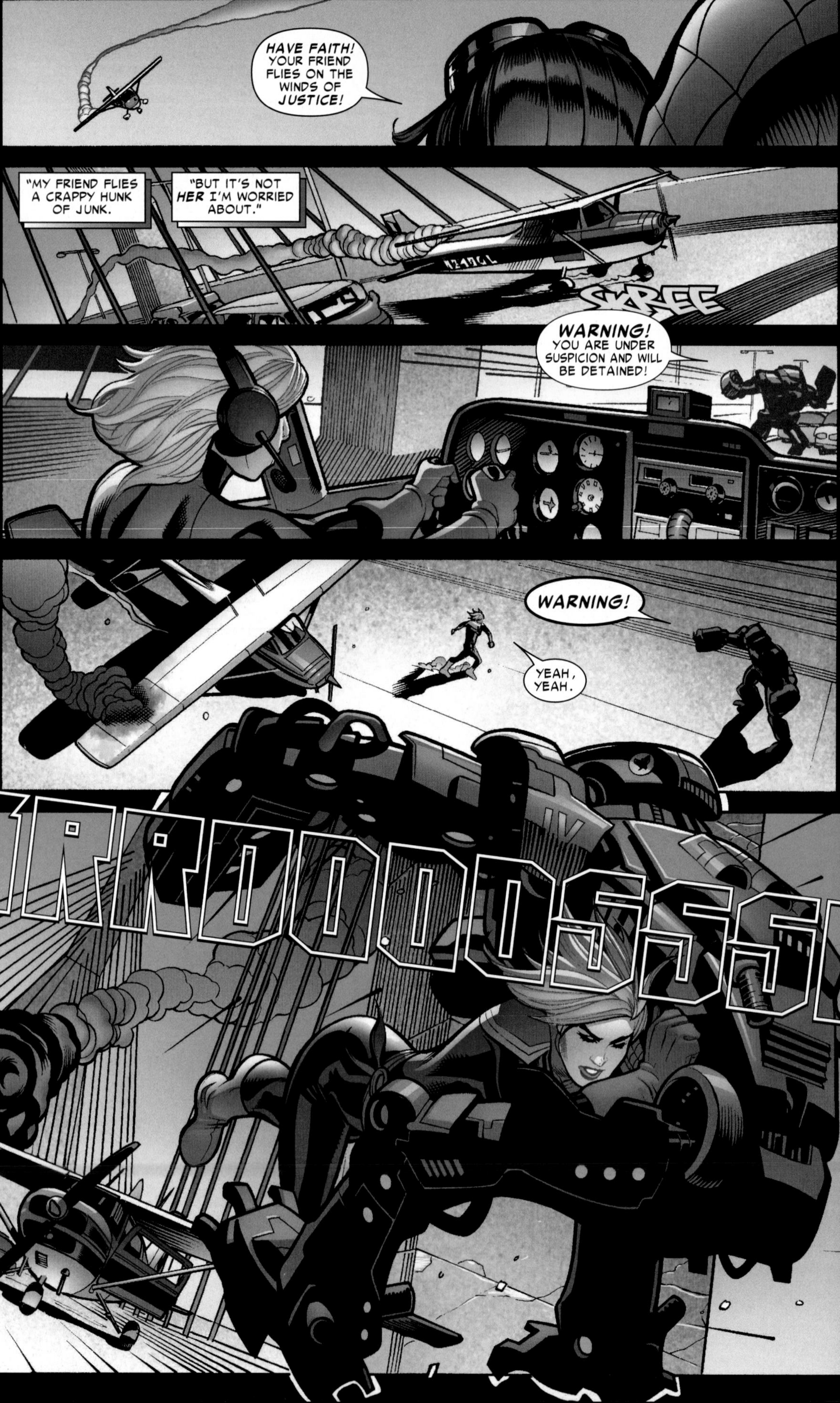

HAVE FAITH! YOUR FRIEND FLIES ON THE WINDS OF JUSTICE!
"MY FRIEND FLIES A CRAPPY HUNK OF JUNK.
"BUT IT'S NOT HER I'M WORRIED ABOUT."
SKREE
WARNING! YOU ARE UNDER SUSPICION AND WILL BE DETAINED!
WARNING!
YEAH, YEAH.

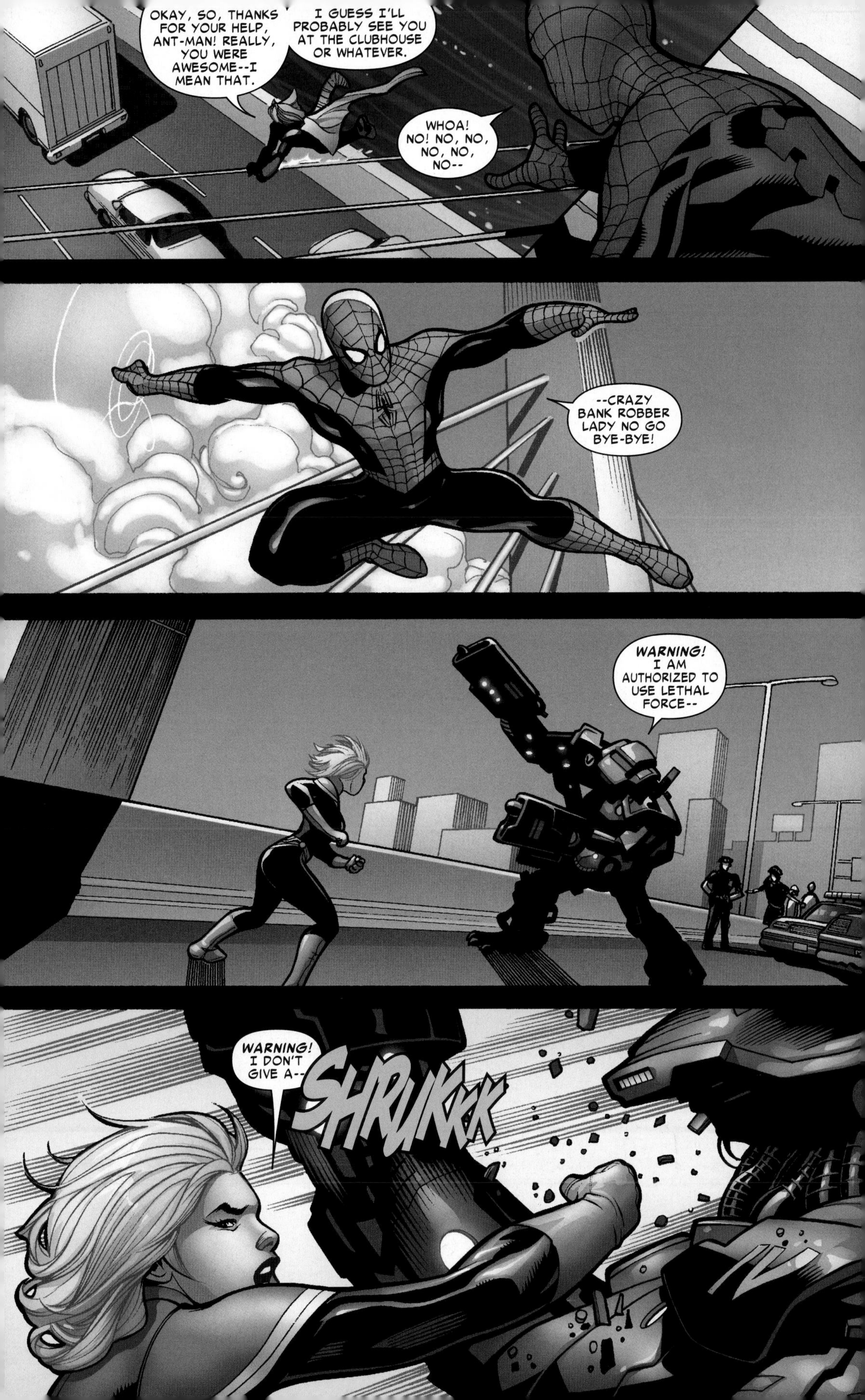
OKAY, SO, THANKS FOR YOUR HELP, ANT-MAN! REALLY, YOU WERE AWESOME--I MEAN THAT.
I GUESS I'LL PROBABLY SEE YOU AT THE CLUBHOUSE OR WHATEVER.
WHOA! NO! NO, NO, NO, NO, NO--
--CRAZY BANK ROBBER LADY NO GO BYE-BYE!
WARNING! I AM AUTHORIZED TO USE LETHAL FORCE--
WARNING! I DON'T GIVE A--
SHRUKKK

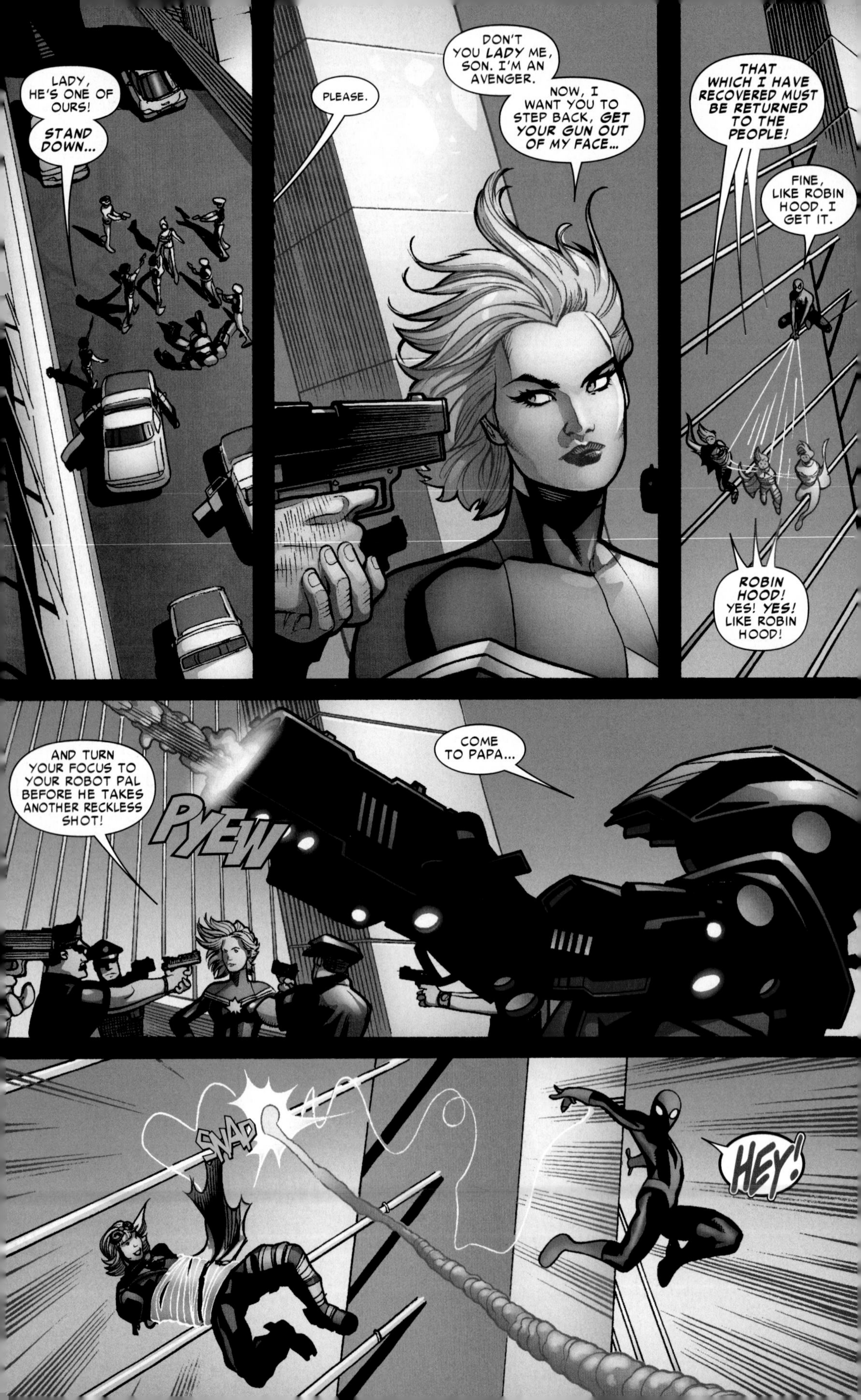

LADY, HE'S ONE OF OURS!
STAND DOWN...
PLEASE.
DON'T YOU LADY ME, SON. I'M AN AVENGER.
NOW, I WANT YOU TO STEP BACK, GET YOUR GUN OUT OF MY FACE...
THAT WHICH I HAVE RECOVERED MUST BE RETURNED TO THE PEOPLE!
FINE, LIKE ROBIN HOOD. I GET IT.
ROBIN HOOD! YES! YES! LIKE ROBIN HOOD!
AND TURN YOUR FOCUS TO YOUR ROBOT PAL BEFORE HE TAKES ANOTHER RECKLESS SHOT!
PYEW
COME TO PAPA...
SNAP
HEY!

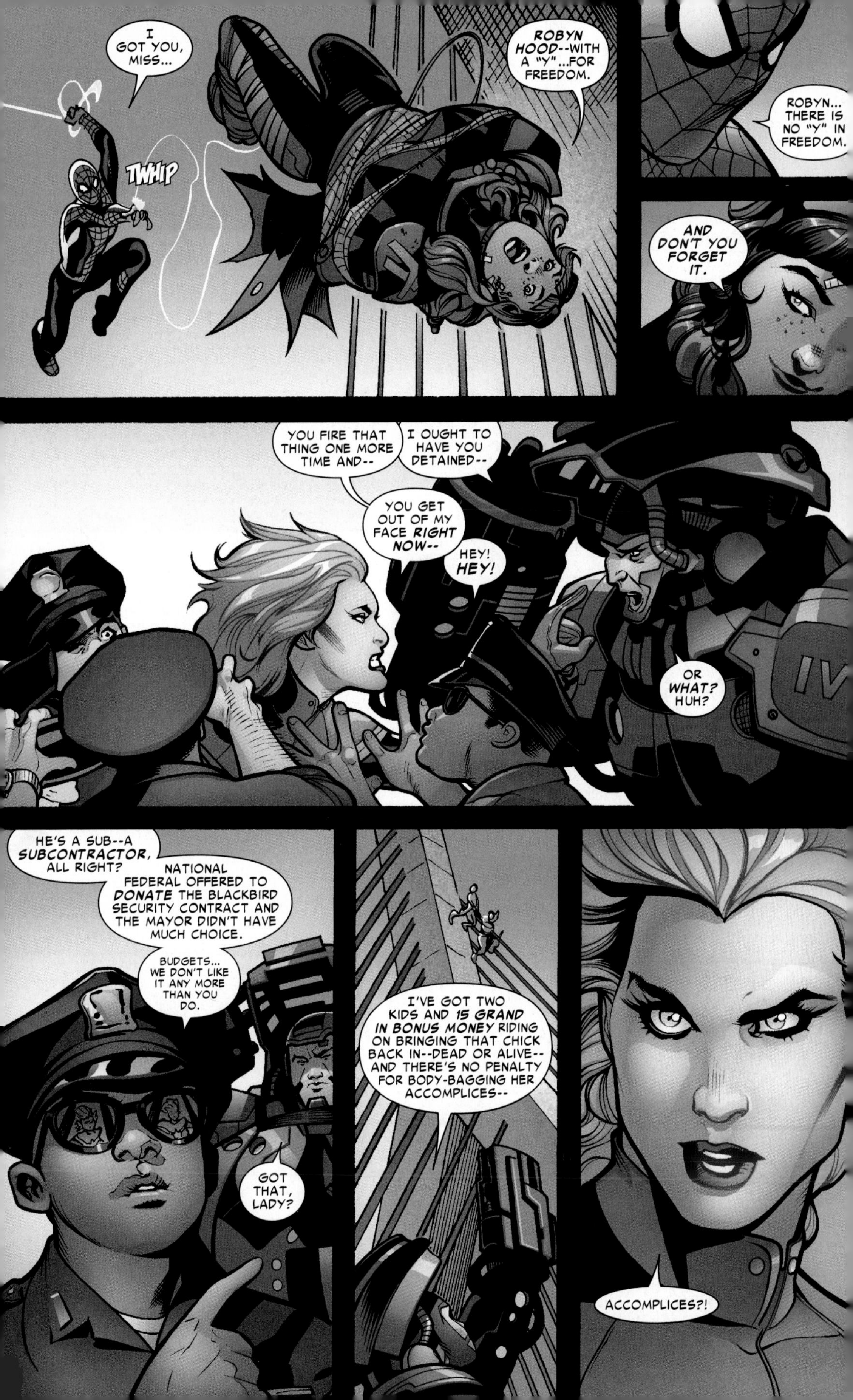
I GOT YOU, MISS...
TWHIP
ROBYN HOOD--WITH A "Y"...FOR FREEDOM.
ROBYN... THERE IS NO "Y" IN FREEDOM.
AND DON'T YOU FORGET IT.
YOU FIRE THAT THING ONE MORE TIME AND--
I OUGHT TO HAVE YOU DETAINED--
YOU GET OUT OF MY FACE RIGHT NOW--
HEY! HEY!
OR WHAT? HUH?
HE'S A SUB--A SUBCONTRACTOR, ALL RIGHT?
NATIONAL FEDERAL OFFERED TO DONATE THE BLACKBIRD SECURITY CONTRACT AND THE MAYOR DIDN'T HAVE MUCH CHOICE.
BUDGETS... WE DON'T LIKE IT ANY MORE THAN YOU DO.
GOT THAT, LADY?
I'VE GOT TWO KIDS AND 15 GRAND IN BONUS MONEY RIDING ON BRINGING THAT CHICK BACK IN--DEAD OR ALIVE--AND THERE'S NO PENALTY FOR BODY-BAGGING HER ACCOMPLICES--
ACCOMPLICES?!

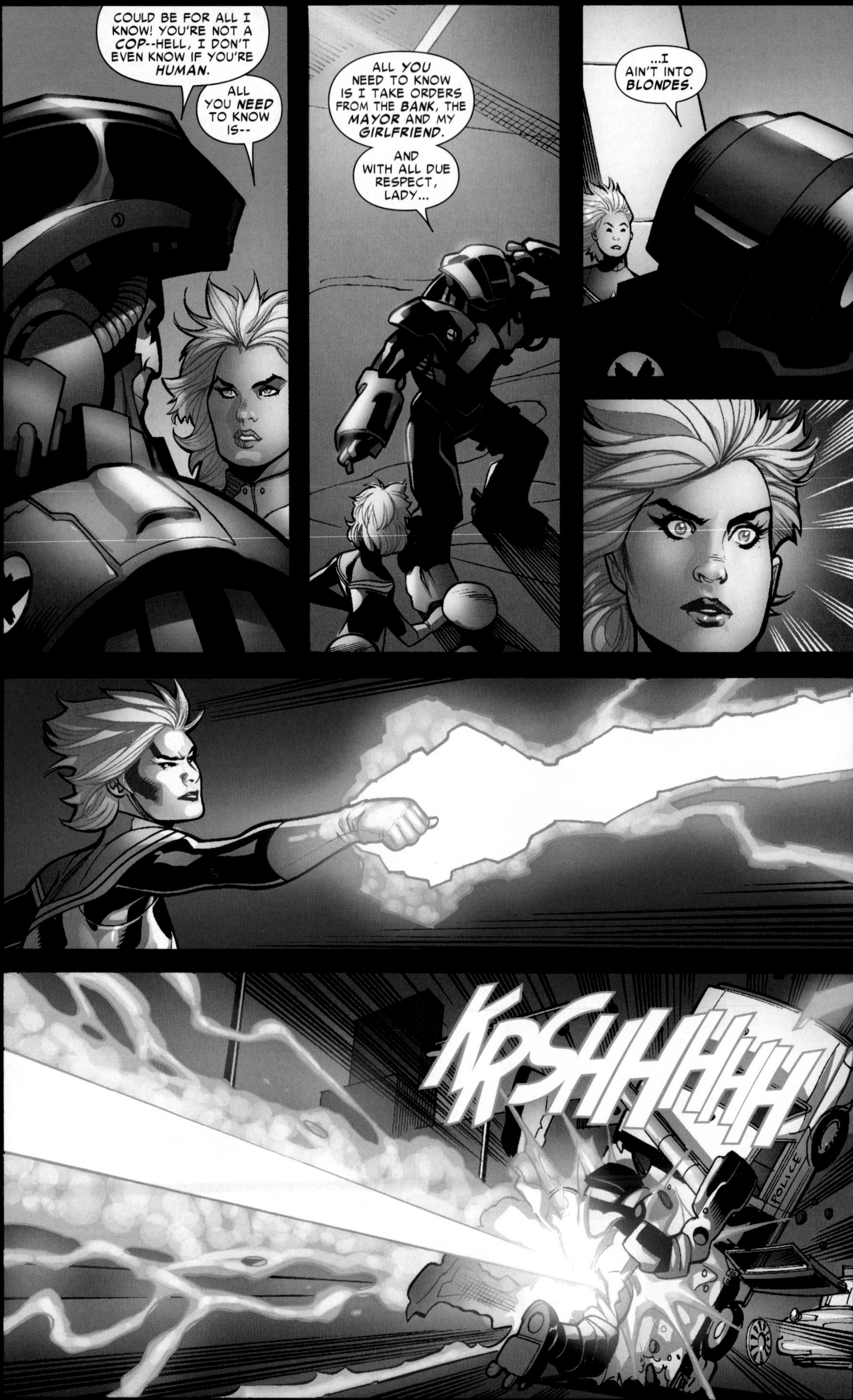
COULD BE FOR ALL I KNOW! YOU'RE NOT A COP--HELL, I DON'T EVEN KNOW IF YOU'RE HUMAN.
ALL YOU NEED TO KNOW IS--
ALL YOU NEED TO KNOW IS I TAKE ORDERS FROM THE BANK, THE MAYOR AND MY GIRLFRIEND.
AND WITH ALL DUE RESPECT, LADY...
...I AIN'T INTO BLONDES.
KRSHHHHHH
POLICE

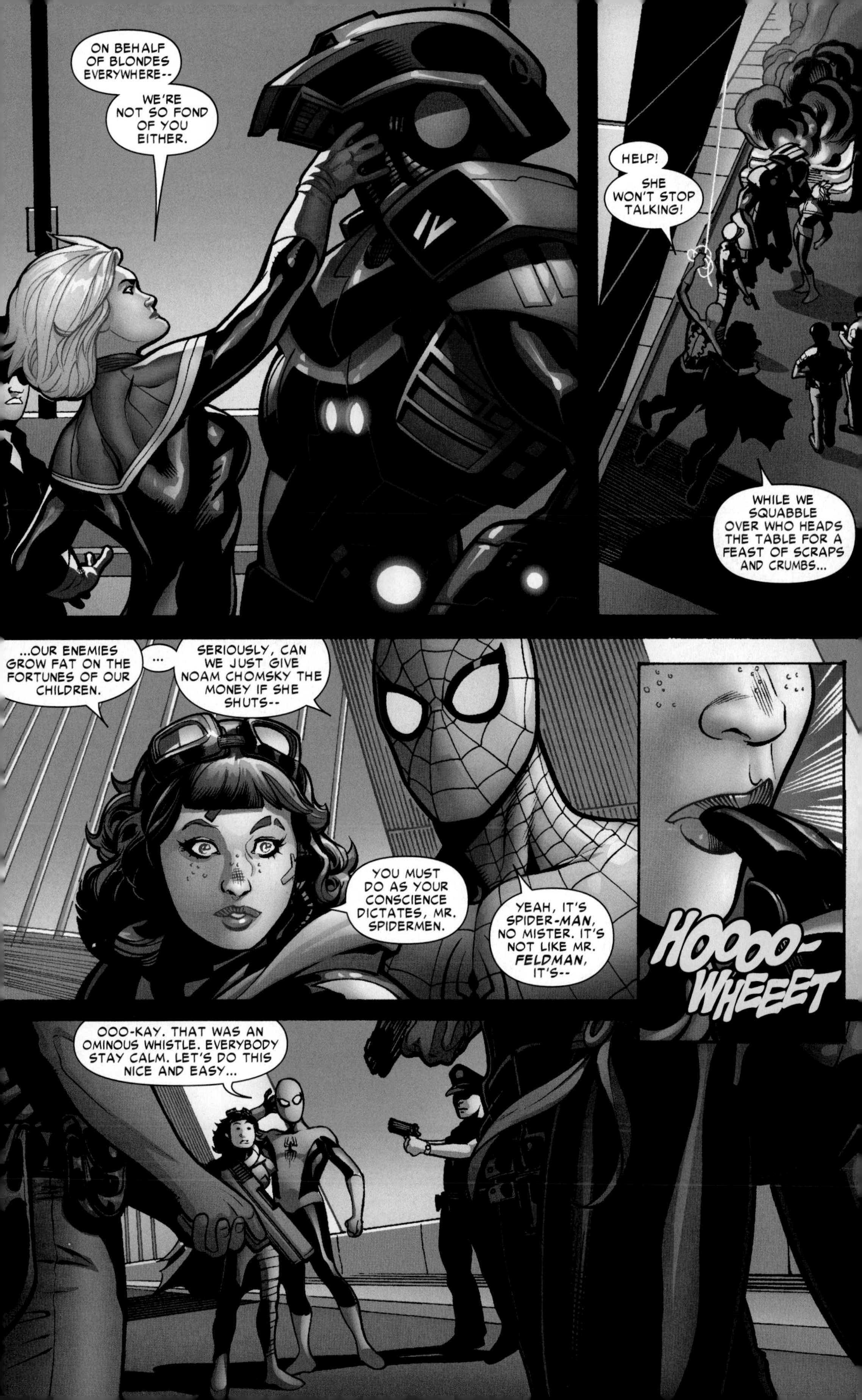
ON BEHALF OF BLONDES EVERYWHERE--
WE'RE NOT SO FOND OF YOU EITHER.
HELP! SHE WON'T STOP TALKING!
WHILE WE SQUABBLE OVER WHO HEADS THE TABLE FOR A FEAST OF SCRAPS AND CRUMBS...
...OUR ENEMIES GROW FAT ON THE FORTUNES OF OUR CHILDREN.
...
SERIOUSLY, CAN WE JUST GIVE NOAM CHOMSKY THE MONEY IF SHE SHUTS--
YOU MUST DO AS YOUR CONSCIENCE DICTATES, MR. SPIDERMEN.
YEAH, IT'S SPIDER-MAN, NO MISTER. IT'S NOT LIKE MR. FELDMAN, IT'S--
HOOOO-WHEEET
OOO-KAY. THAT WAS AN OMINOUS WHISTLE. EVERYBODY STAY CALM. LET'S DO THIS NICE AND EASY...

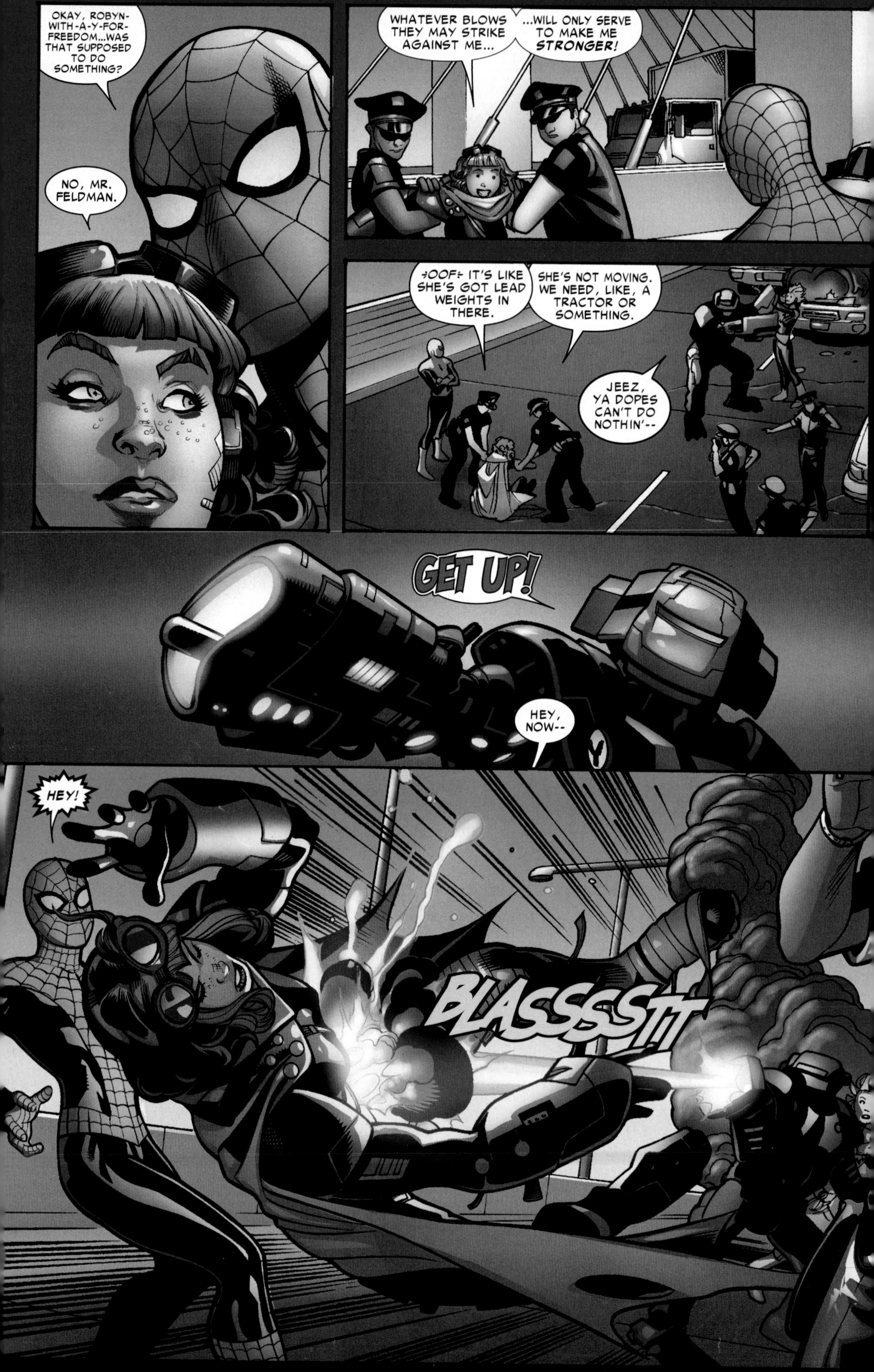
OKAY, ROBYN-WITH-A-Y-FOR-FREEDOM...WAS THAT SUPPOSED TO DO SOMETHING?
NO, MR. FELDMAN.
WHATEVER BLOWS THEY MAY STRIKE AGAINST ME...
...WILL ONLY SERVE TO MAKE ME STRONGER!
=OOF= IT'S LIKE SHE'S GOT LEAD WEIGHTS IN THERE.
SHE'S NOT MOVING. WE NEED, LIKE, A TRACTOR OR SOMETHING.
JEEZ, YA DOPES CAN'T DO NOTHIN'--
GET UP!
HEY, NOW--
HEY!
BLASSSSTT

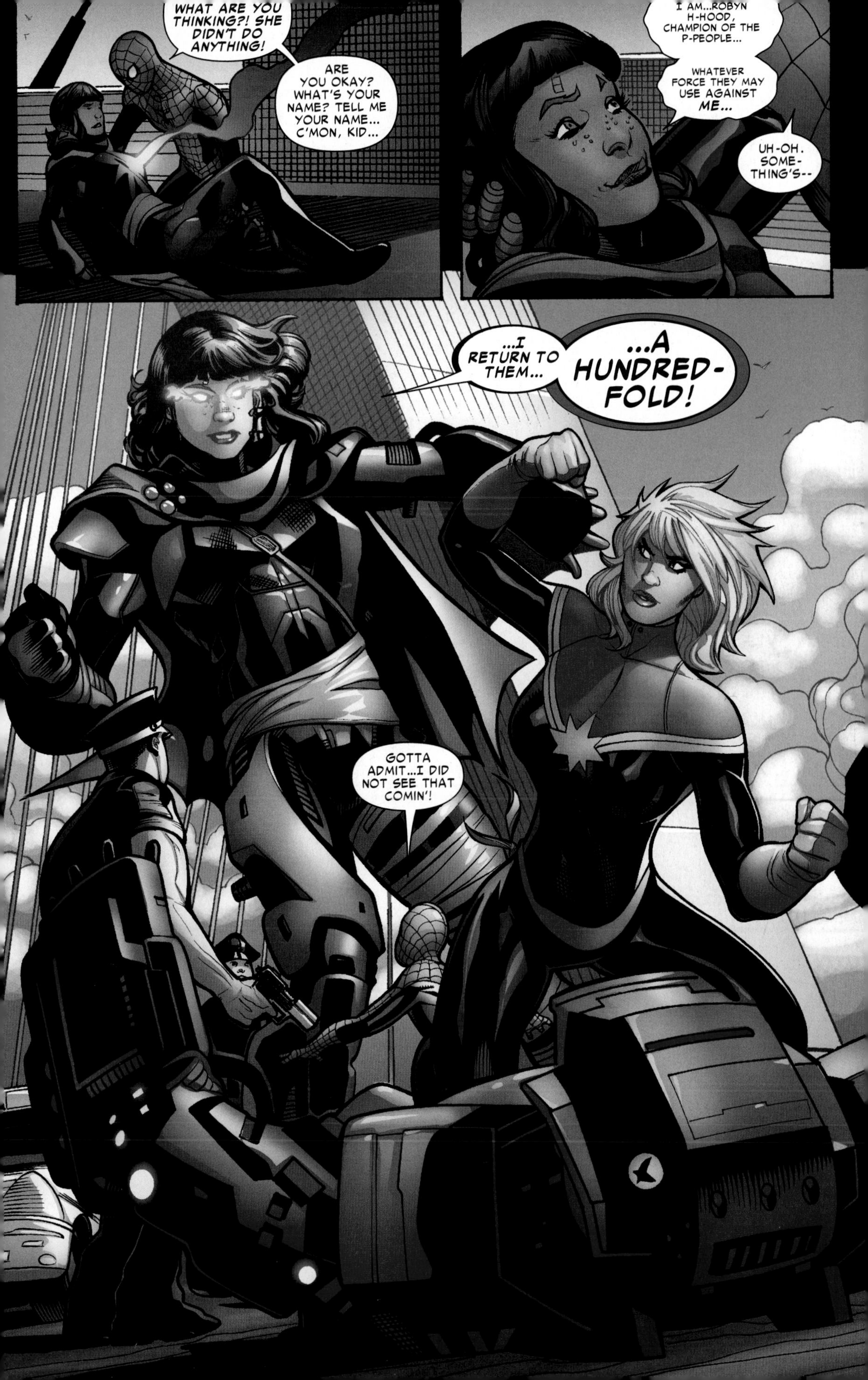
WHAT ARE YOU THINKING?! SHE DIDN'T DO ANYTHING!
ARE YOU OKAY? WHAT'S YOUR NAME? TELL ME YOUR NAME... C'MON, KID...
I AM...ROBYN H-HOOD, CHAMPION OF THE P-PEOPLE...
WHATEVER FORCE THEY MAY USE AGAINST ME...
UH-OH. SOME-THING'S--
...I RETURN TO THEM...
...A HUNDRED-FOLD!
GOTTA ADMIT...I DID NOT SEE THAT COMIN'!

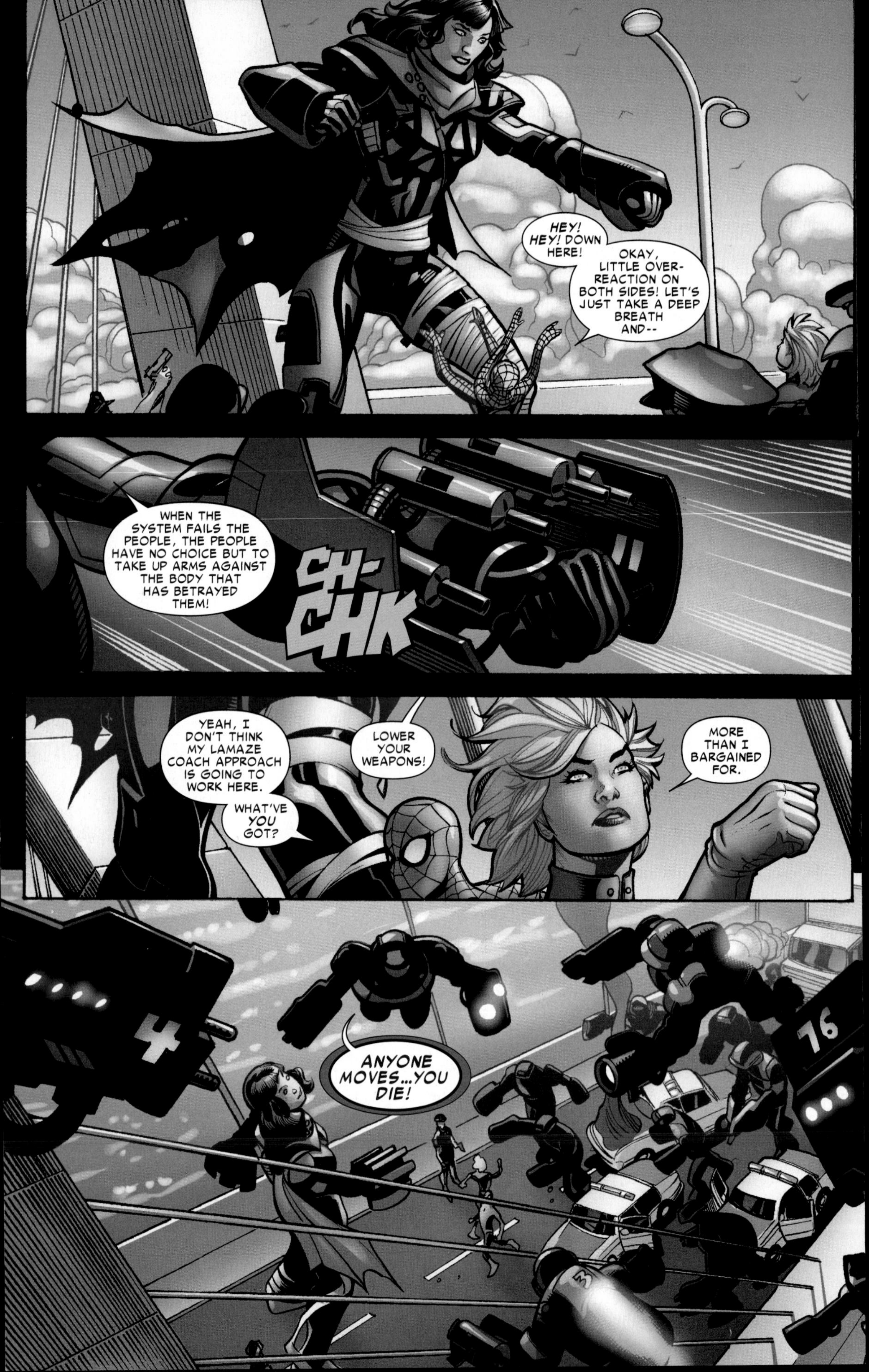
HEY! HEY! DOWN HERE!
OKAY, LITTLE OVER-REACTION ON BOTH SIDES! LET'S JUST TAKE A DEEP BREATH AND--
WHEN THE SYSTEM FAILS THE PEOPLE, THE PEOPLE HAVE NO CHOICE BUT TO TAKE UP ARMS AGAINST THE BODY THAT HAS BETRAYED THEM!
CH-CHK
YEAH, I DON'T THINK MY LAMAZE COACH APPROACH IS GOING TO WORK HERE.
WHAT'VE YOU GOT?
LOWER YOUR WEAPONS!
MORE THAN I BARGAINED FOR.
ANYONE MOVES...YOU DIE!
4
76

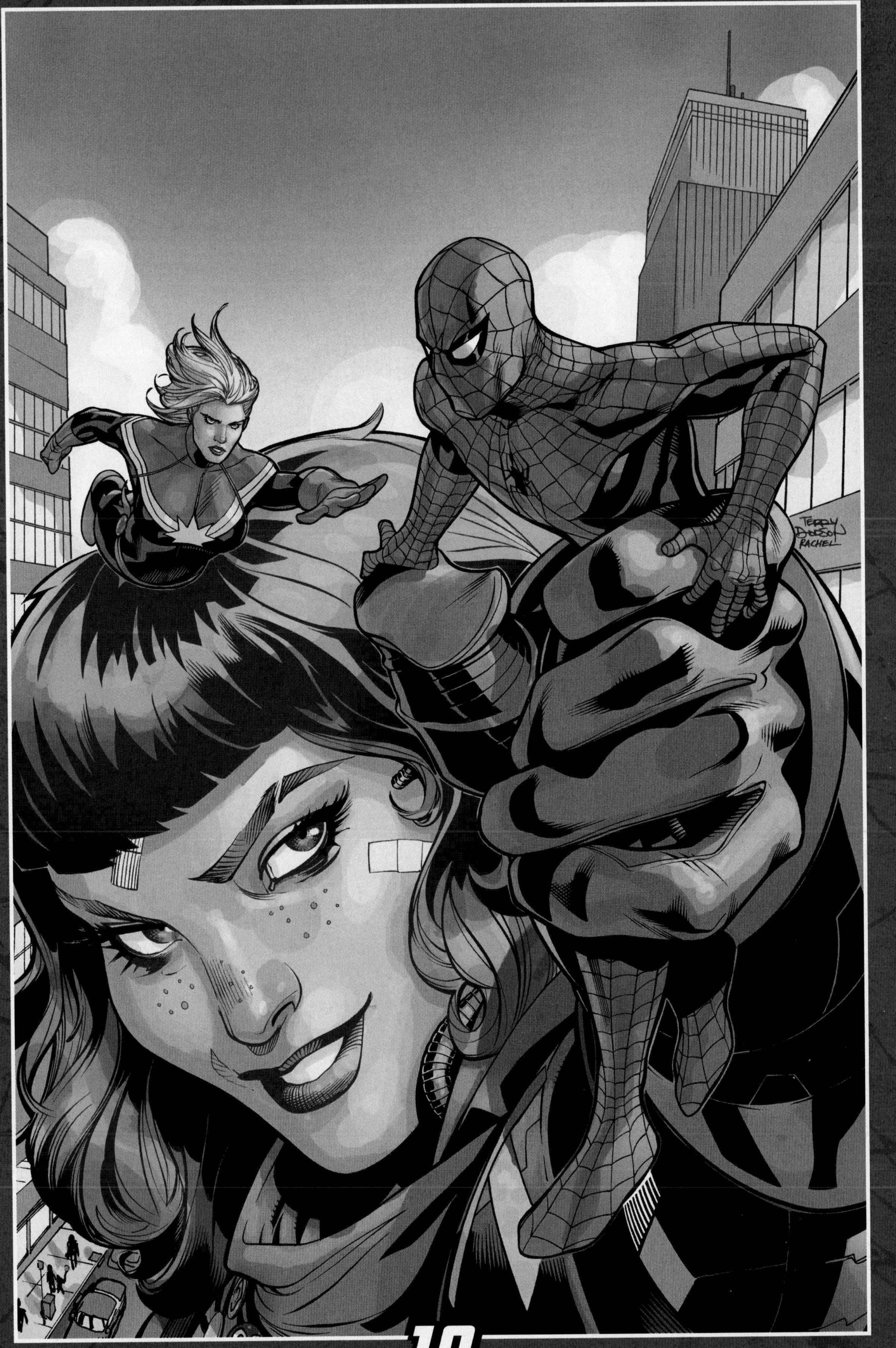
TERRY
DODSON
RACHEL

10

While attending a demonstration in radiology, high school student Peter Parker was bitten by a spider which had accidentally been exposed to radioactive rays. Through a miracle of science, Peter soon found that he had gained the spider's powers…and had, in effect, become a human spider! Later he joined the Avengers. And now he is the…

AVENGING SPIDER-MAN

When U.S. Air Force officer Col. Carol Danvers was caught in the explosion of an alien device with the Kree warrior Captain Marvel, Carol's genetic code was irreversibly altered, granting her the power to fly, incredibl strength, and an ability to harness and project energy. The two were allies for a time, until Captain Marvel lost h life. Now, Carol has chosen to take up the mantle in his honor. She's an intergalactic adventurer, a space-farin super heroine, and an Avenger. She's Earth's Mightiest Hero, the all-new…

CAPTAIN MARVEL

I don't know who I am or where I came from but I will take back what has been taken by those that have too much and return it to those that have too little! I am…

ROBYN HOOD

AVENGING SPIDER-MAN

PREVIOUSLY…

Ace pilot Carol Danvers was flying Peter Parker to Boston to visit his Aunt May when they collided midair with Robyn Hood! Robyn (with-a-Y-for-freedom) is a suspected bank robber on the run from National Federal Bank. Now Captain Marvel and Mr. Spider-Man are trying to sort things out between Robyn, the evil Bank and their private security team of ~~men in robot suits~~ oppressors of the people but they just learned that shooting Robyn causes her to absorb the energy and grow ~~50 feet tall!~~ bigger and stronger than ever before!

WRITER: **KELLY SUE DeCONNICK**   PENCILS: **TERRY DODSON**

INKER: **RACHEL DODSON**   COLORS: **EDGAR DELGADO**

LETTERER: **VC's JOE CARAMAGNA**   COVER: **TERRY AND RACHEL DODSON**

EDITOR: **ELLIE PYLE**   SENIOR EDITOR: **STEPHEN WACKER**

EXECUTIVE EDITOR: **TOM BREVOORT**   EDITOR IN CHIEF: **AXEL ALONSO**

CHIEF CREATIVE OFFICER: **JOE QUESADA**   PUBLISHER: **DAN BUCKLEY**   EXECUTIVE PRODUCER: **ALAN FINE**

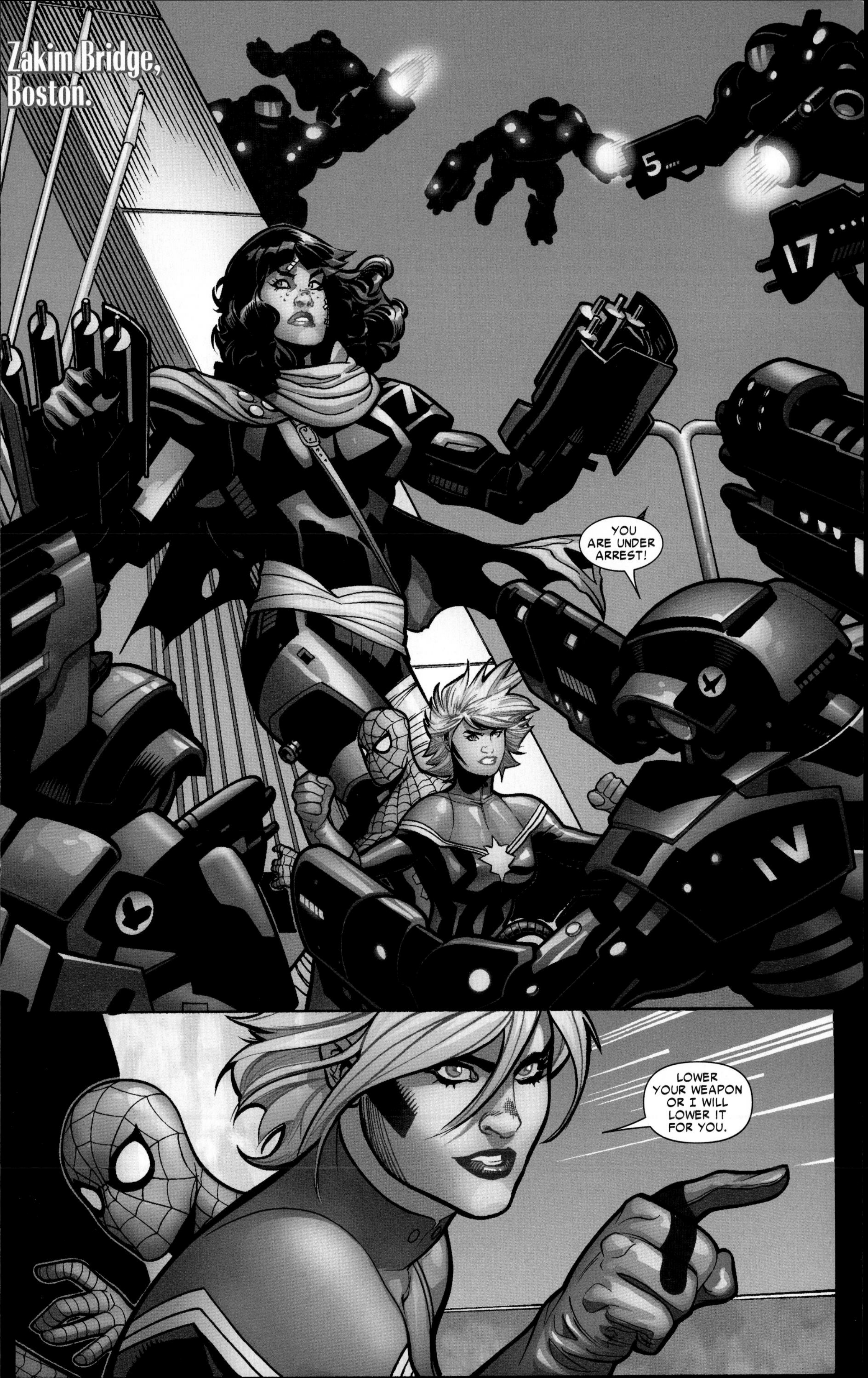
Zakim Bridge, Boston.
5
17
YOU ARE UNDER ARREST!
IV
LOWER YOUR WEAPON OR I WILL LOWER IT FOR YOU.

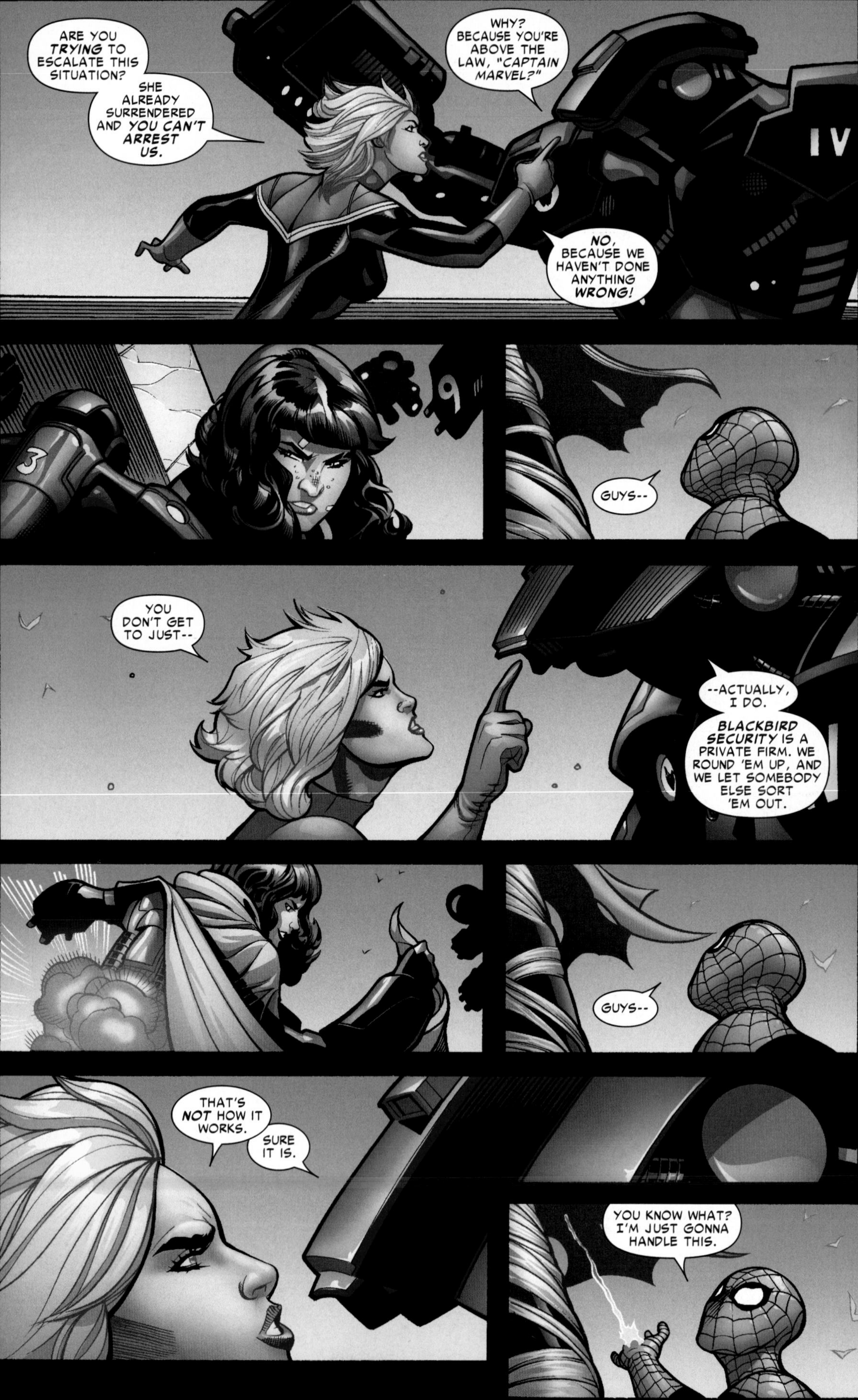
ARE YOU TRYING TO ESCALATE THIS SITUATION?
SHE ALREADY SURRENDERED AND YOU CAN'T ARREST US.
WHY? BECAUSE YOU'RE ABOVE THE LAW, "CAPTAIN MARVEL?"
NO, BECAUSE WE HAVEN'T DONE ANYTHING WRONG!
GUYS--
YOU DON'T GET TO JUST--
--ACTUALLY, I DO.
BLACKBIRD SECURITY IS A PRIVATE FIRM. WE ROUND 'EM UP, AND WE LET SOMEBODY ELSE SORT 'EM OUT.
GUYS--
THAT'S NOT HOW IT WORKS.
SURE IT IS.
YOU KNOW WHAT? I'M JUST GONNA HANDLE THIS.

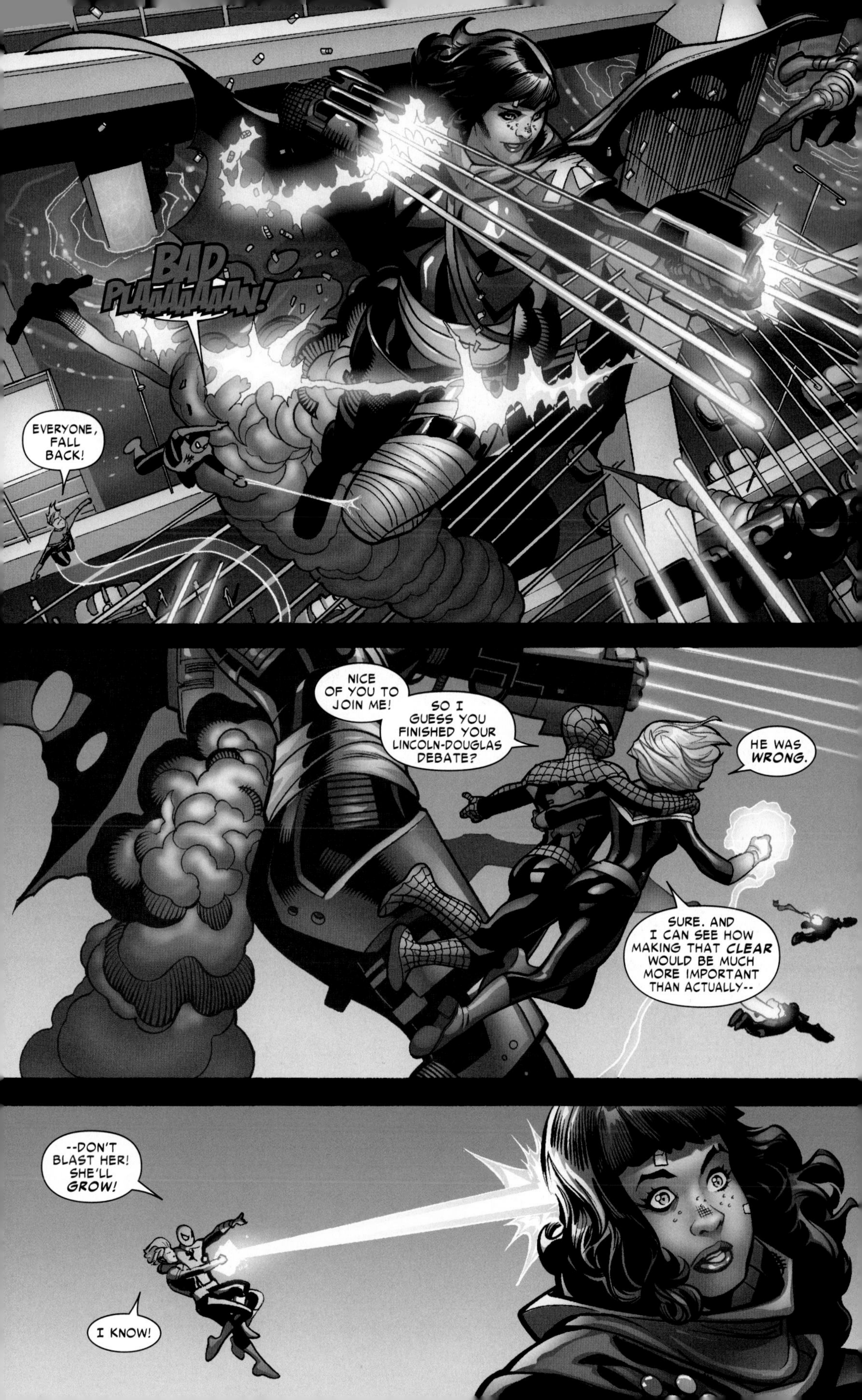
BAD PLAAAAAAAN!
EVERYONE, FALL BACK!
NICE OF YOU TO JOIN ME!
SO I GUESS YOU FINISHED YOUR LINCOLN-DOUGLAS DEBATE?
HE WAS WRONG.
SURE. AND I CAN SEE HOW MAKING THAT CLEAR WOULD BE MUCH MORE IMPORTANT THAN ACTUALLY--
--DON'T BLAST HER! SHE'LL GROW!
I KNOW!

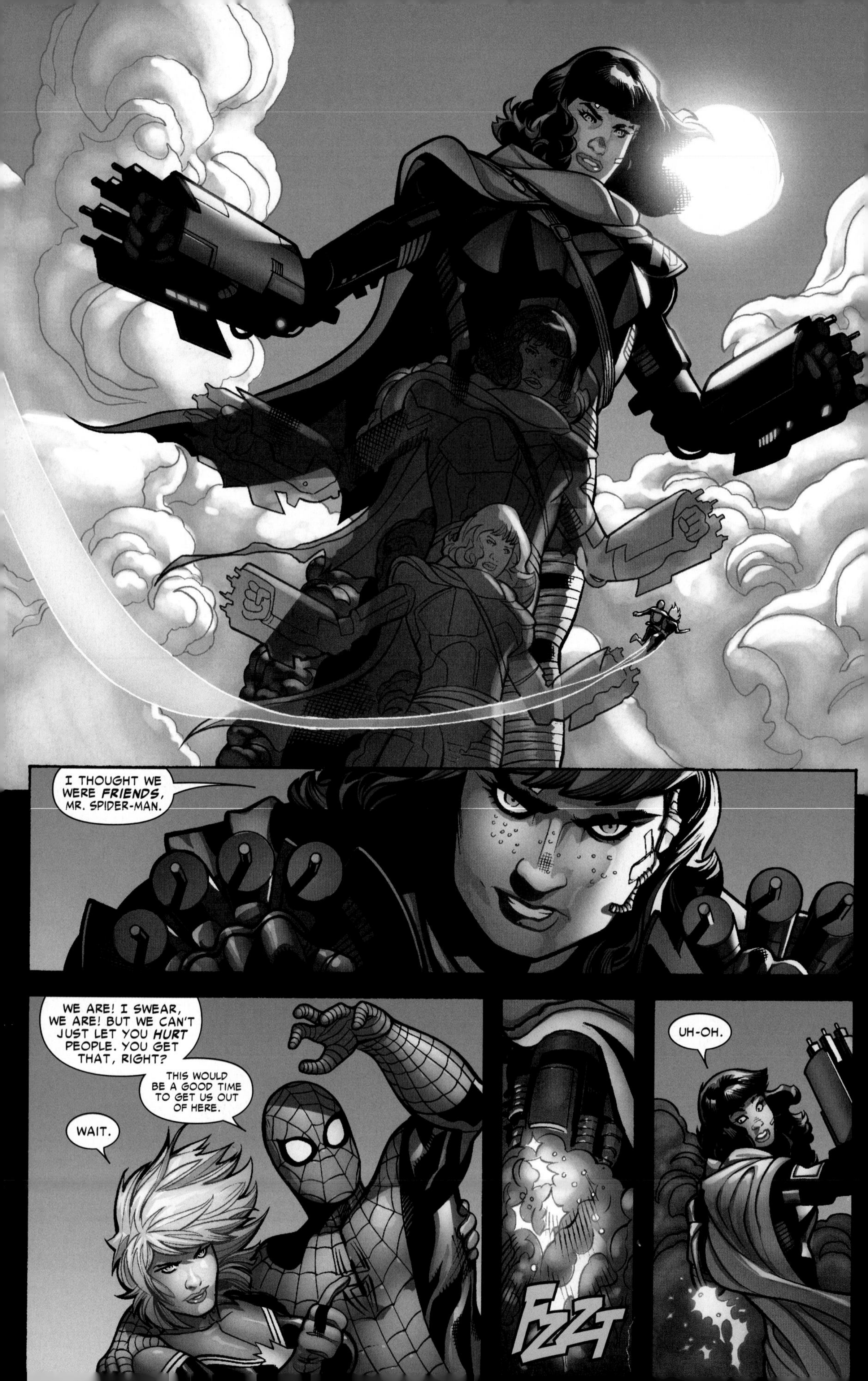
I THOUGHT WE WERE FRIENDS, MR. SPIDER-MAN.
WE ARE! I SWEAR, WE ARE! BUT WE CAN'T JUST LET YOU HURT PEOPLE. YOU GET THAT, RIGHT?
THIS WOULD BE A GOOD TIME TO GET US OUT OF HERE.
WAIT.
FZZT
UH-OH.

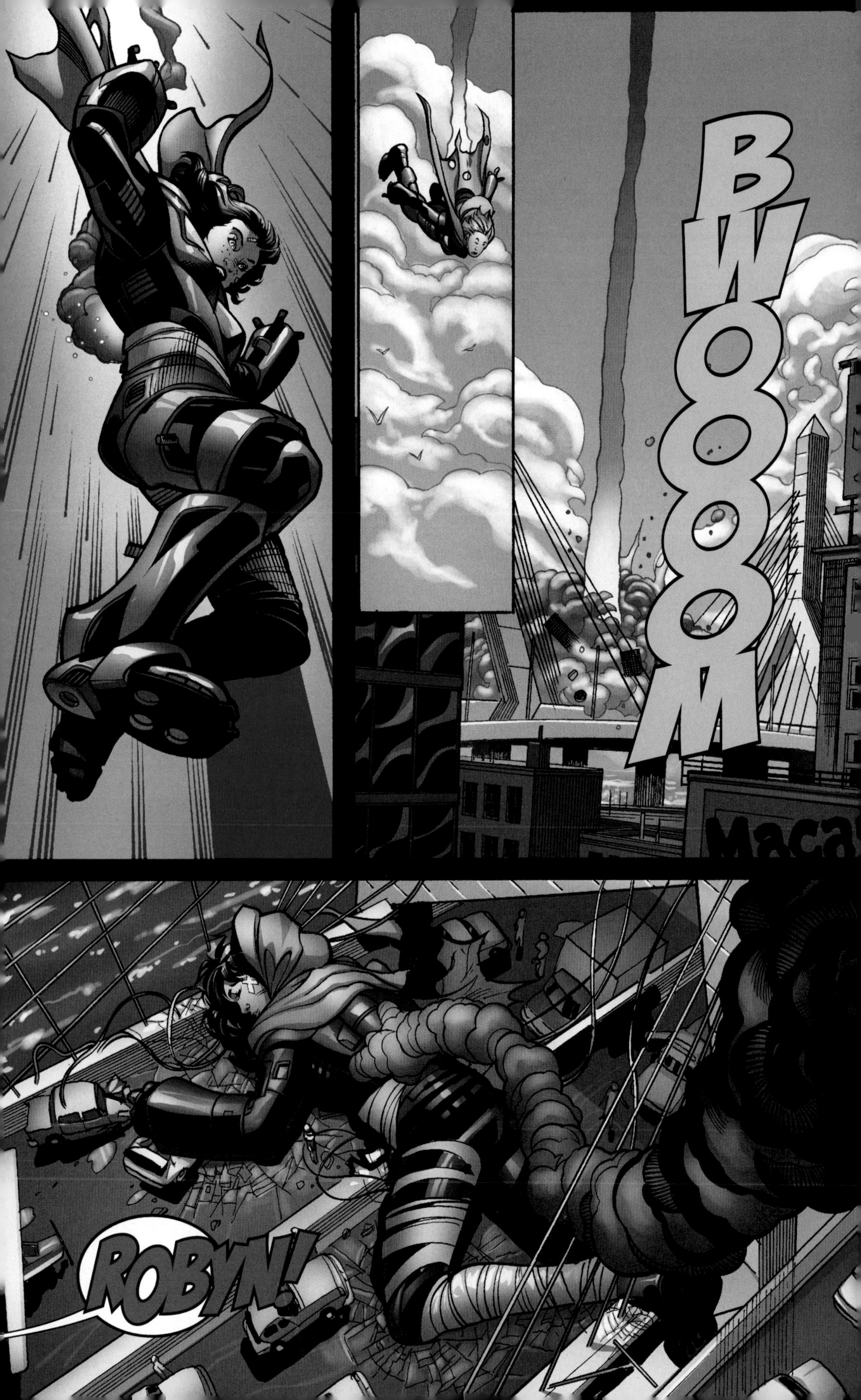
BWOOOOM
Maca
ROBYN!

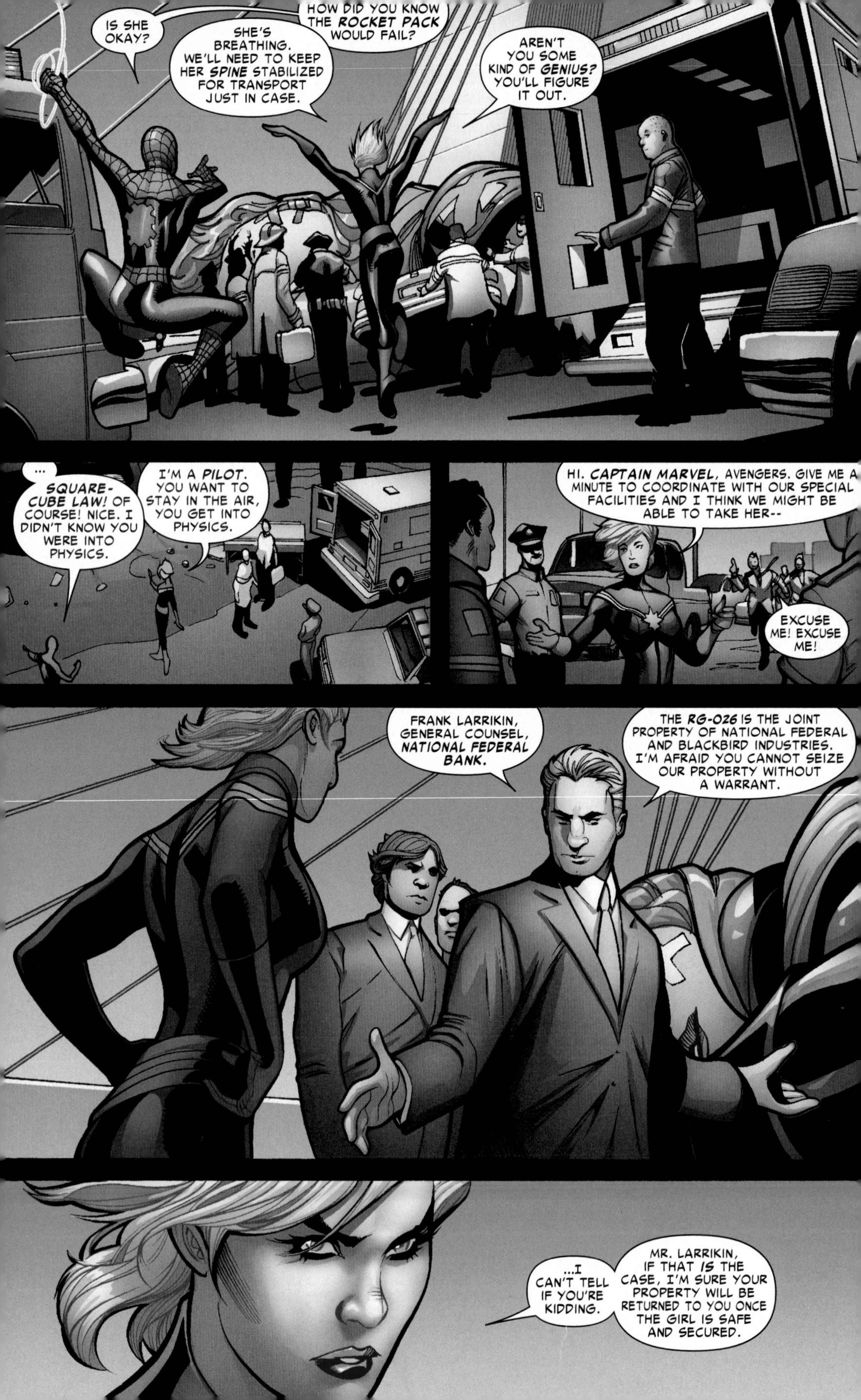
IS SHE OKAY?
SHE'S BREATHING. WE'LL NEED TO KEEP HER SPINE STABILIZED FOR TRANSPORT JUST IN CASE.
HOW DID YOU KNOW THE ROCKET PACK WOULD FAIL?
AREN'T YOU SOME KIND OF GENIUS? YOU'LL FIGURE IT OUT.
... SQUARE-CUBE LAW! OF COURSE! NICE. I DIDN'T KNOW YOU WERE INTO PHYSICS.
I'M A PILOT. YOU WANT TO STAY IN THE AIR, YOU GET INTO PHYSICS.
HI. CAPTAIN MARVEL, AVENGERS. GIVE ME A MINUTE TO COORDINATE WITH OUR SPECIAL FACILITIES AND I THINK WE MIGHT BE ABLE TO TAKE HER--
EXCUSE ME! EXCUSE ME!
FRANK LARRIKIN, GENERAL COUNSEL, NATIONAL FEDERAL BANK.
THE RG-026 IS THE JOINT PROPERTY OF NATIONAL FEDERAL AND BLACKBIRD INDUSTRIES. I'M AFRAID YOU CANNOT SEIZE OUR PROPERTY WITHOUT A WARRANT.
MR. LARRIKIN, IF THAT IS THE CASE, I'M SURE YOUR PROPERTY WILL BE RETURNED TO YOU ONCE THE GIRL IS SAFE AND SECURED.
...I CAN'T TELL IF YOU'RE KIDDING.

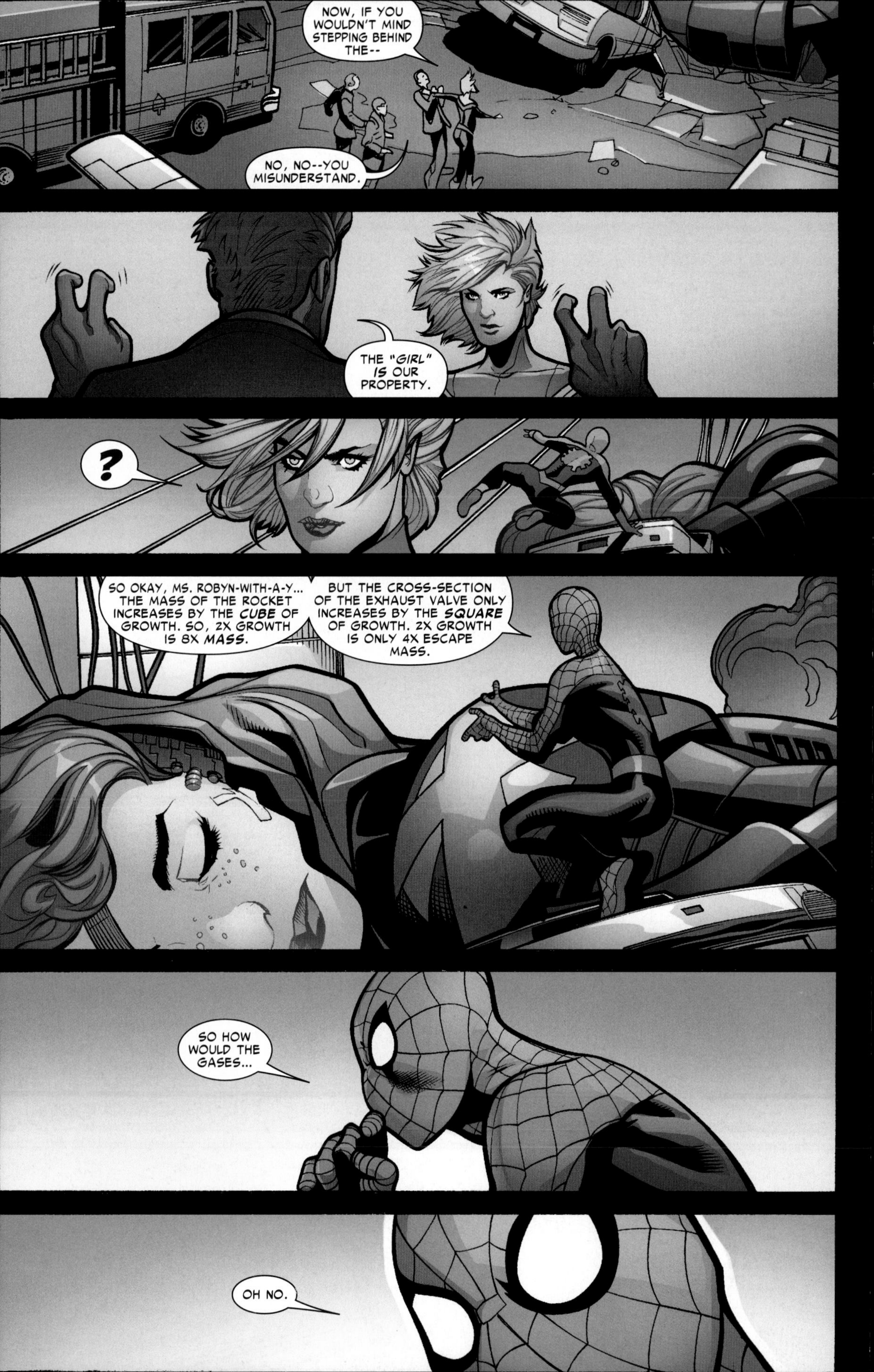
NOW, IF YOU WOULDN'T MIND STEPPING BEHIND THE--
NO, NO--YOU MISUNDERSTAND.
THE "GIRL" IS OUR PROPERTY.
?
SO OKAY, MS. ROBYN-WITH-A-Y... THE MASS OF THE ROCKET INCREASES BY THE CUBE OF GROWTH. SO, 2X GROWTH IS 8X MASS.
BUT THE CROSS-SECTION OF THE EXHAUST VALVE ONLY INCREASES BY THE SQUARE OF GROWTH. 2X GROWTH IS ONLY 4X ESCAPE MASS.
SO HOW WOULD THE GASES...
OH NO.

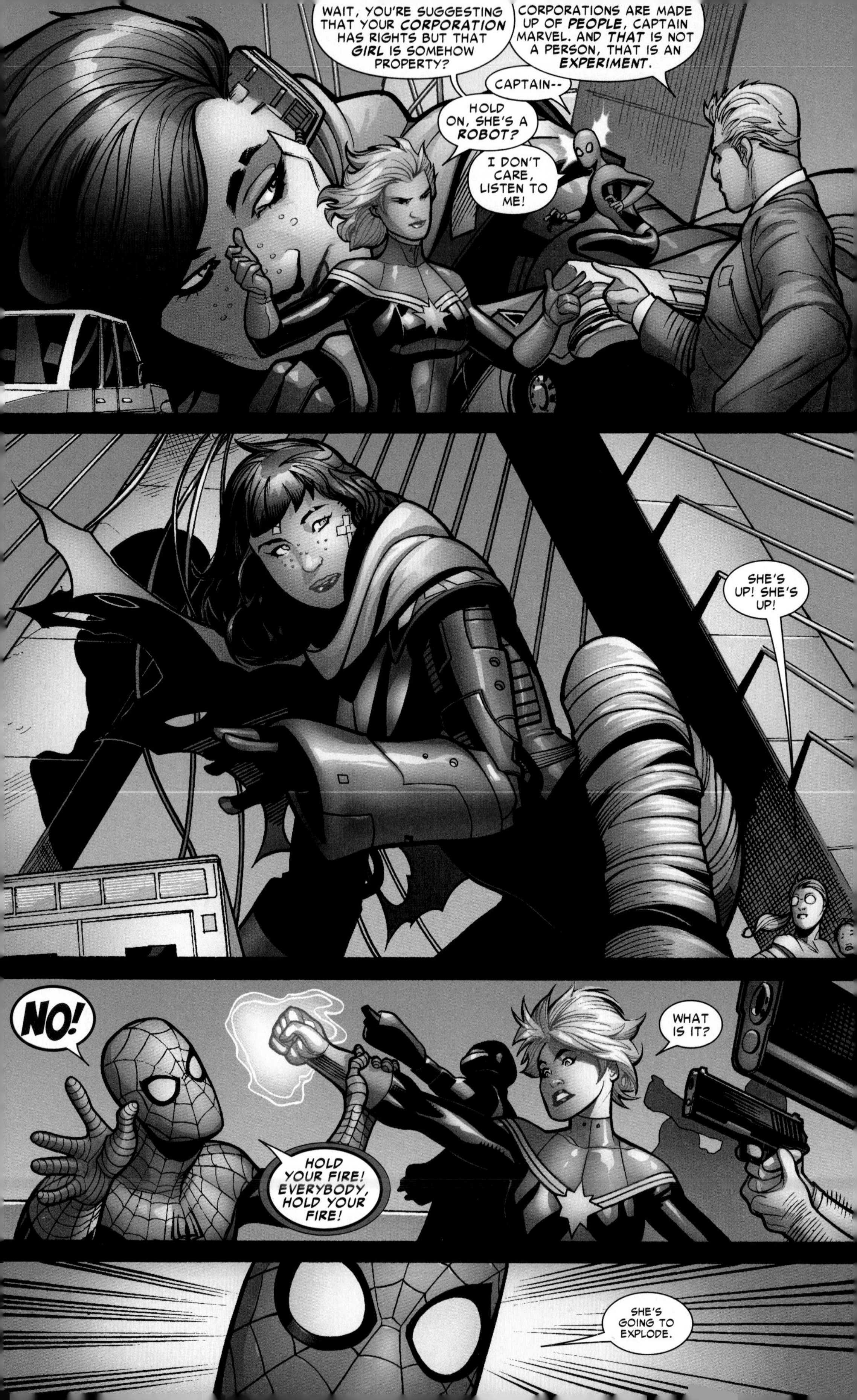
WAIT, YOU'RE SUGGESTING THAT YOUR CORPORATION HAS RIGHTS BUT THAT GIRL IS SOMEHOW PROPERTY?
CORPORATIONS ARE MADE UP OF PEOPLE, CAPTAIN MARVEL. AND THAT IS NOT A PERSON, THAT IS AN EXPERIMENT.
CAPTAIN--
HOLD ON, SHE'S A ROBOT?
I DON'T CARE, LISTEN TO ME!
SHE'S UP! SHE'S UP!
NO!
WHAT IS IT?
HOLD YOUR FIRE! EVERYBODY, HOLD YOUR FIRE!
SHE'S GOING TO EXPLODE.

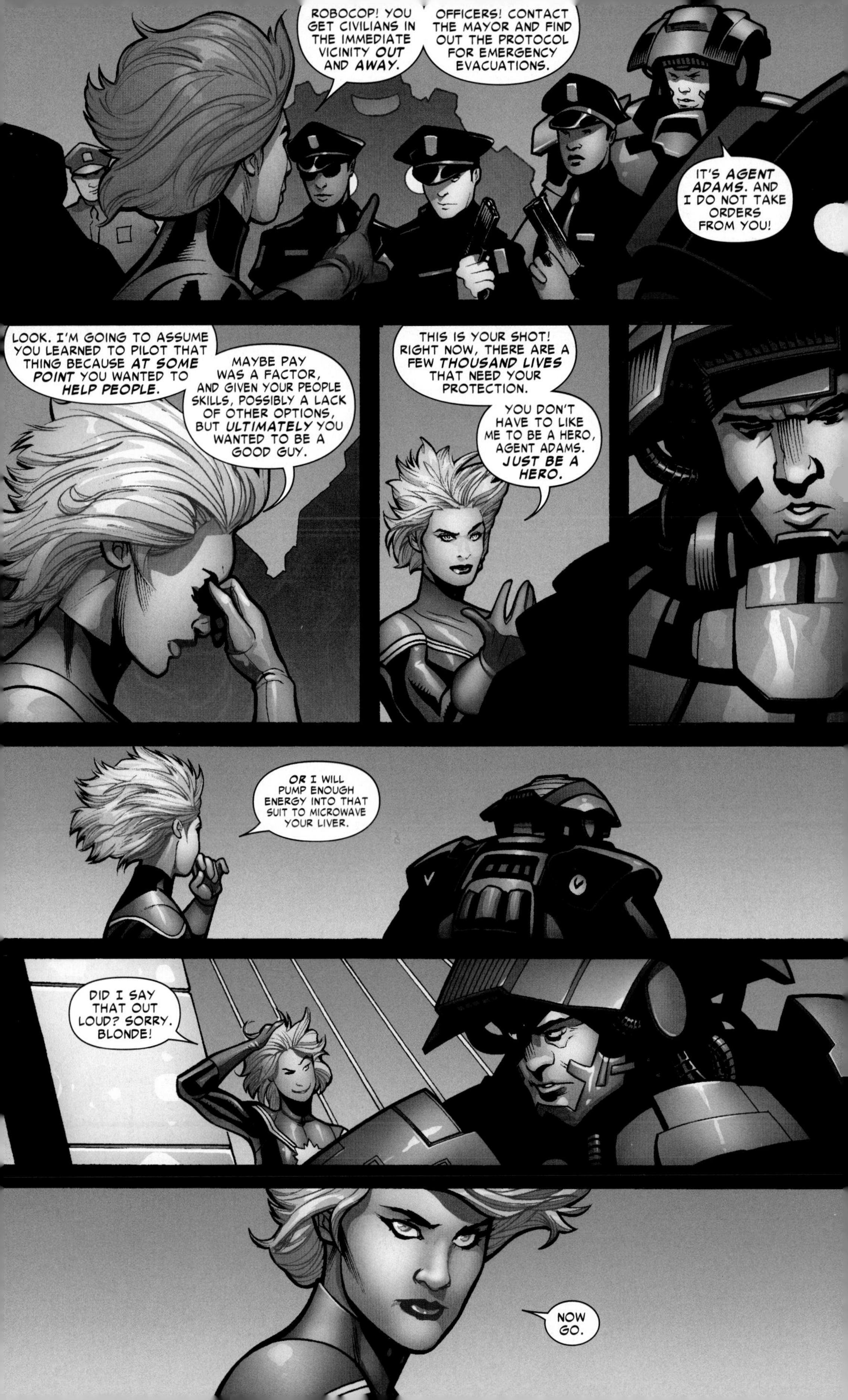
ROBOCOP! YOU GET CIVILIANS IN THE IMMEDIATE VICINITY OUT AND AWAY.
OFFICERS! CONTACT THE MAYOR AND FIND OUT THE PROTOCOL FOR EMERGENCY EVACUATIONS.
IT'S AGENT ADAMS. AND I DO NOT TAKE ORDERS FROM YOU!
LOOK. I'M GOING TO ASSUME YOU LEARNED TO PILOT THAT THING BECAUSE AT SOME POINT YOU WANTED TO HELP PEOPLE.
MAYBE PAY WAS A FACTOR, AND GIVEN YOUR PEOPLE SKILLS, POSSIBLY A LACK OF OTHER OPTIONS, BUT ULTIMATELY YOU WANTED TO BE A GOOD GUY.
THIS IS YOUR SHOT! RIGHT NOW, THERE ARE A FEW THOUSAND LIVES THAT NEED YOUR PROTECTION.
YOU DON'T HAVE TO LIKE ME TO BE A HERO, AGENT ADAMS. JUST BE A HERO.
OR I WILL PUMP ENOUGH ENERGY INTO THAT SUIT TO MICROWAVE YOUR LIVER.
DID I SAY THAT OUT LOUD? SORRY. BLONDE!
NOW GO.

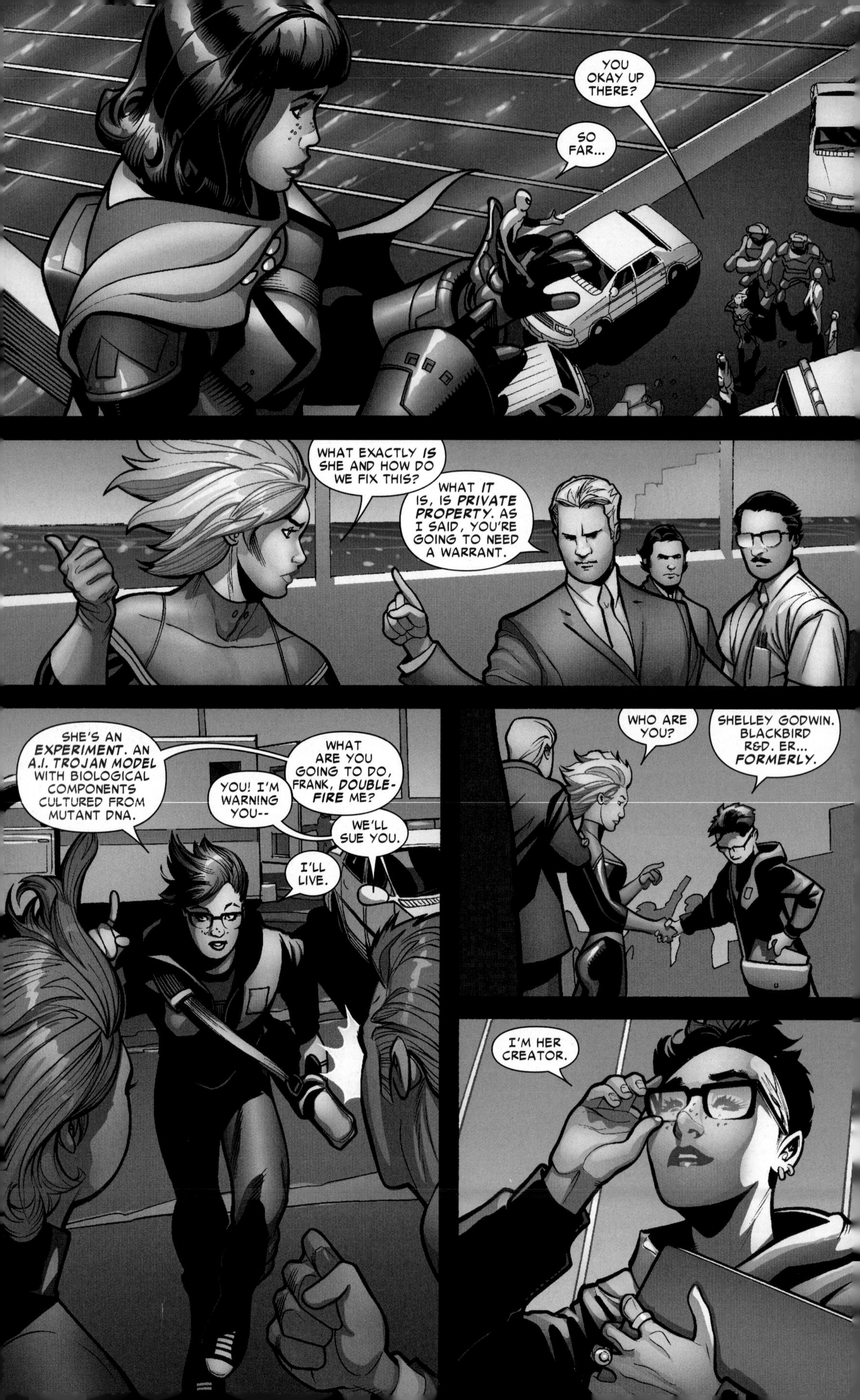

YOU OKAY UP THERE?
SO FAR...
WHAT EXACTLY IS SHE AND HOW DO WE FIX THIS?
WHAT IT IS, IS PRIVATE PROPERTY. AS I SAID, YOU'RE GOING TO NEED A WARRANT.
SHE'S AN EXPERIMENT. AN A.I. TROJAN MODEL WITH BIOLOGICAL COMPONENTS CULTURED FROM MUTANT DNA.
WHAT ARE YOU GOING TO DO, FRANK, DOUBLE-FIRE ME?
YOU! I'M WARNING YOU--
WE'LL SUE YOU.
I'LL LIVE.
WHO ARE YOU?
SHELLEY GODWIN. BLACKBIRD R&D. ER... FORMERLY.
I'M HER CREATOR.

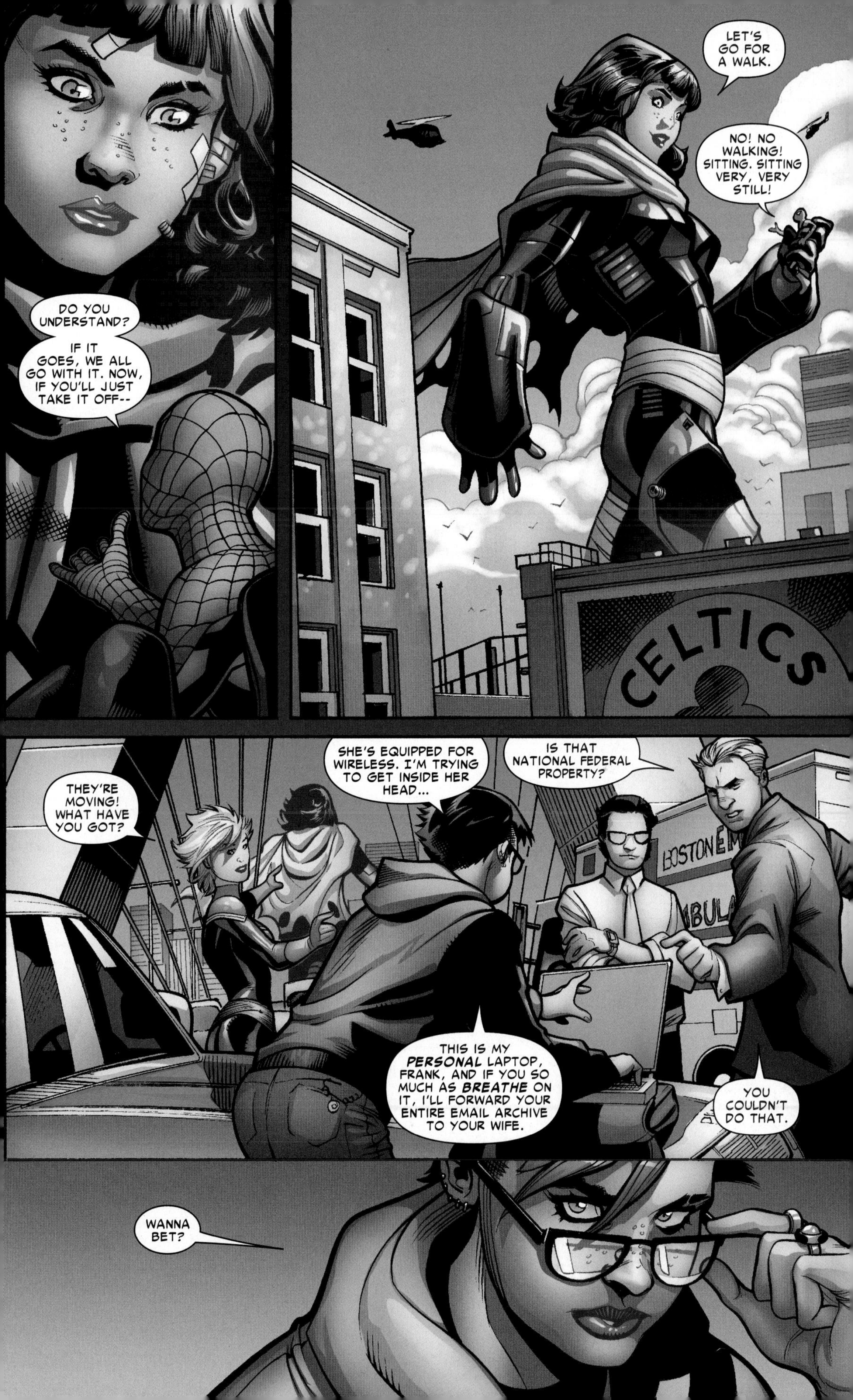
DO YOU UNDERSTAND?
IF IT GOES, WE ALL GO WITH IT. NOW, IF YOU'LL JUST TAKE IT OFF--
LET'S GO FOR A WALK.
NO! NO WALKING! SITTING. SITTING VERY, VERY STILL!
CELTICS
THEY'RE MOVING! WHAT HAVE YOU GOT?
SHE'S EQUIPPED FOR WIRELESS. I'M TRYING TO GET INSIDE HER HEAD...
IS THAT NATIONAL FEDERAL PROPERTY?
BOSTON
THIS IS MY *PERSONAL* LAPTOP, FRANK, AND IF YOU SO MUCH AS *BREATHE* ON IT, I'LL FORWARD YOUR ENTIRE EMAIL ARCHIVE TO YOUR WIFE.
YOU COULDN'T DO THAT.
WANNA BET?

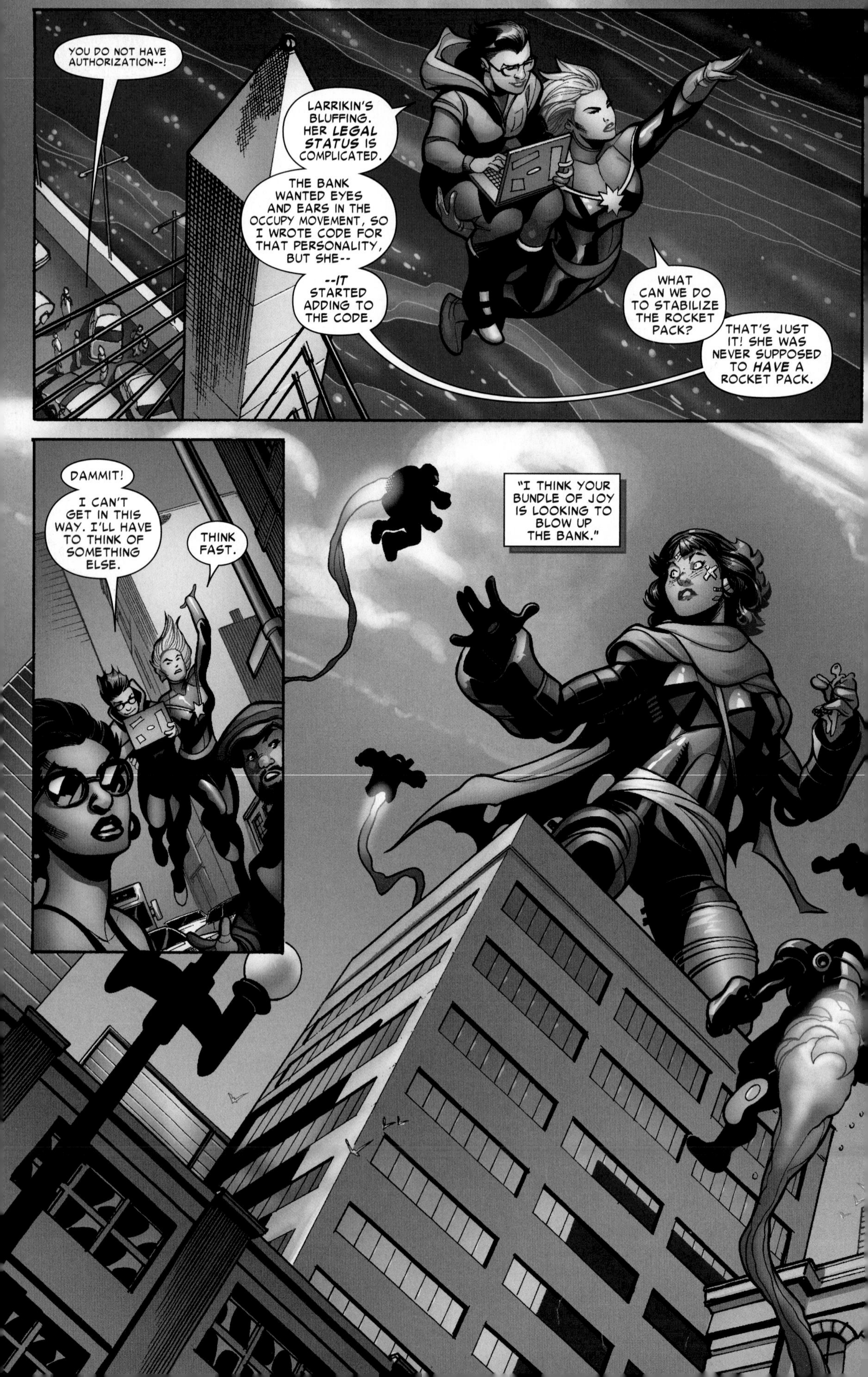
YOU DO NOT HAVE AUTHORIZATION--!
LARRIKIN'S BLUFFING. HER *LEGAL STATUS* IS COMPLICATED.
THE BANK WANTED EYES AND EARS IN THE OCCUPY MOVEMENT, SO I WROTE CODE FOR THAT PERSONALITY, BUT SHE--
--*IT* STARTED ADDING TO THE CODE.
WHAT CAN WE DO TO STABILIZE THE ROCKET PACK?
THAT'S JUST IT! SHE WAS NEVER SUPPOSED TO *HAVE* A ROCKET PACK.
DAMMIT!
I CAN'T GET IN THIS WAY. I'LL HAVE TO THINK OF SOMETHING ELSE.
THINK FAST.
"I THINK YOUR BUNDLE OF JOY IS LOOKING TO BLOW UP THE BANK."

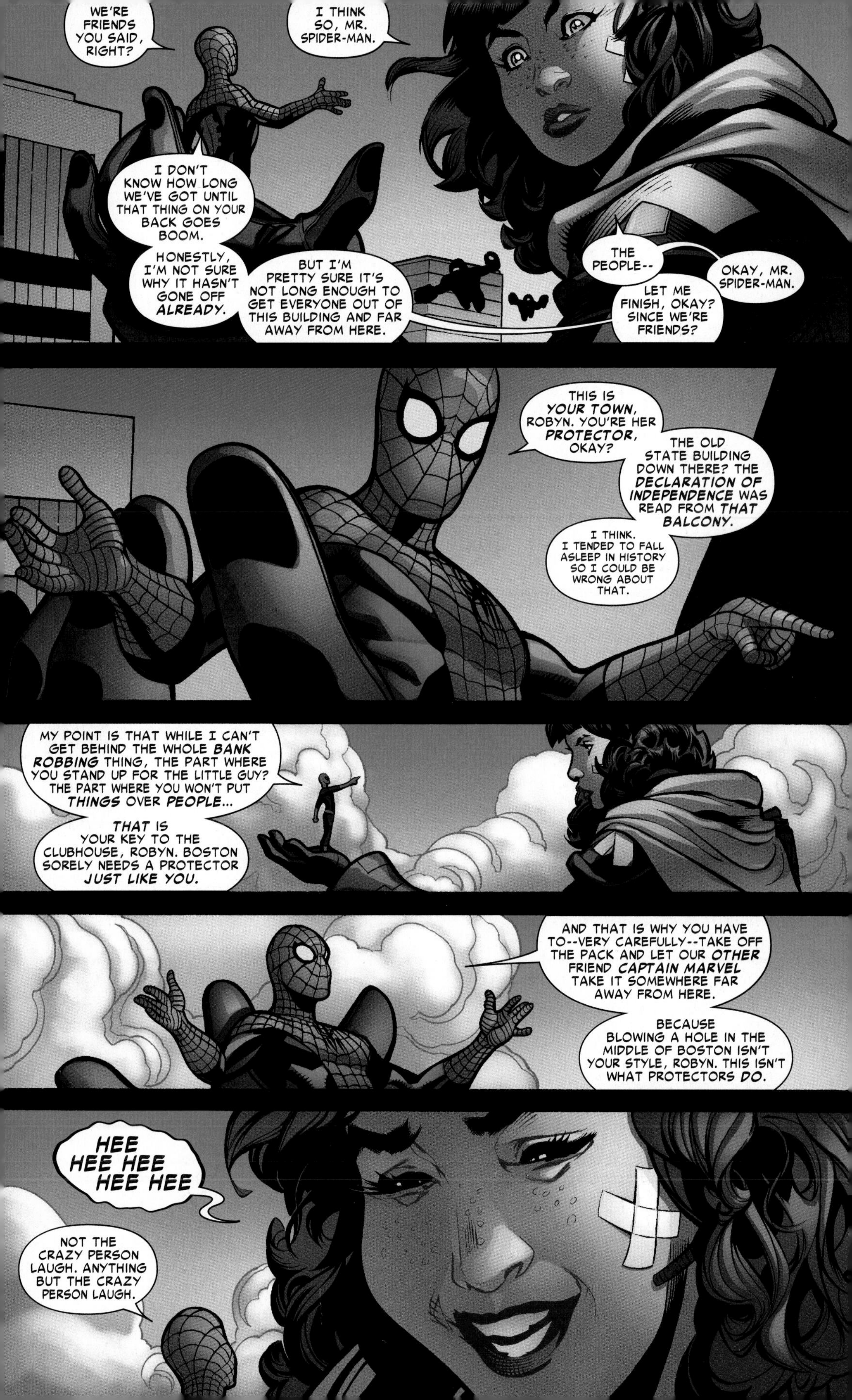
WE'RE FRIENDS YOU SAID, RIGHT?
I THINK SO, MR. SPIDER-MAN.
I DON'T KNOW HOW LONG WE'VE GOT UNTIL THAT THING ON YOUR BACK GOES BOOM.
HONESTLY, I'M NOT SURE WHY IT HASN'T GONE OFF ALREADY.
BUT I'M PRETTY SURE IT'S NOT LONG ENOUGH TO GET EVERYONE OUT OF THIS BUILDING AND FAR AWAY FROM HERE.
THE PEOPLE--
LET ME FINISH, OKAY? SINCE WE'RE FRIENDS?
OKAY, MR. SPIDER-MAN.
THIS IS YOUR TOWN, ROBYN. YOU'RE HER PROTECTOR, OKAY?
THE OLD STATE BUILDING DOWN THERE? THE DECLARATION OF INDEPENDENCE WAS READ FROM THAT BALCONY.
I THINK. I TENDED TO FALL ASLEEP IN HISTORY SO I COULD BE WRONG ABOUT THAT.
MY POINT IS THAT WHILE I CAN'T GET BEHIND THE WHOLE BANK ROBBING THING, THE PART WHERE YOU STAND UP FOR THE LITTLE GUY? THE PART WHERE YOU WON'T PUT THINGS OVER PEOPLE...
THAT IS YOUR KEY TO THE CLUBHOUSE, ROBYN. BOSTON SORELY NEEDS A PROTECTOR JUST LIKE YOU.
AND THAT IS WHY YOU HAVE TO--VERY CAREFULLY--TAKE OFF THE PACK AND LET OUR OTHER FRIEND CAPTAIN MARVEL TAKE IT SOMEWHERE FAR AWAY FROM HERE.
BECAUSE BLOWING A HOLE IN THE MIDDLE OF BOSTON ISN'T YOUR STYLE, ROBYN. THIS ISN'T WHAT PROTECTORS DO.
HEE HEE HEE HEE HEE
NOT THE CRAZY PERSON LAUGH. ANYTHING BUT THE CRAZY PERSON LAUGH.

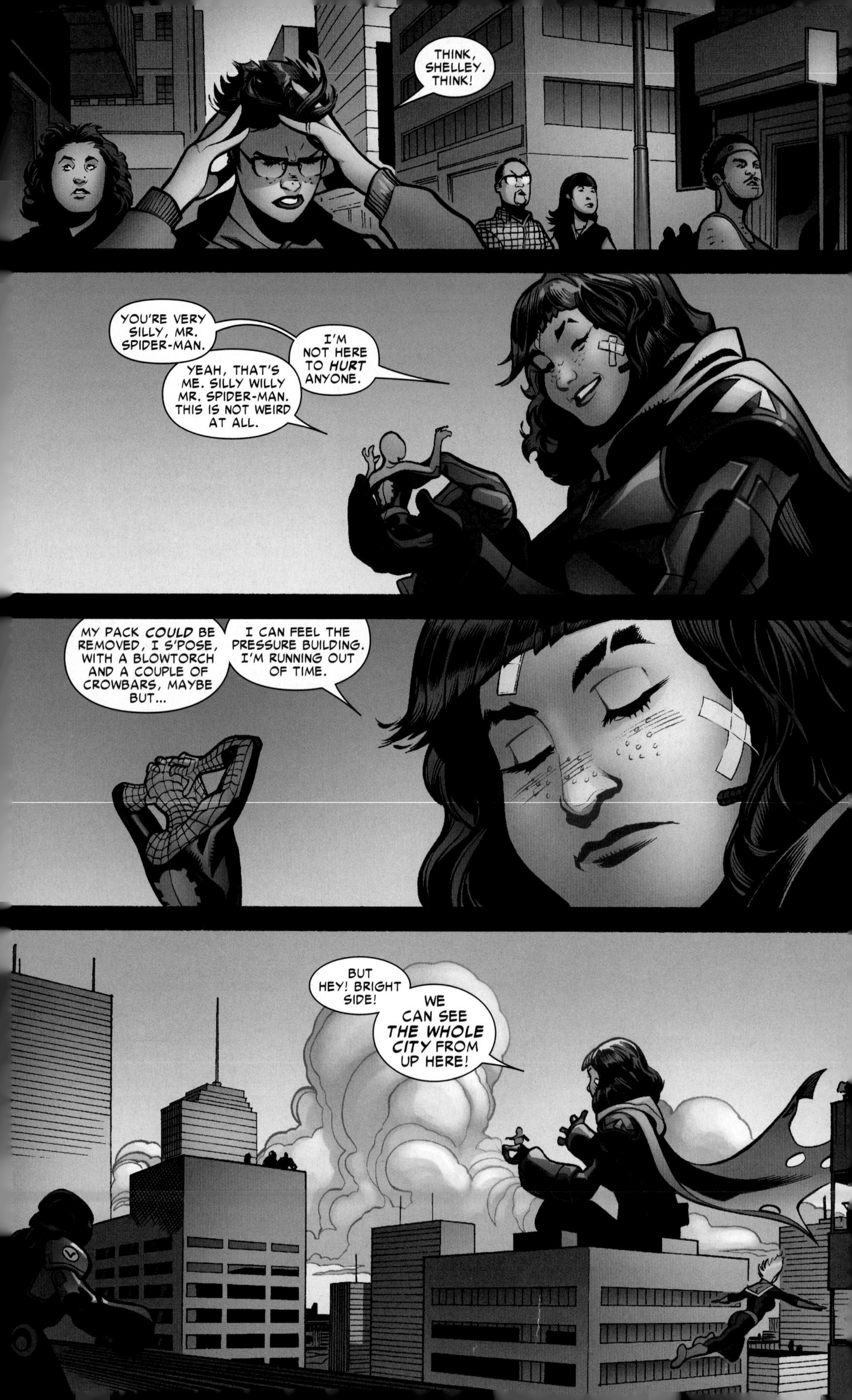
THINK, SHELLEY. THINK!
YOU'RE VERY SILLY, MR. SPIDER-MAN.
I'M NOT HERE TO *HURT* ANYONE.
YEAH, THAT'S ME. SILLY WILLY MR. SPIDER-MAN. THIS IS NOT WEIRD AT ALL.
MY PACK *COULD* BE REMOVED, I S'POSE, WITH A BLOWTORCH AND A COUPLE OF CROWBARS, MAYBE BUT...
I CAN FEEL THE PRESSURE BUILDING. I'M RUNNING OUT OF TIME.
BUT HEY! BRIGHT SIDE!
WE CAN SEE *THE WHOLE CITY* FROM UP HERE!

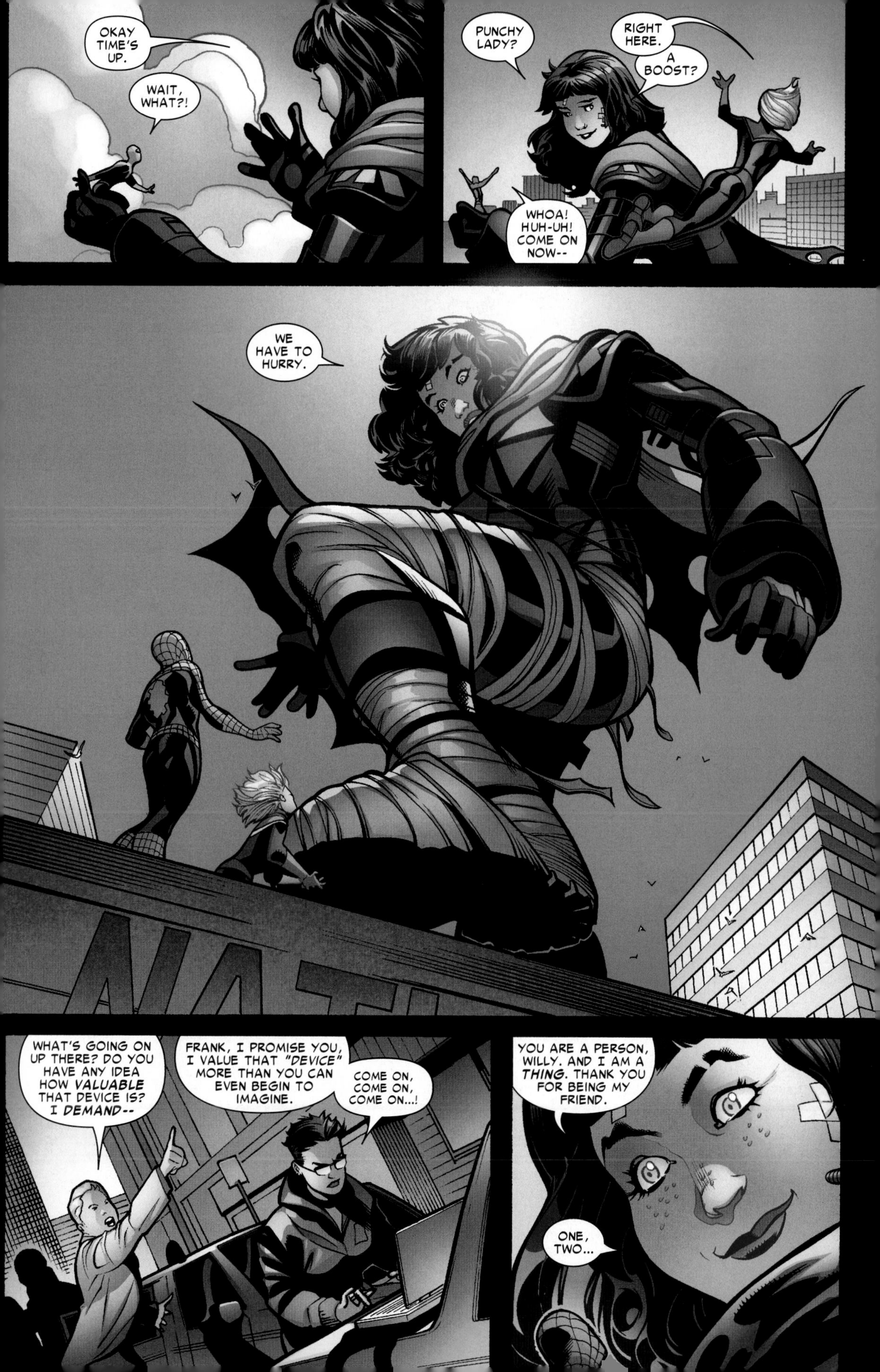
OKAY TIME'S UP.
WAIT, WHAT?!
PUNCHY LADY?
RIGHT HERE.
A BOOST?
WHOA! HUH-UH! COME ON NOW--
WE HAVE TO HURRY.
WHAT'S GOING ON UP THERE? DO YOU HAVE ANY IDEA HOW VALUABLE THAT DEVICE IS? I DEMAND--
FRANK, I PROMISE YOU, I VALUE THAT "DEVICE" MORE THAN YOU CAN EVEN BEGIN TO IMAGINE.
COME ON, COME ON, COME ON...!
YOU ARE A PERSON, WILLY. AND I AM A THING. THANK YOU FOR BEING MY FRIEND.
ONE, TWO...

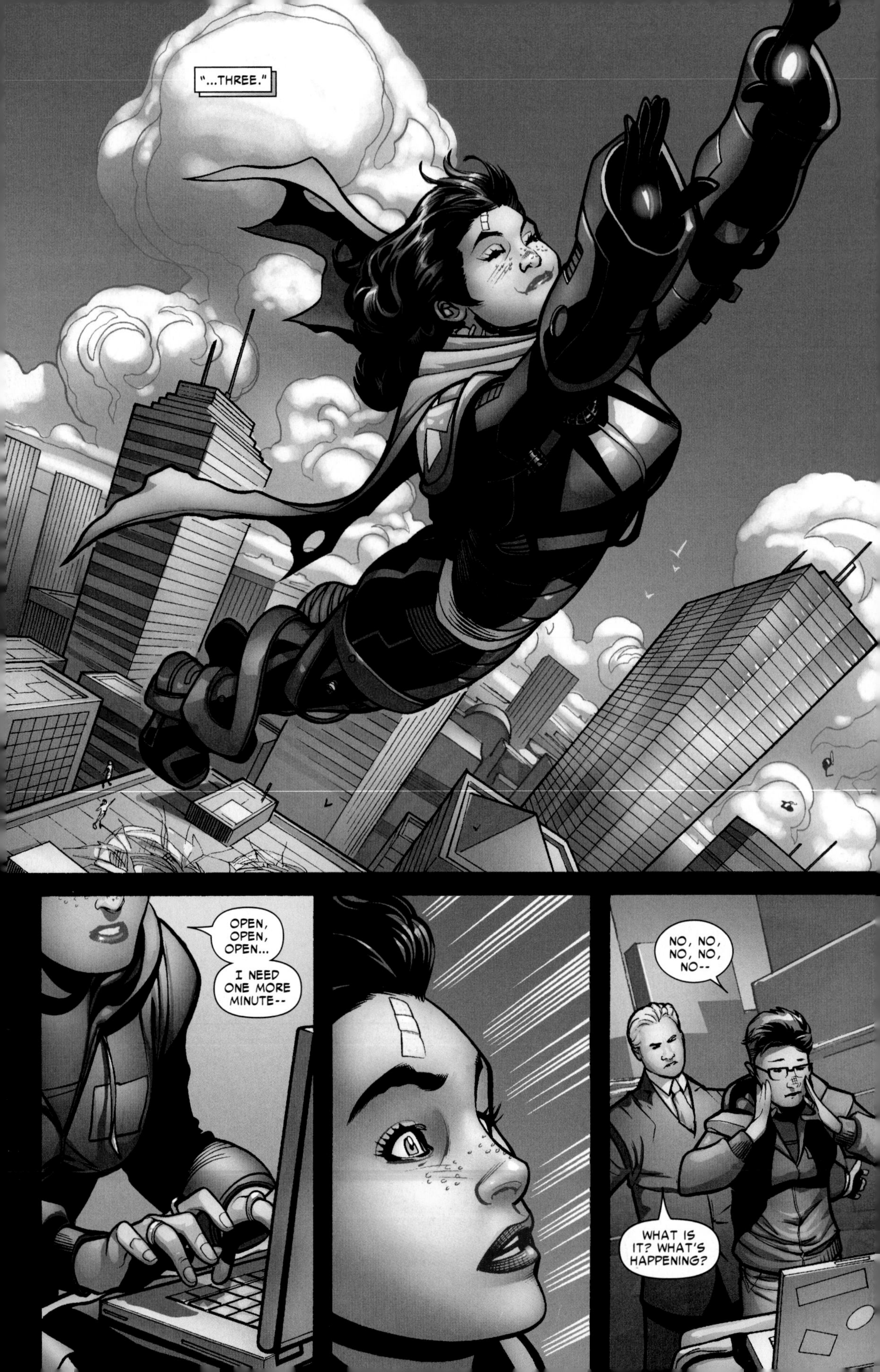
"...THREE."
OPEN, OPEN, OPEN...
I NEED ONE MORE MINUTE--
NO, NO, NO, NO, NO--
WHAT IS IT? WHAT'S HAPPENING?

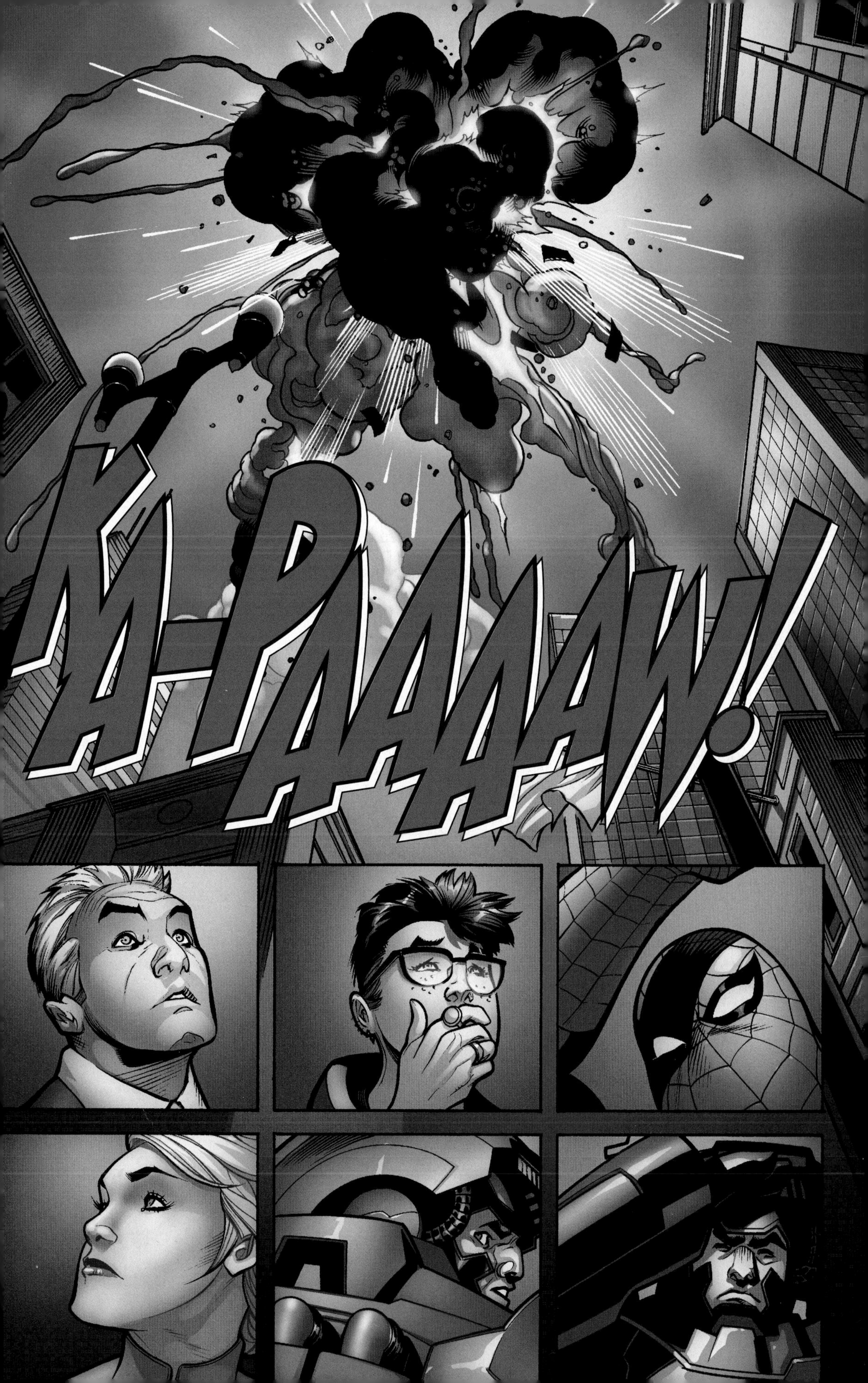
KA-PAAAAW!

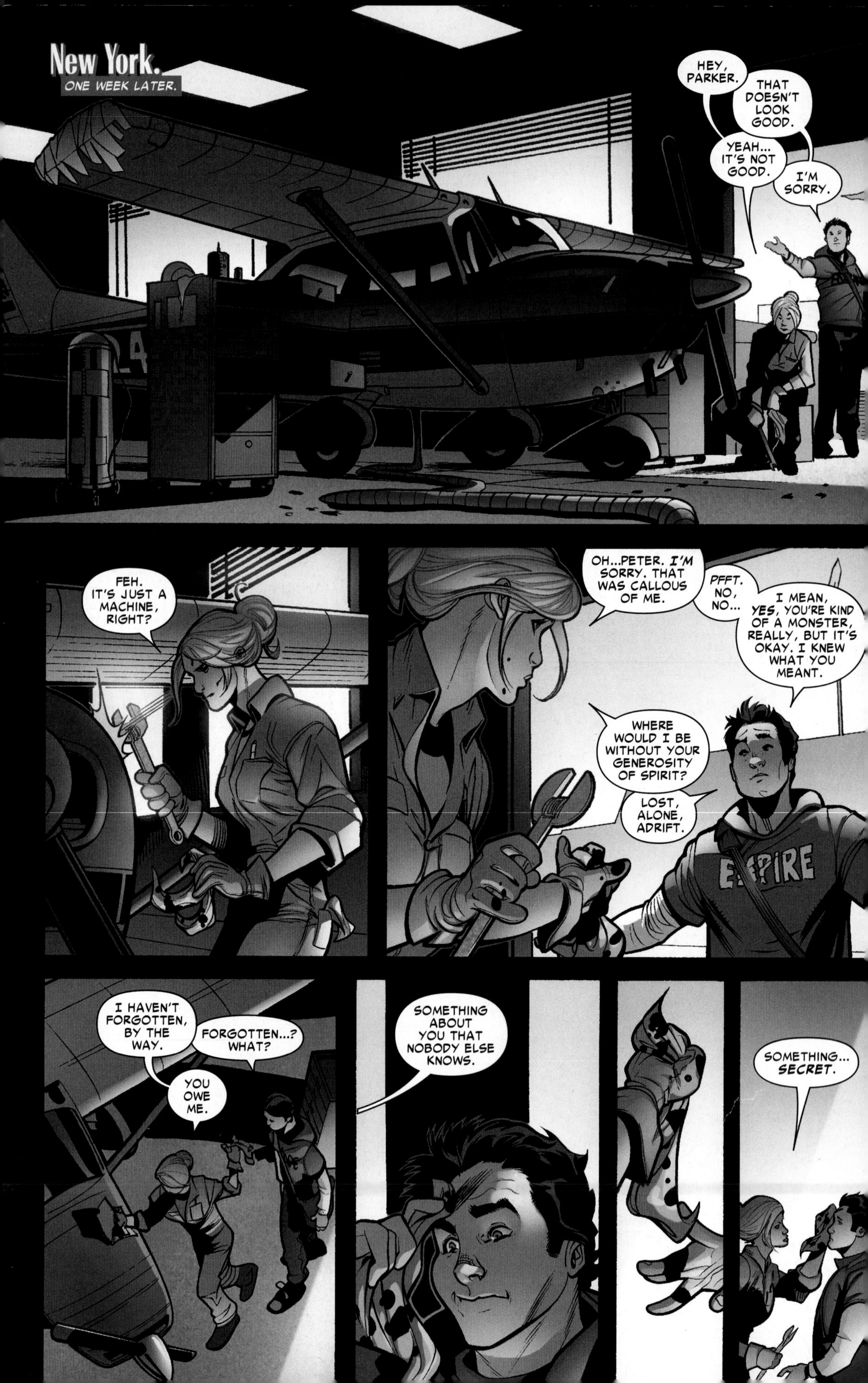
New York.
ONE WEEK LATER.
HEY, PARKER.
THAT DOESN'T LOOK GOOD.
YEAH... IT'S NOT GOOD.
I'M SORRY.
FEH. IT'S JUST A MACHINE, RIGHT?
OH...PETER. I'M SORRY. THAT WAS CALLOUS OF ME.
PFFT. NO, NO...
I MEAN, YES, YOU'RE KIND OF A MONSTER, REALLY, BUT IT'S OKAY. I KNEW WHAT YOU MEANT.
WHERE WOULD I BE WITHOUT YOUR GENEROSITY OF SPIRIT?
LOST, ALONE, ADRIFT.
EMPIRE
I HAVEN'T FORGOTTEN, BY THE WAY.
FORGOTTEN...? WHAT?
YOU OWE ME.
SOMETHING ABOUT YOU THAT NOBODY ELSE KNOWS.
SOMETHING... SECRET.

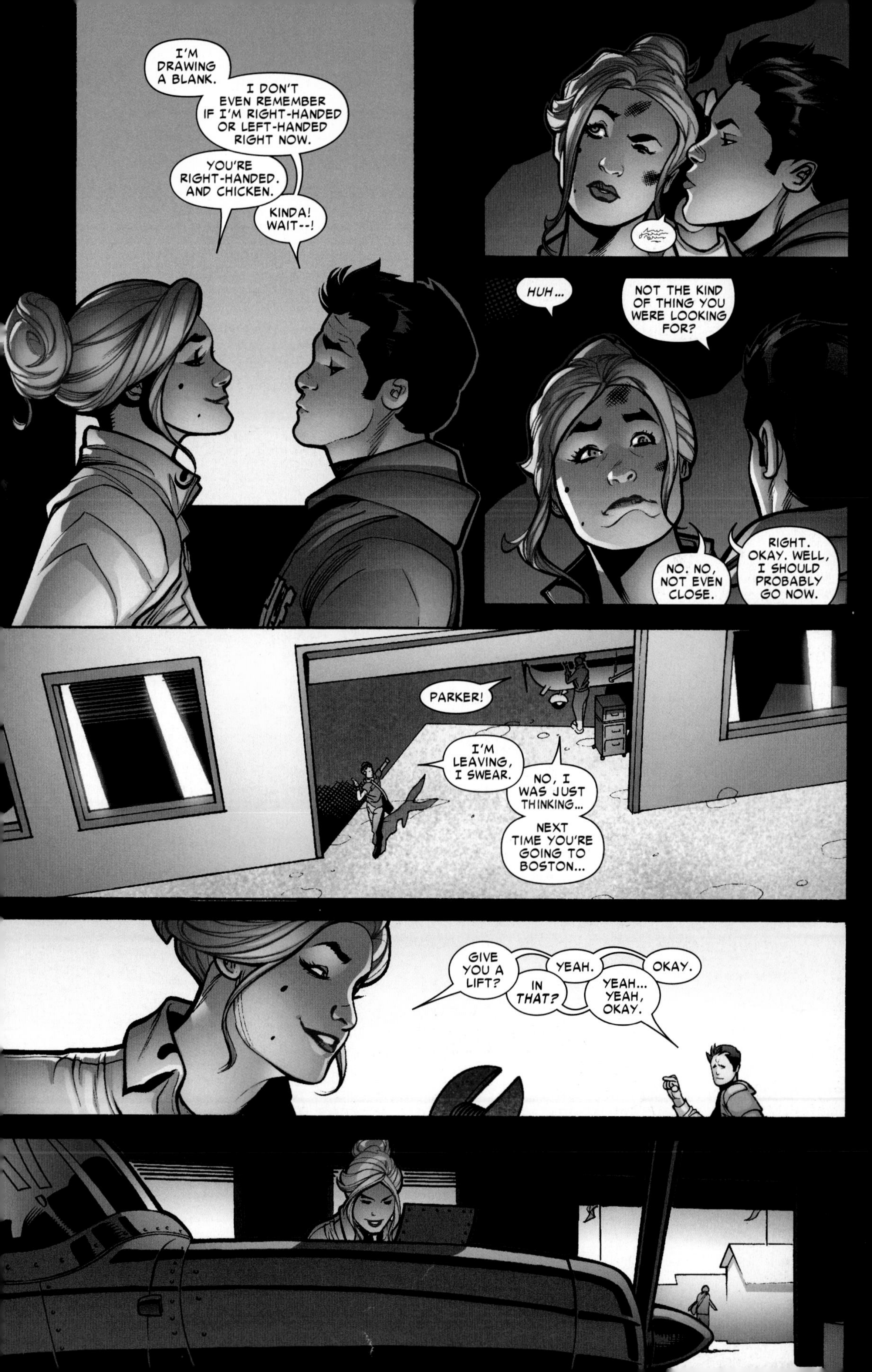
I'M DRAWING A BLANK.
I DON'T EVEN REMEMBER IF I'M RIGHT-HANDED OR LEFT-HANDED RIGHT NOW.
YOU'RE RIGHT-HANDED. AND CHICKEN.
KINDA! WAIT--!
HUH...
NOT THE KIND OF THING YOU WERE LOOKING FOR?
NO. NO, NOT EVEN CLOSE.
RIGHT. OKAY. WELL, I SHOULD PROBABLY GO NOW.
PARKER!
I'M LEAVING, I SWEAR.
NO, I WAS JUST THINKING...
NEXT TIME YOU'RE GOING TO BOSTON...
GIVE YOU A LIFT?
IN *THAT?*
YEAH.
YEAH... YEAH, OKAY.
OKAY.

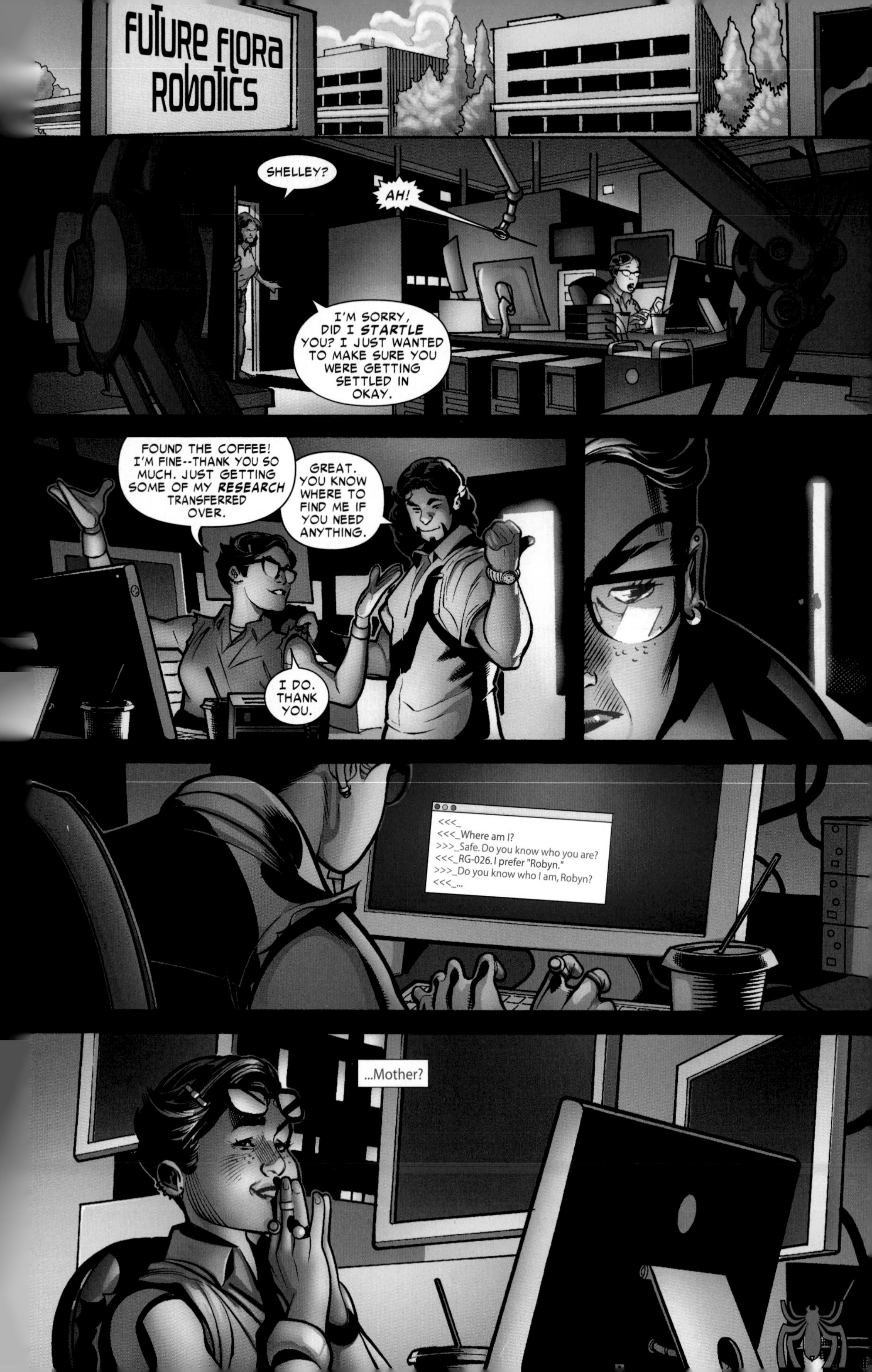
FUTURE FLORA ROBOTICS
SHELLEY?
AH!
I'M SORRY, DID I STARTLE YOU? I JUST WANTED TO MAKE SURE YOU WERE GETTING SETTLED IN OKAY.
FOUND THE COFFEE! I'M FINE--THANK YOU SO MUCH. JUST GETTING SOME OF MY RESEARCH TRANSFERRED OVER.
GREAT. YOU KNOW WHERE TO FIND ME IF YOU NEED ANYTHING.
I DO. THANK YOU.
<<<_
<<<_Where am I?
>>>_Safe. Do you know who you are?
<<<_RG-026. I prefer "Robyn."
>>>_Do you know who I am, Robyn?
<<<_...
...Mother?

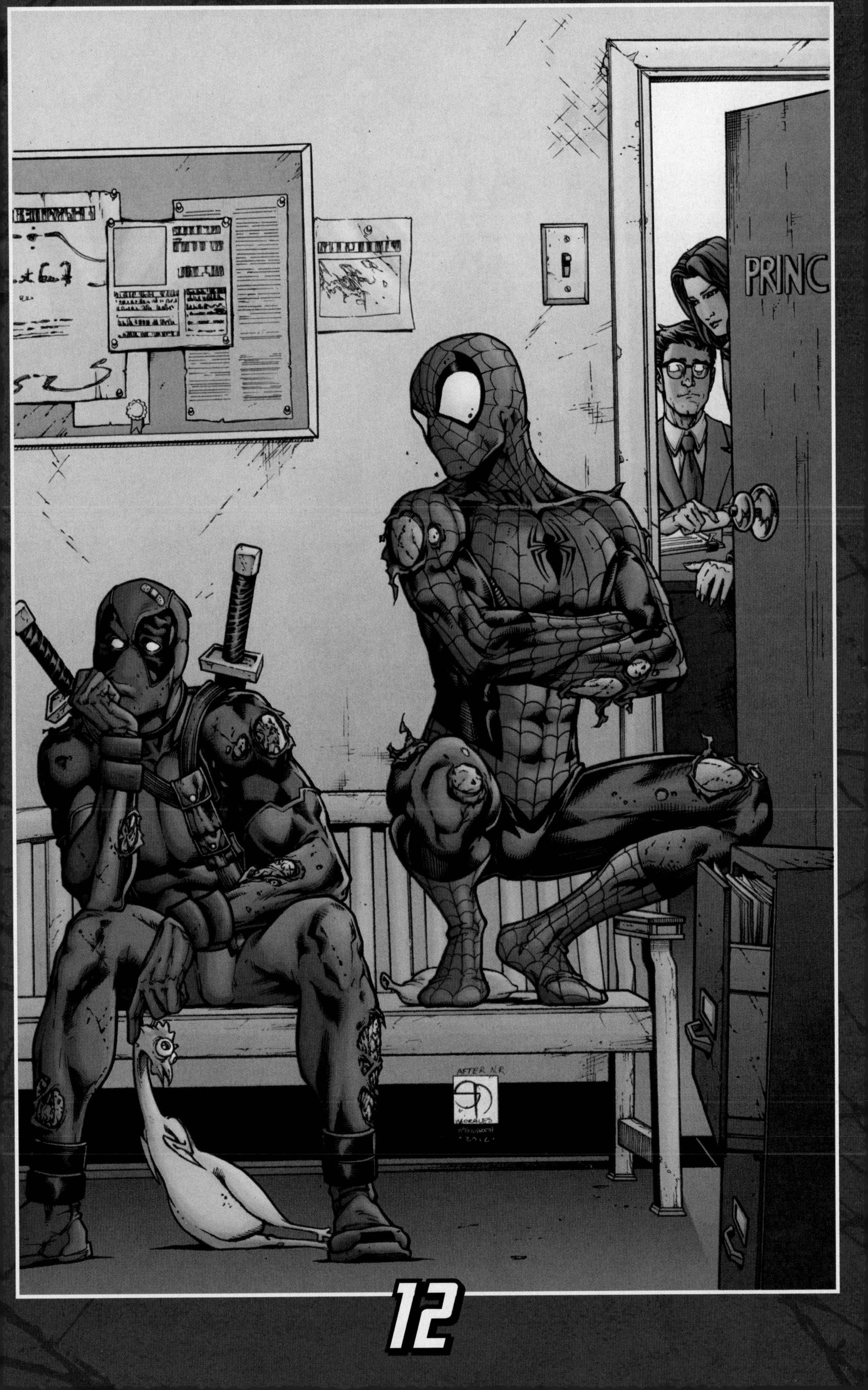
PRINC
AFTER N.R.

12

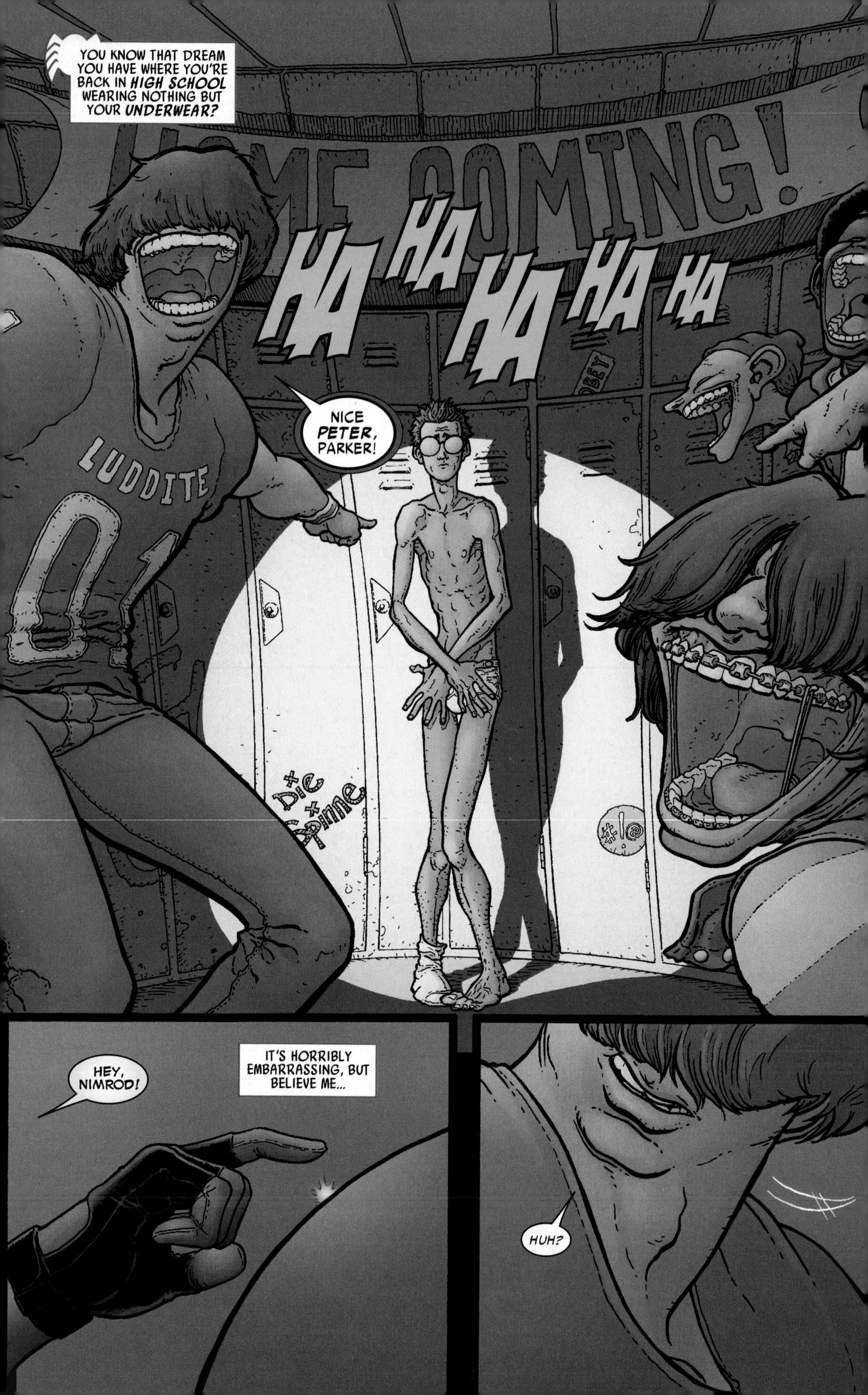
YOU KNOW THAT DREAM YOU HAVE WHERE YOU'RE BACK IN HIGH SCHOOL WEARING NOTHING BUT YOUR UNDERWEAR?
HOMECOMING!
HA HA HA HA HA HA
NICE PETER, PARKER!
LUDDITE
01
OBEY
Die Spinne
#!@
HEY, NIMROD!
IT'S HORRIBLY EMBARRASSING, BUT BELIEVE ME...
HUH?

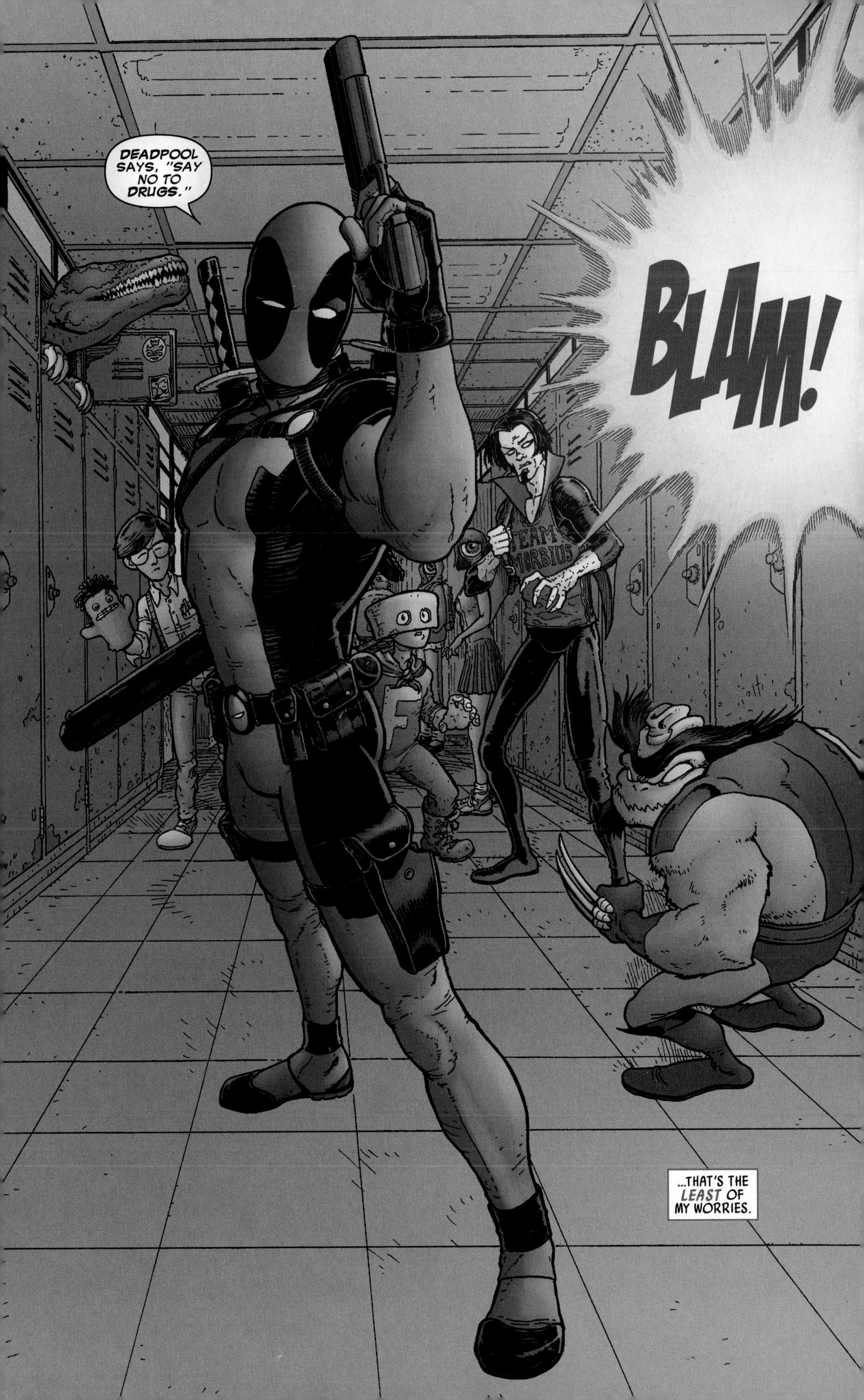
DEADPOOL SAYS, "SAY NO TO DRUGS."
BLAM!
TEAM MORBIUS
...THAT'S THE LEAST OF MY WORRIES.

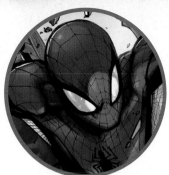

While attending a demonstration in radiology, high school student Peter Parker was bitten by a spider which had accidentally been exposed to radioactive rays. Through a miracle of science Peter soon found that he had gained the spider's powers…and had, in effect, become a human spider! Later he joined the Avengers. And now he is the…

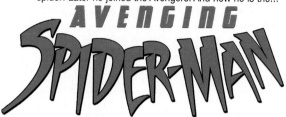

AVENGING SPIDER-MAN

After being diagnosed with cancer, the deadly mercenary Wade Wilson volunteered for the Weapon X program hoping that they would be able to give him a cure. Their solution was to give him a healing factor similar to Wolverine's. Now, he's the Merc with a Mouth, the Regeneratin' Degenerate. He's…

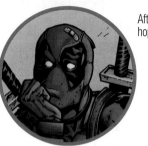

DEADPOOL

AVENGING SPIDER-MAN

PREVIOUSLY...

Spider-Man celebrated the 50th anniversary of his debu…

…y.

Before that, Spider-Man teamed up with Captain Marve…

on a failed … s the

tim… because this story probably takes

place before both…

WHY DO THEY NEED TO KNOW WHAT HAPPENED PREVIOUSLY? I WASN'T HERE, IT COULDN'T HAVE BEEN THAT IMPORTANT.

Well, sometimes, Deadpool, readers are new, either to comics or reading this book, and they need to know things upfront so that they can jump right in and feel included.

LIKE THE FACT THAT I TALK TO MYSELF IN CAPTIONS?

Yes, and sometimes there are things even long-standing readers need to know.

LIKE THE FACT THAT THIS STORY TAKES PLACE BEFORE DEADPOOL #50?

Exactly!

CAN I START SHOOTING PEOPLE YET?

Probably not, it is a Spider-Man book.

WRITER: KEVIN SHINICK ART: AARON KUDER

COLOR ART: MATT HOLLINGSWORTH LETTERER: VC's JOE CARAMAGNA

COVER: DAVIS, MORALES AND HOLLINGSWORTH

ASSISTANT EDITOR: ELLIE PYLE ASSOCIATE EDITOR: SANA AMANAT EDITOR: STEPHEN WACKER

OMG! THIS DUDE'S LAST NAME IS "WACKER"!

EXECUTIVE EDITOR: TOM BREVOORT EDITOR IN CHIEF: AXEL ALONSO

CHIEF CREATIVE OFFICER: JOE QUESADA PUBLISHER: DAN BUCKLEY EXECUTIVE PRODUCER: ALAN FINE

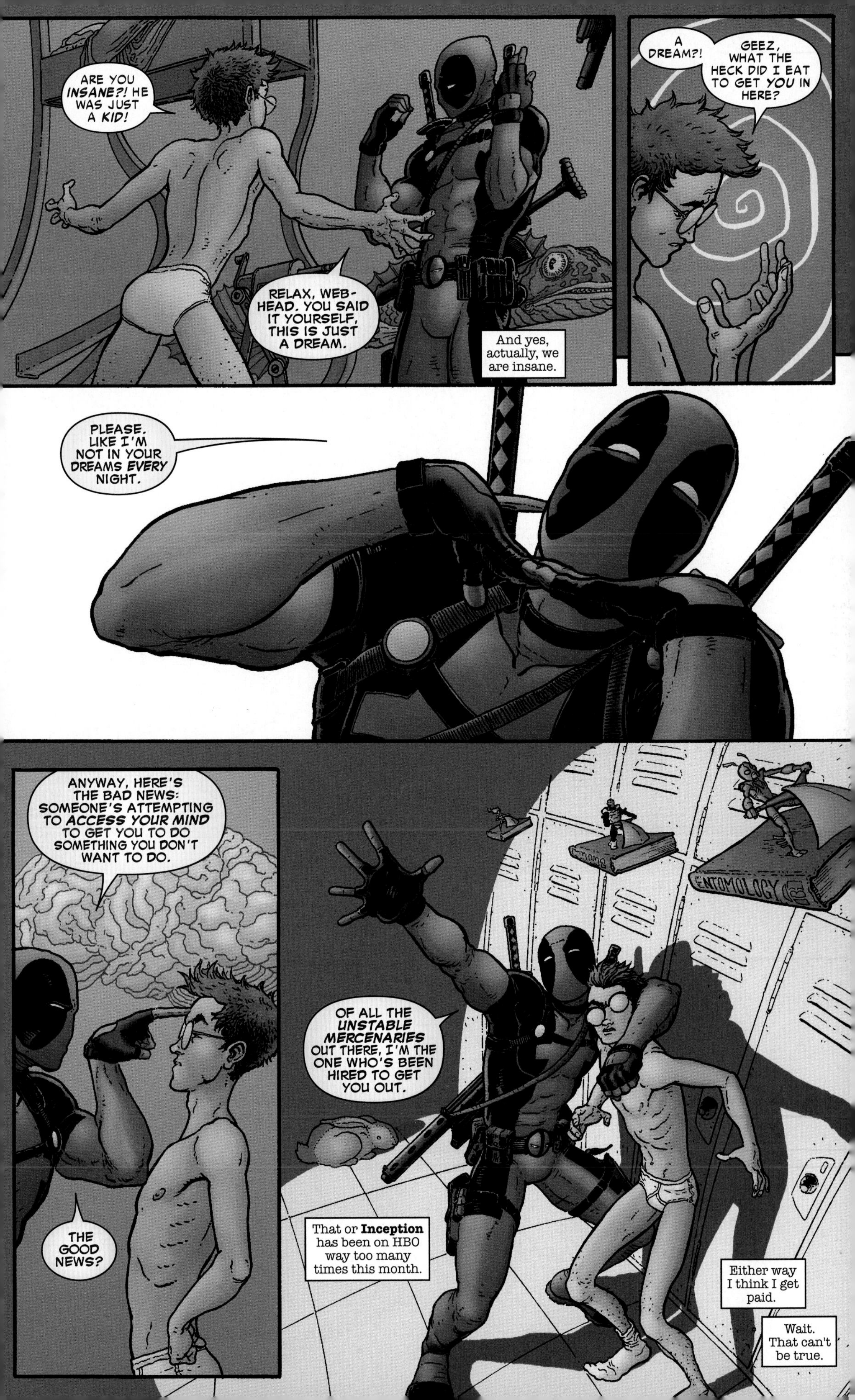
ARE YOU INSANE?! HE WAS JUST A KID!
RELAX, WEB-HEAD. YOU SAID IT YOURSELF, THIS IS JUST A DREAM.
And yes, actually, we are insane.
A DREAM?!
GEEZ, WHAT THE HECK DID I EAT TO GET YOU IN HERE?
PLEASE. LIKE I'M NOT IN YOUR DREAMS EVERY NIGHT.
ANYWAY, HERE'S THE BAD NEWS: SOMEONE'S ATTEMPTING TO ACCESS YOUR MIND TO GET YOU TO DO SOMETHING YOU DON'T WANT TO DO.
THE GOOD NEWS?
OF ALL THE UNSTABLE MERCENARIES OUT THERE, I'M THE ONE WHO'S BEEN HIRED TO GET YOU OUT.
ENTOMOLOGY
That or Inception has been on HBO way too many times this month.
Either way I think I get paid.
Wait. That can't be true.

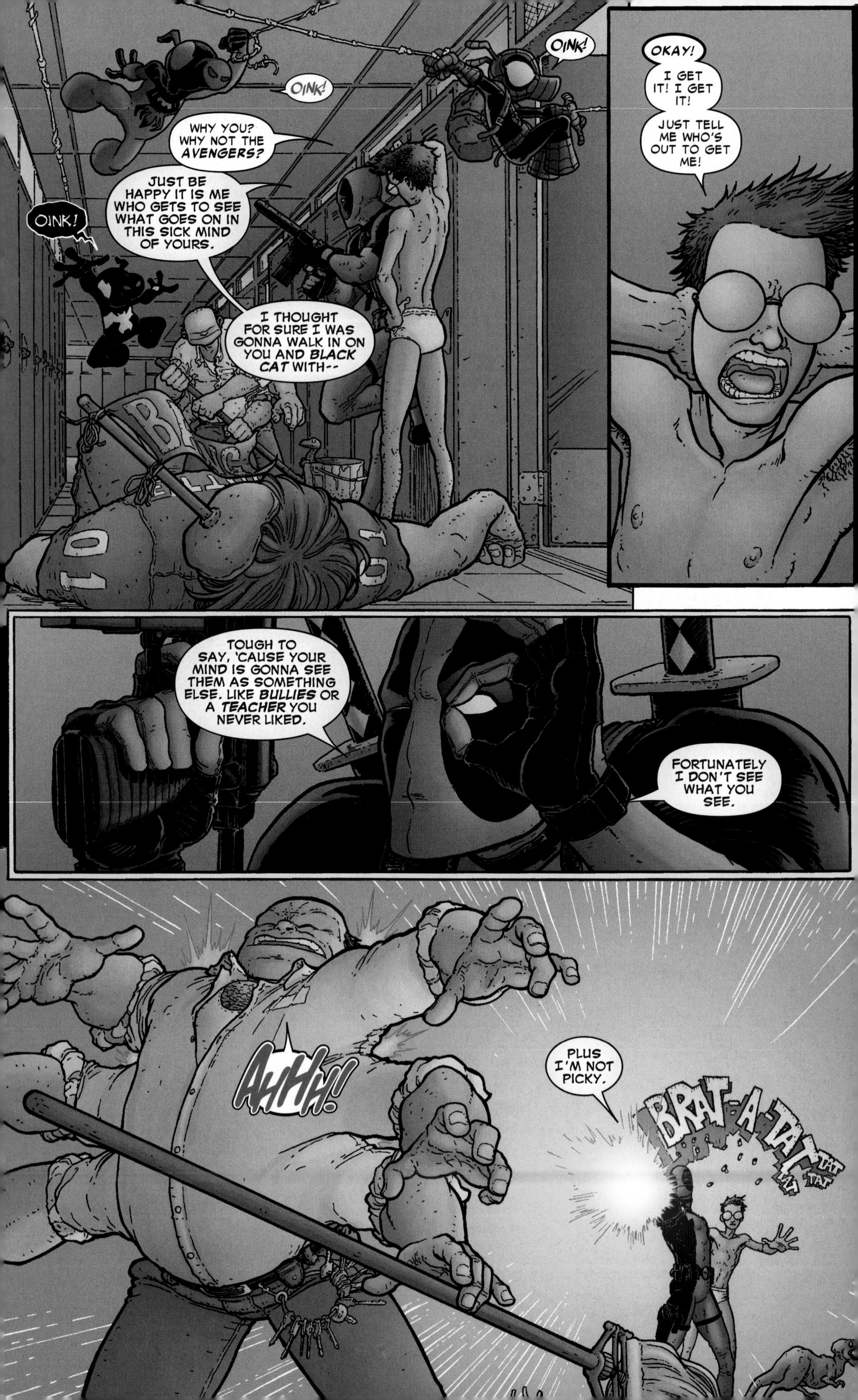
OINK!
OINK!
WHY YOU? WHY NOT THE AVENGERS?
OINK!
JUST BE HAPPY IT IS ME WHO GETS TO SEE WHAT GOES ON IN THIS SICK MIND OF YOURS.
I THOUGHT FOR SURE I WAS GONNA WALK IN ON YOU AND BLACK CAT WITH--
OINK!
OKAY!
I GET IT! I GET IT!
JUST TELL ME WHO'S OUT TO GET ME!
TOUGH TO SAY, 'CAUSE YOUR MIND IS GONNA SEE THEM AS SOMETHING ELSE. LIKE BULLIES OR A TEACHER YOU NEVER LIKED.
FORTUNATELY I DON'T SEE WHAT YOU SEE.
AHHH!
PLUS I'M NOT PICKY.
BRAT-A-TAT TAT TAT TAT

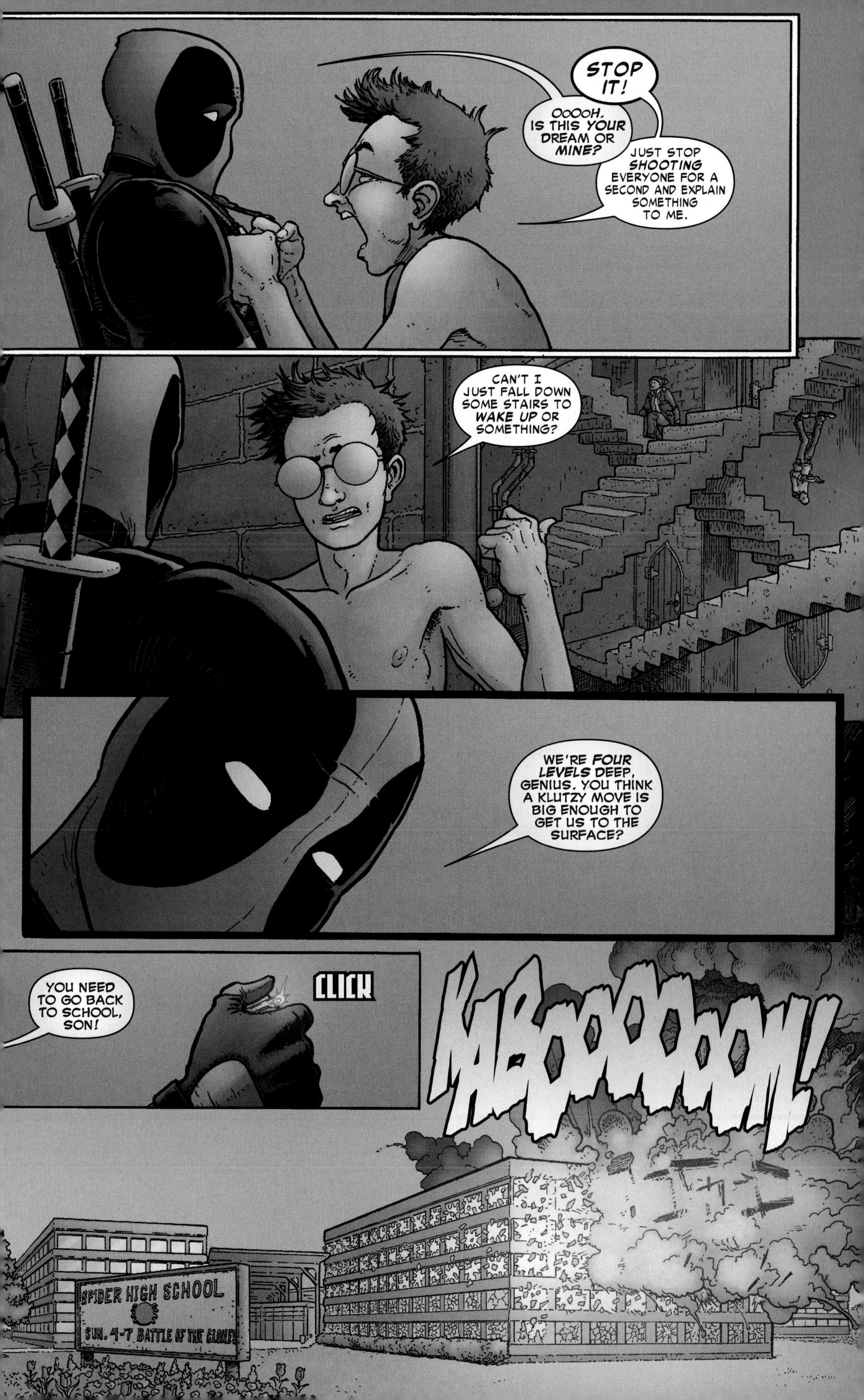
STOP IT!
OOOOH. IS THIS YOUR DREAM OR MINE?
JUST STOP SHOOTING EVERYONE FOR A SECOND AND EXPLAIN SOMETHING TO ME.
CAN'T I JUST FALL DOWN SOME STAIRS TO WAKE UP OR SOMETHING?
WE'RE FOUR LEVELS DEEP, GENIUS. YOU THINK A KLUTZY MOVE IS BIG ENOUGH TO GET US TO THE SURFACE?
YOU NEED TO GO BACK TO SCHOOL, SON!
CLICK
KABOOOOOOM!
SPIDER HIGH SCHOOL
SUN. 4-7 BATTLE OF THE GLOVES

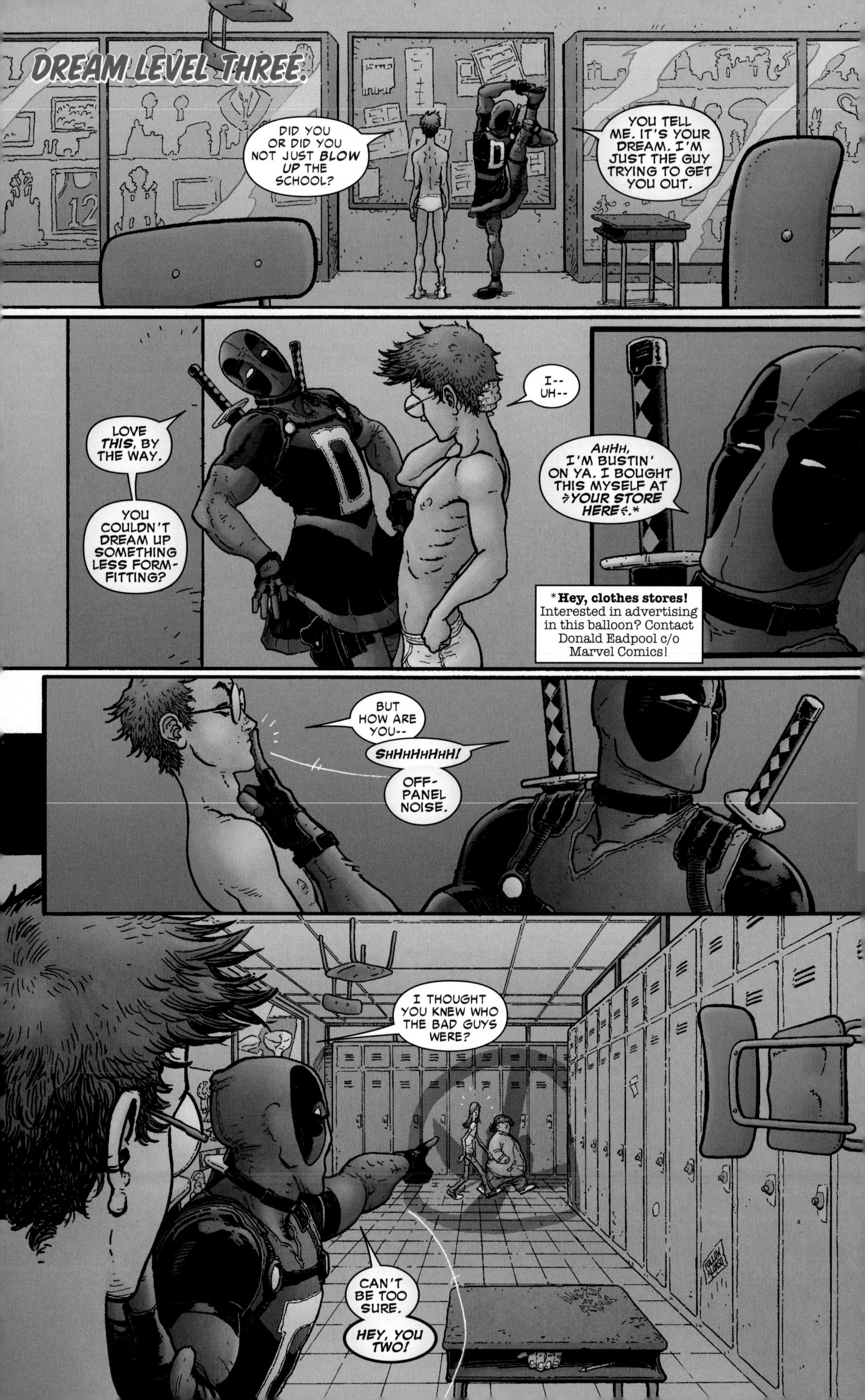
DREAM LEVEL THREE.
DID YOU OR DID YOU NOT JUST BLOW UP THE SCHOOL?
YOU TELL ME. IT'S YOUR DREAM. I'M JUST THE GUY TRYING TO GET YOU OUT.
LOVE THIS, BY THE WAY.
YOU COULDN'T DREAM UP SOMETHING LESS FORM-FITTING?
I-- UH--
AHHH, I'M BUSTIN' ON YA. I BOUGHT THIS MYSELF AT ⇒YOUR STORE HERE⇐.*
*Hey, clothes stores! Interested in advertising in this balloon? Contact Donald Eadpool c/o Marvel Comics!
BUT HOW ARE YOU--
SHHHHHHHH!
OFF-PANEL NOISE.
I THOUGHT YOU KNEW WHO THE BAD GUYS WERE?
CAN'T BE TOO SURE.
HEY, YOU TWO!

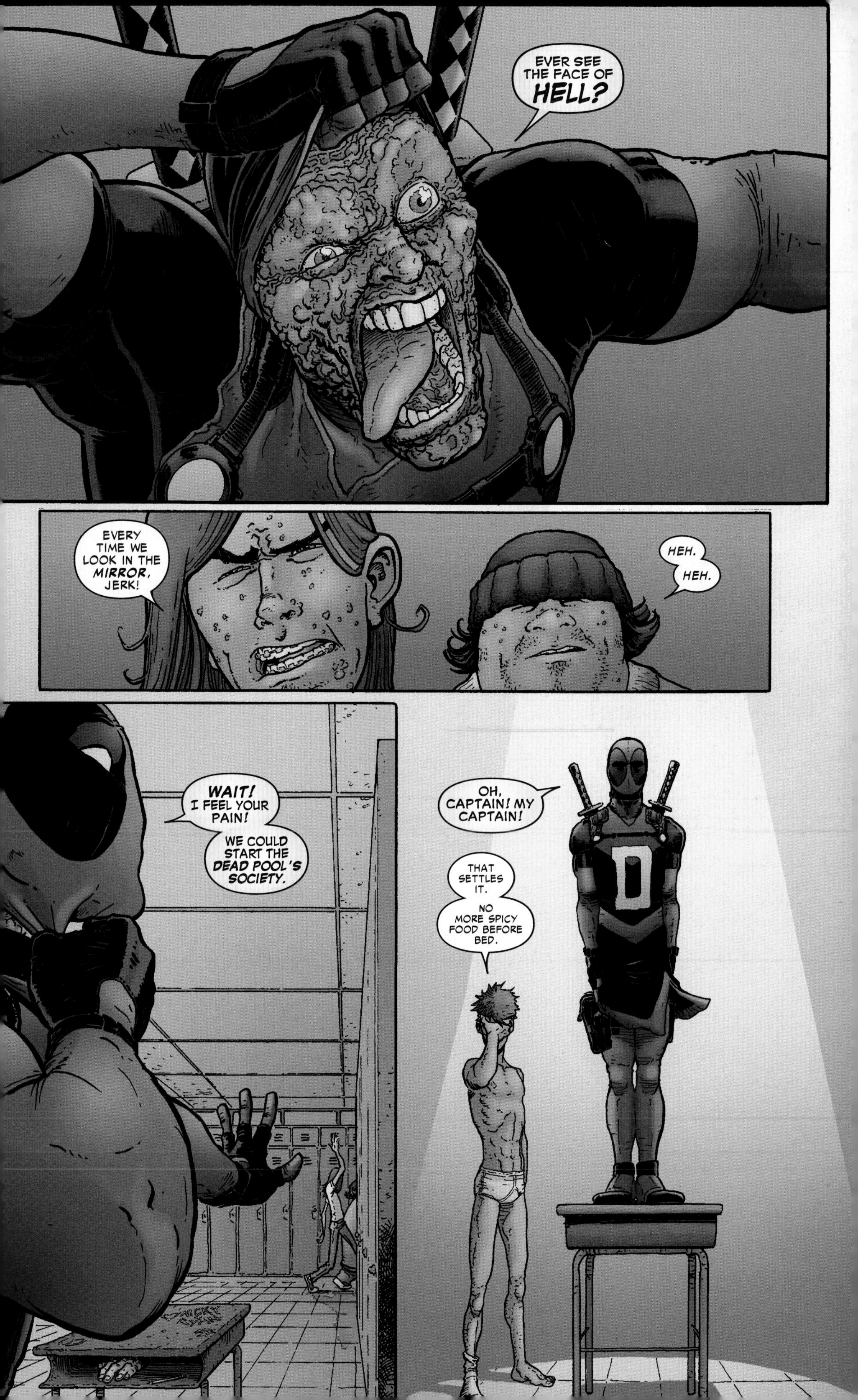
EVER SEE THE FACE OF HELL?
EVERY TIME WE LOOK IN THE MIRROR, JERK!
HEH. HEH.
WAIT! I FEEL YOUR PAIN!
WE COULD START THE DEAD POOL'S SOCIETY.
OH, CAPTAIN! MY CAPTAIN!
THAT SETTLES IT.
NO MORE SPICY FOOD BEFORE BED.

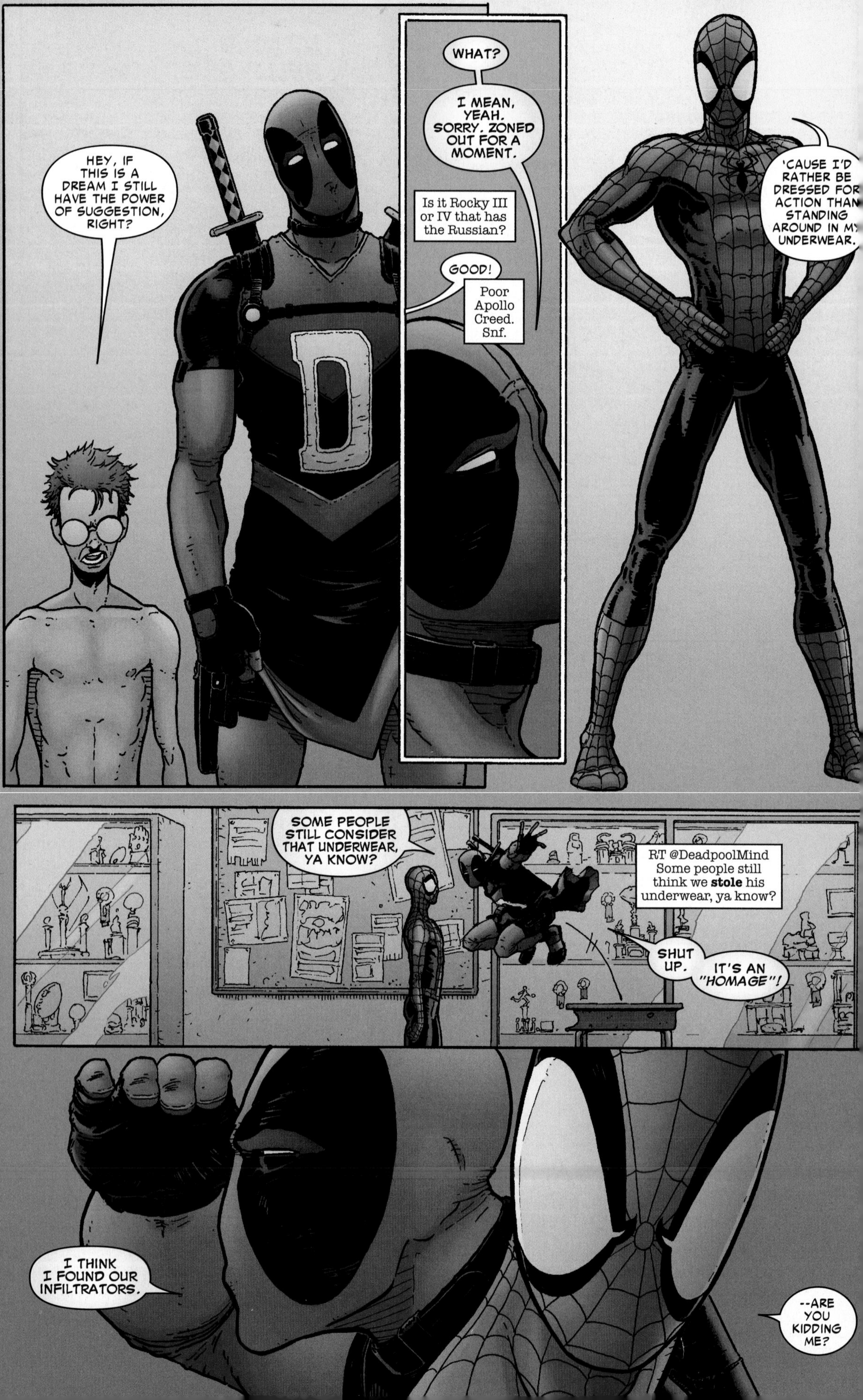
HEY, IF THIS IS A DREAM I STILL HAVE THE POWER OF SUGGESTION, RIGHT?
WHAT?
I MEAN, YEAH. SORRY. ZONED OUT FOR A MOMENT.
Is it Rocky III or IV that has the Russian?
GOOD!
Poor Apollo Creed. Snf.
'CAUSE I'D RATHER BE DRESSED FOR ACTION THAN STANDING AROUND IN MY UNDERWEAR.
SOME PEOPLE STILL CONSIDER THAT UNDERWEAR, YA KNOW?
RT @DeadpoolMind Some people still think we **stole** his underwear, ya know?
SHUT UP.
IT'S AN "HOMAGE"!
I THINK I FOUND OUR INFILTRATORS.
--ARE YOU KIDDING ME?

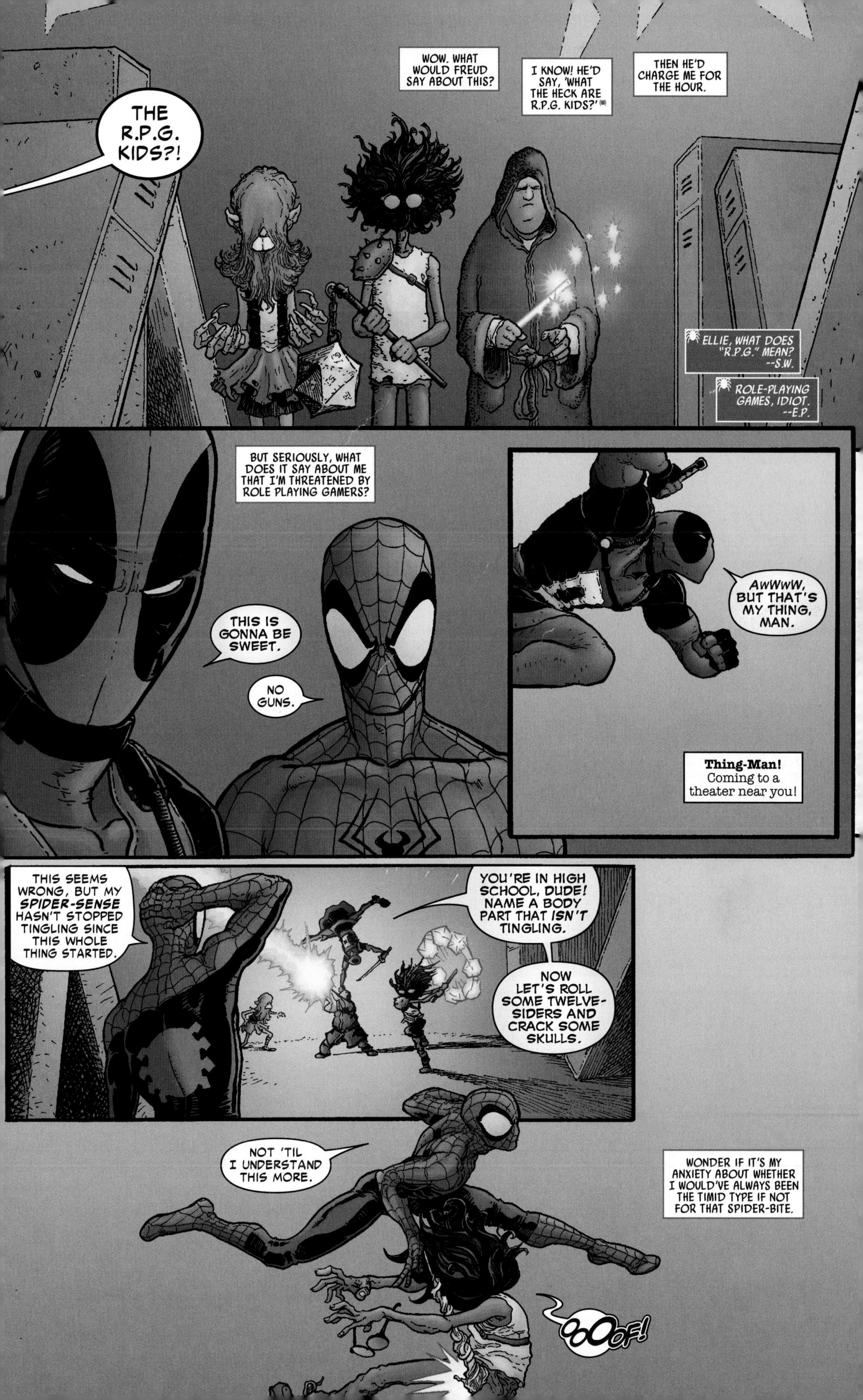
THE R.P.G. KIDS?!
WOW. WHAT WOULD FREUD SAY ABOUT THIS?
I KNOW! HE'D SAY, 'WHAT THE HECK ARE R.P.G. KIDS?'
THEN HE'D CHARGE ME FOR THE HOUR.
ELLIE, WHAT DOES "R.P.G." MEAN? --S.W.
ROLE-PLAYING GAMES, IDIOT. --E.P.
BUT SERIOUSLY, WHAT DOES IT SAY ABOUT ME THAT I'M THREATENED BY ROLE PLAYING GAMERS?
THIS IS GONNA BE SWEET.
NO GUNS.
AwWwW, BUT THAT'S MY THING, MAN.
Thing-Man! Coming to a theater near you!
THIS SEEMS WRONG, BUT MY SPIDER-SENSE HASN'T STOPPED TINGLING SINCE THIS WHOLE THING STARTED.
YOU'RE IN HIGH SCHOOL, DUDE! NAME A BODY PART THAT ISN'T TINGLING.
NOW LET'S ROLL SOME TWELVE-SIDERS AND CRACK SOME SKULLS.
NOT 'TIL I UNDERSTAND THIS MORE.
WONDER IF IT'S MY ANXIETY ABOUT WHETHER I WOULD'VE ALWAYS BEEN THE TIMID TYPE IF NOT FOR THAT SPIDER-BITE.
OOOOF!

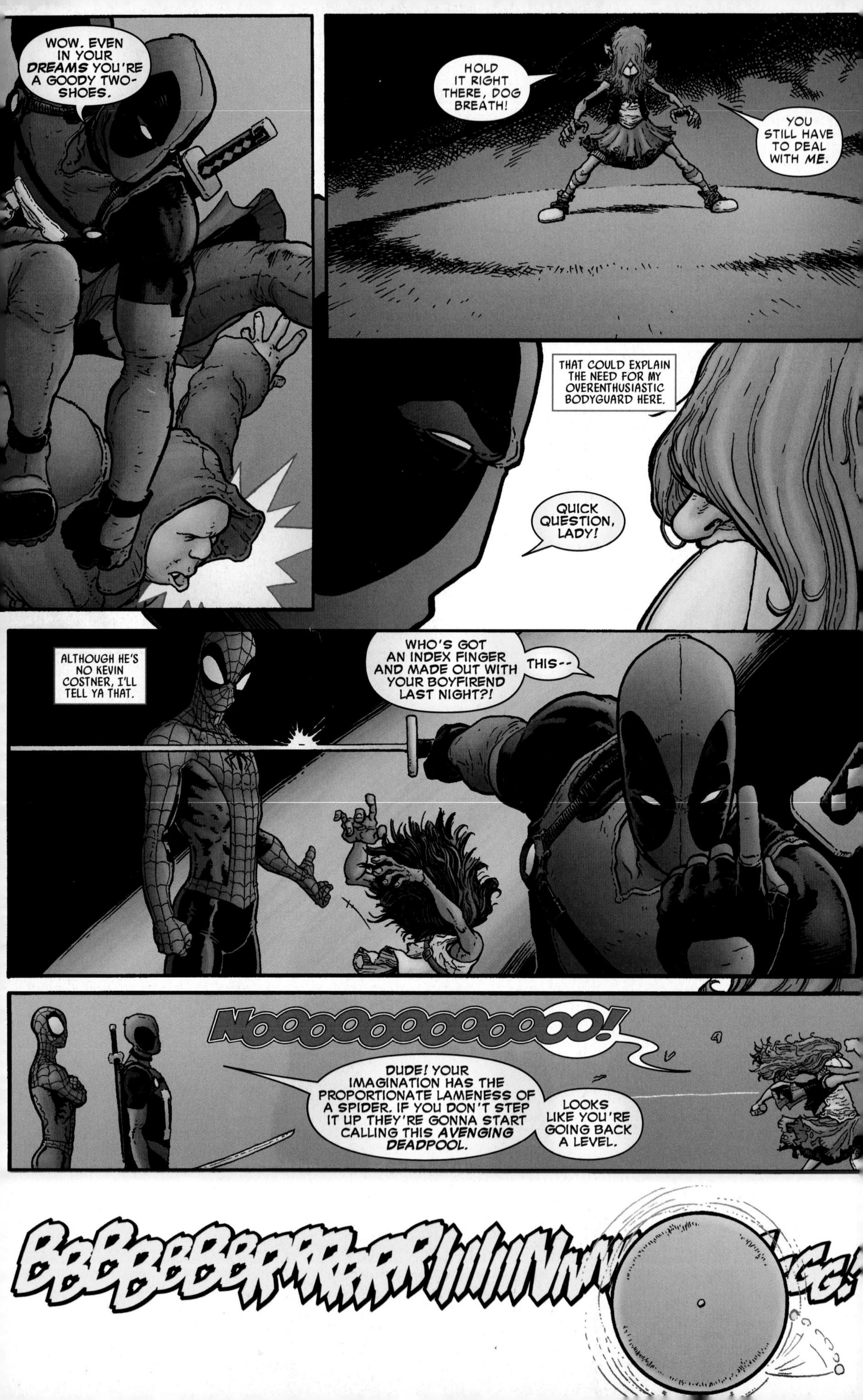
WOW. EVEN IN YOUR DREAMS YOU'RE A GOODY TWO-SHOES.
HOLD IT RIGHT THERE, DOG BREATH!
YOU STILL HAVE TO DEAL WITH ME.
THAT COULD EXPLAIN THE NEED FOR MY OVERENTHUSIASTIC BODYGUARD HERE.
QUICK QUESTION, LADY!
ALTHOUGH HE'S NO KEVIN COSTNER, I'LL TELL YA THAT.
WHO'S GOT AN INDEX FINGER AND MADE OUT WITH YOUR BOYFIREND LAST NIGHT?!
THIS--
NOOOOOOOOOOOOO!
DUDE! YOUR IMAGINATION HAS THE PROPORTIONATE LAMENESS OF A SPIDER. IF YOU DON'T STEP IT UP THEY'RE GONNA START CALLING THIS AVENGING DEADPOOL.
LOOKS LIKE YOU'RE GOING BACK A LEVEL.
BBBBBBBRRRRRRRIIIIIINNN

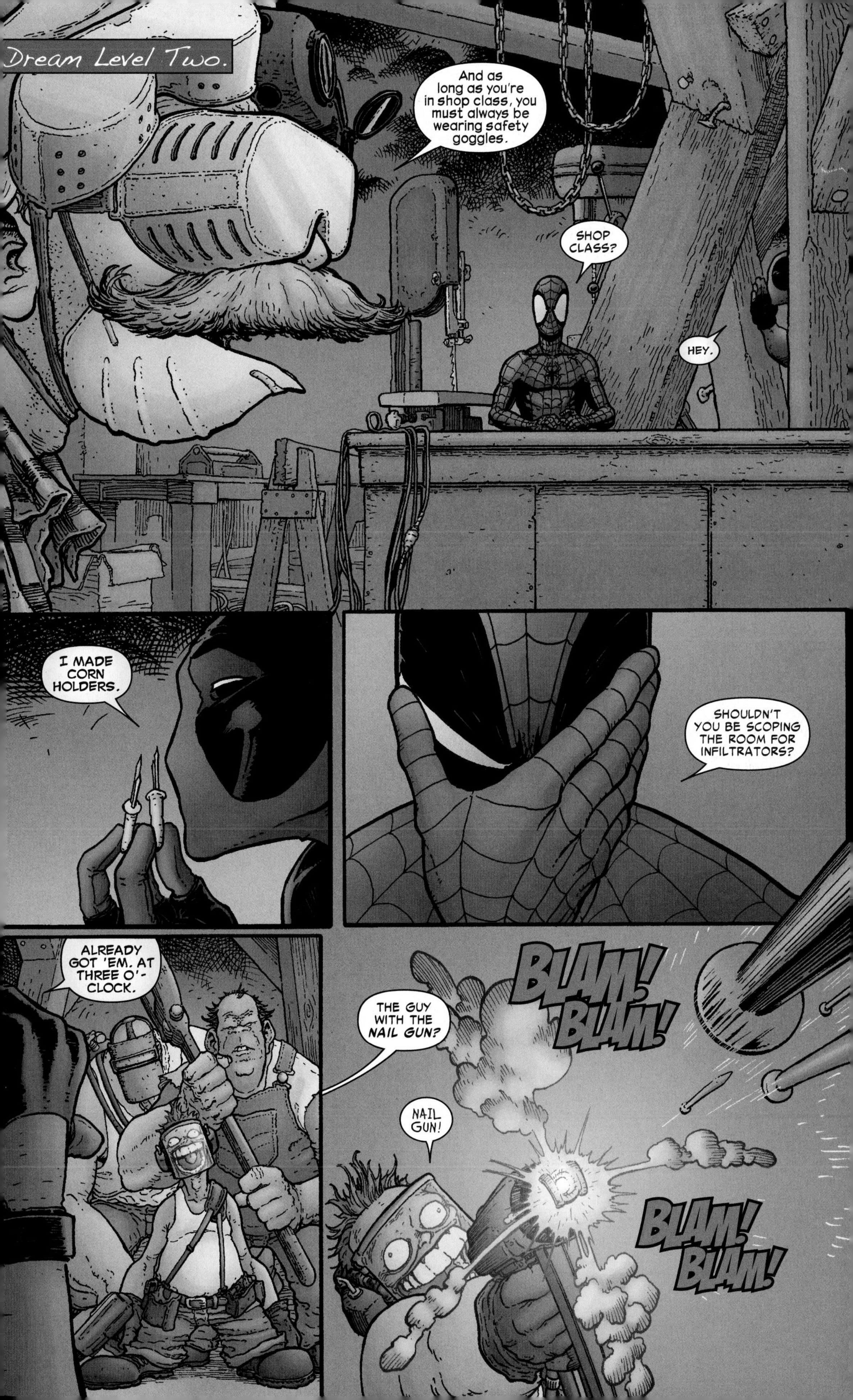
Dream Level Two.
And as long as you're in shop class, you must always be wearing safety goggles.
SHOP CLASS?
HEY.
I MADE CORN HOLDERS.
SHOULDN'T YOU BE SCOPING THE ROOM FOR INFILTRATORS?
ALREADY GOT 'EM. AT THREE O'-CLOCK.
THE GUY WITH THE NAIL GUN?
BLAM! BLAM!
NAIL GUN!
BLAM! BLAM!

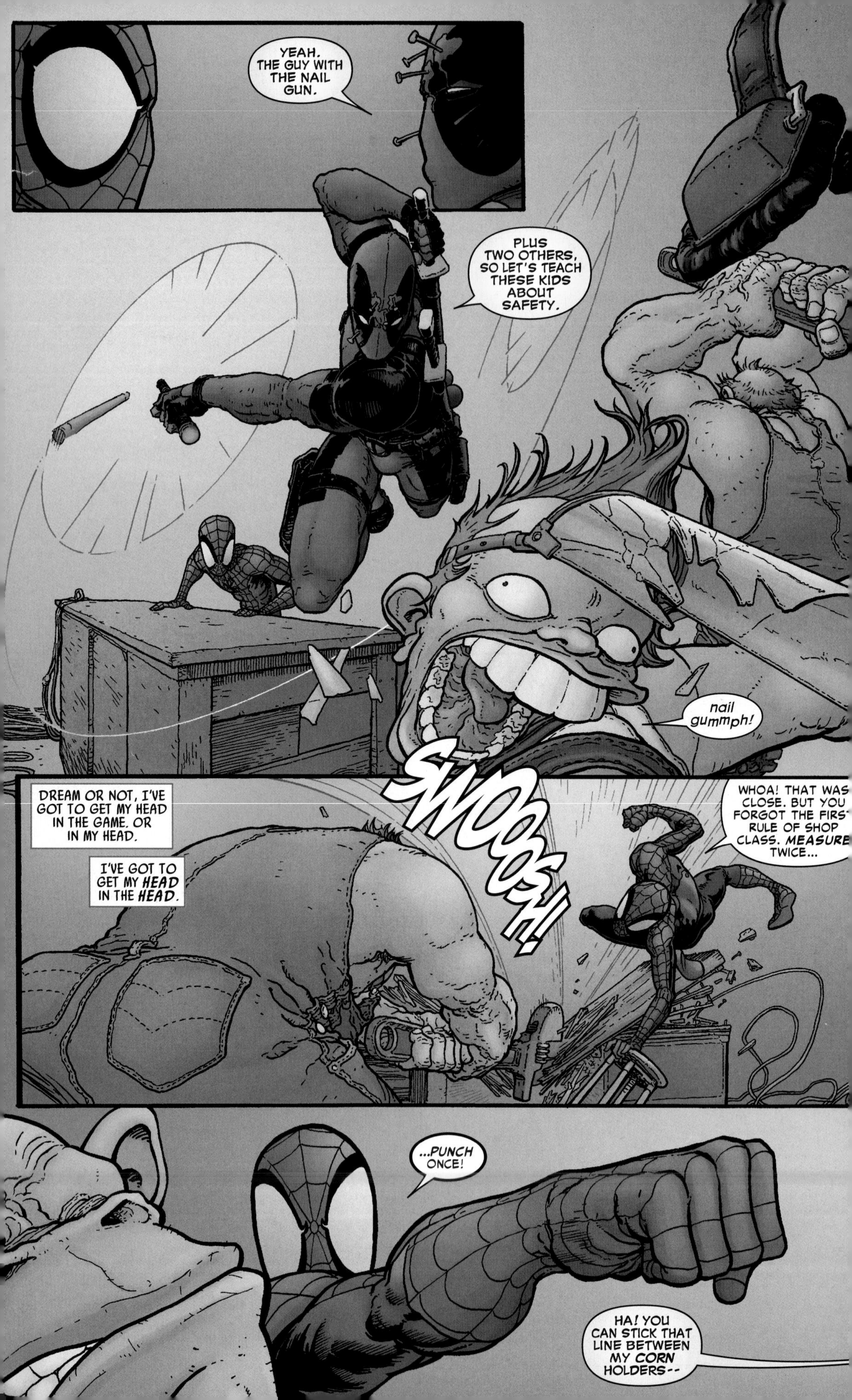

YEAH. THE GUY WITH THE NAIL GUN.
PLUS TWO OTHERS, SO LET'S TEACH THESE KIDS ABOUT SAFETY.
nail gummph!
SWOOOSH!
DREAM OR NOT, I'VE GOT TO GET MY HEAD IN THE GAME. OR IN MY HEAD.
I'VE GOT TO GET MY HEAD IN THE HEAD.
WHOA! THAT WAS CLOSE. BUT YOU FORGOT THE FIRST RULE OF SHOP CLASS. MEASURE TWICE...
...PUNCH ONCE!
HA! YOU CAN STICK THAT LINE BETWEEN MY CORN HOLDERS--

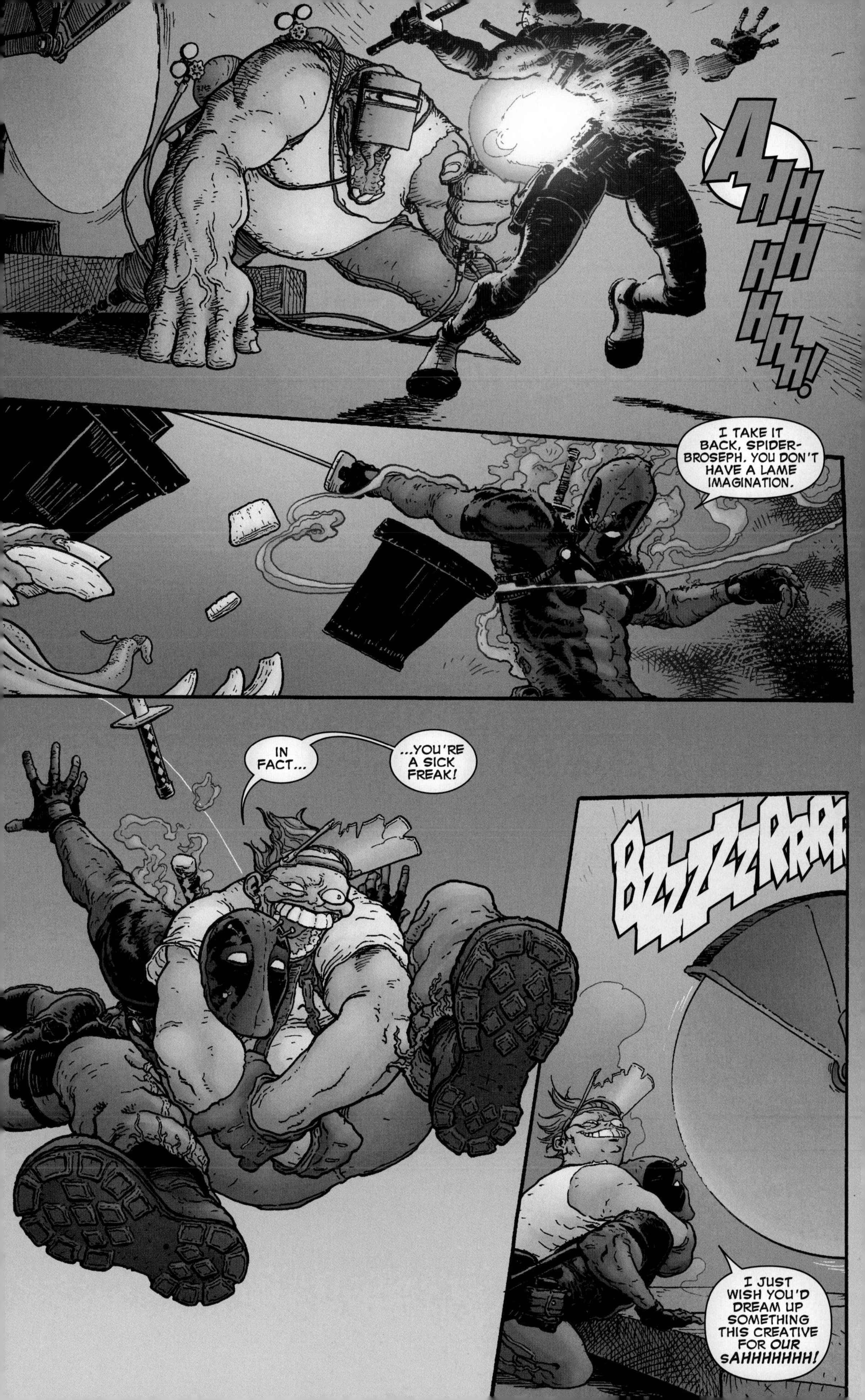
AHHHHHHHH!
I TAKE IT BACK, SPIDER-BROSEPH. YOU DON'T HAVE A LAME IMAGINATION.
IN FACT...
...YOU'RE A SICK FREAK!
BZZZZRRRR
I JUST WISH YOU'D DREAM UP SOMETHING THIS CREATIVE FOR OUR SAHHHHHHH!

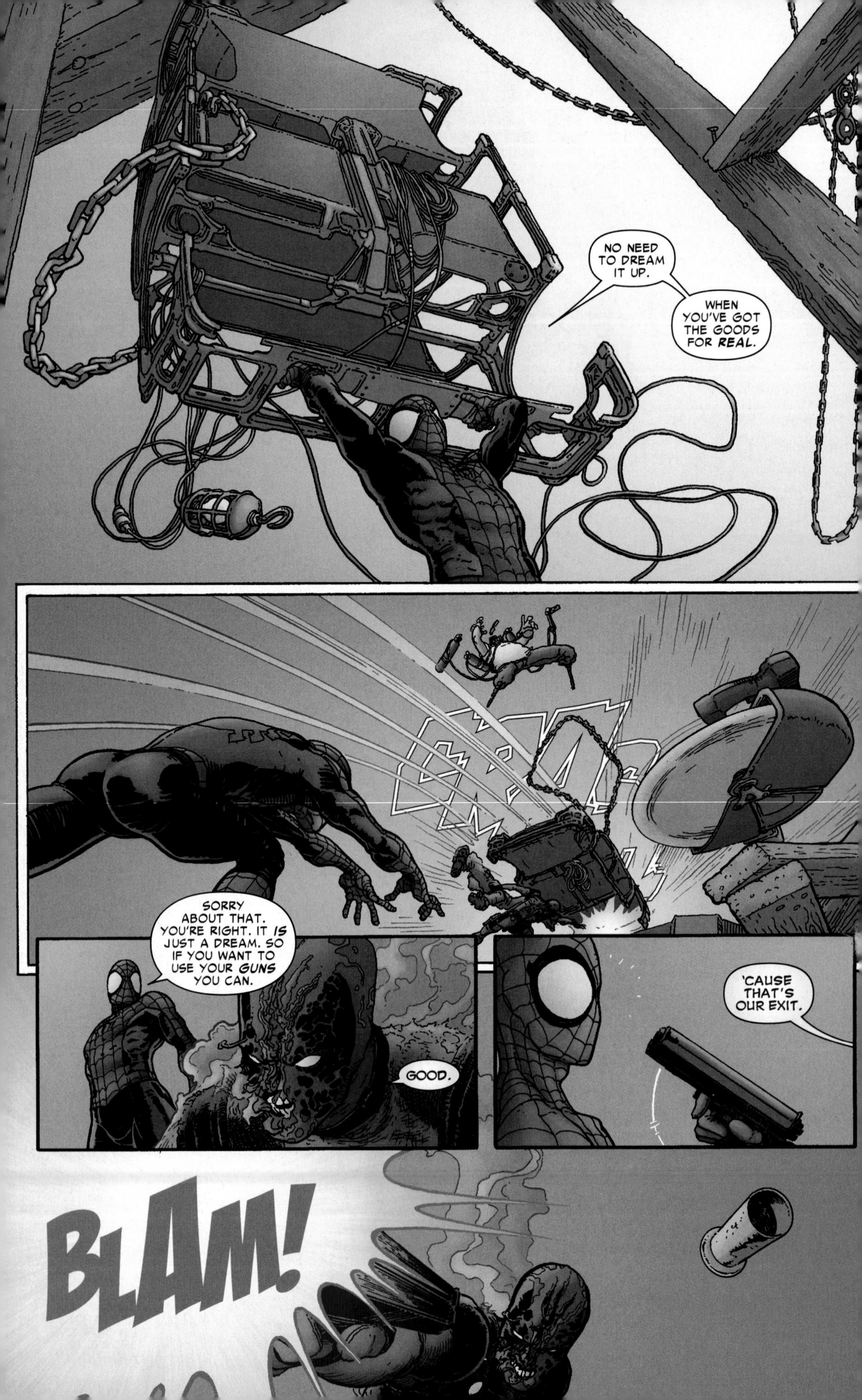
NO NEED TO DREAM IT UP.
WHEN YOU'VE GOT THE GOODS FOR *REAL*.
SORRY ABOUT THAT. YOU'RE RIGHT. IT *IS* JUST A DREAM. SO IF YOU WANT TO USE YOUR *GUNS* YOU CAN.
GOOD.
'CAUSE THAT'S OUR EXIT.
BLAM!

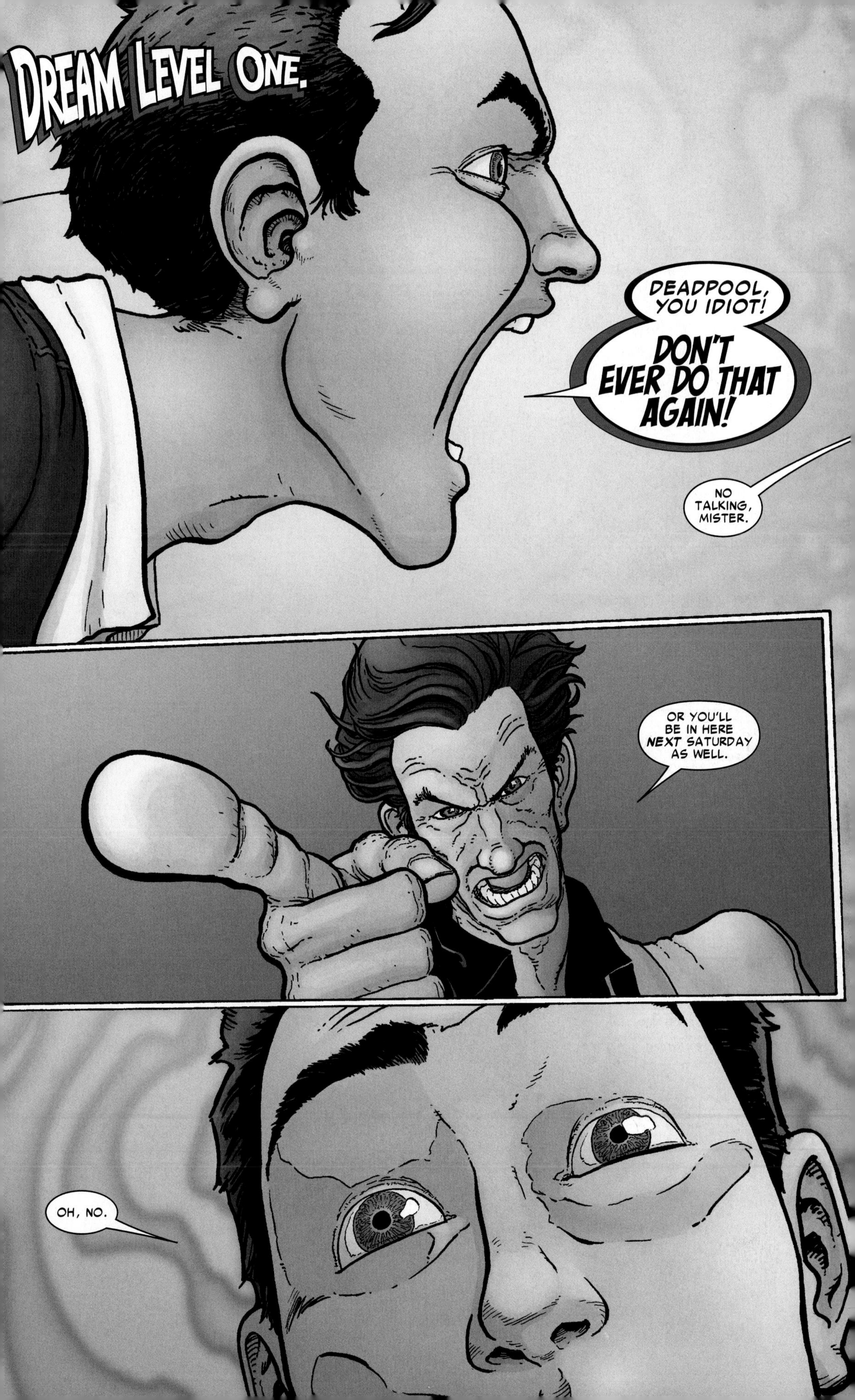
DREAM LEVEL ONE.
DEADPOOL, YOU IDIOT!
DON'T EVER DO THAT AGAIN!
NO TALKING, MISTER.
OR YOU'LL BE IN HERE NEXT SATURDAY AS WELL.
OH, NO.

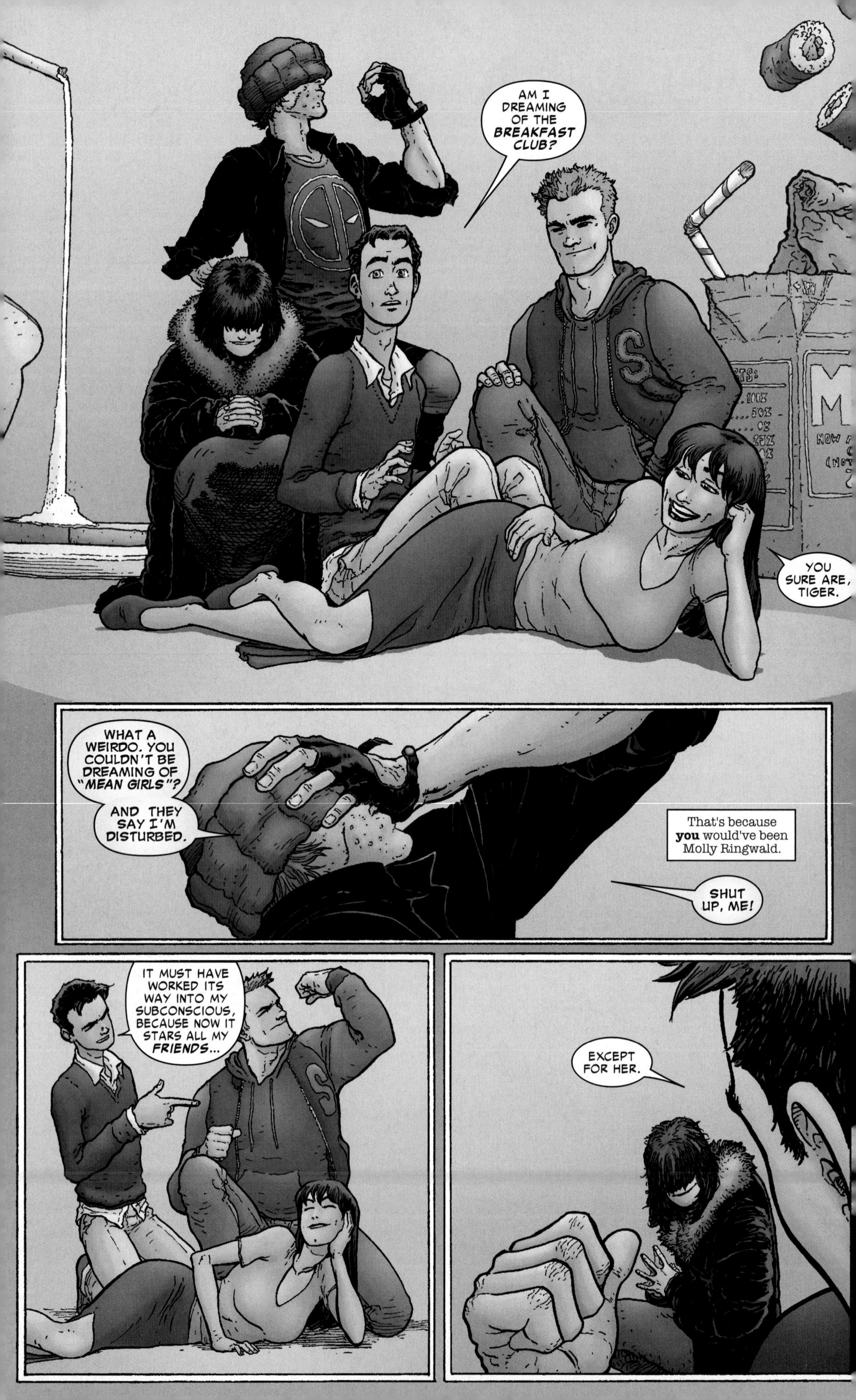
AM I DREAMING OF THE BREAKFAST CLUB?
YOU SURE ARE, TIGER.
WHAT A WEIRDO. YOU COULDN'T BE DREAMING OF "MEAN GIRLS"?
AND THEY SAY I'M DISTURBED.
That's because you would've been Molly Ringwald.
SHUT UP, ME!
IT MUST HAVE WORKED ITS WAY INTO MY SUBCONSCIOUS, BECAUSE NOW IT STARS ALL MY FRIENDS...
EXCEPT FOR HER.

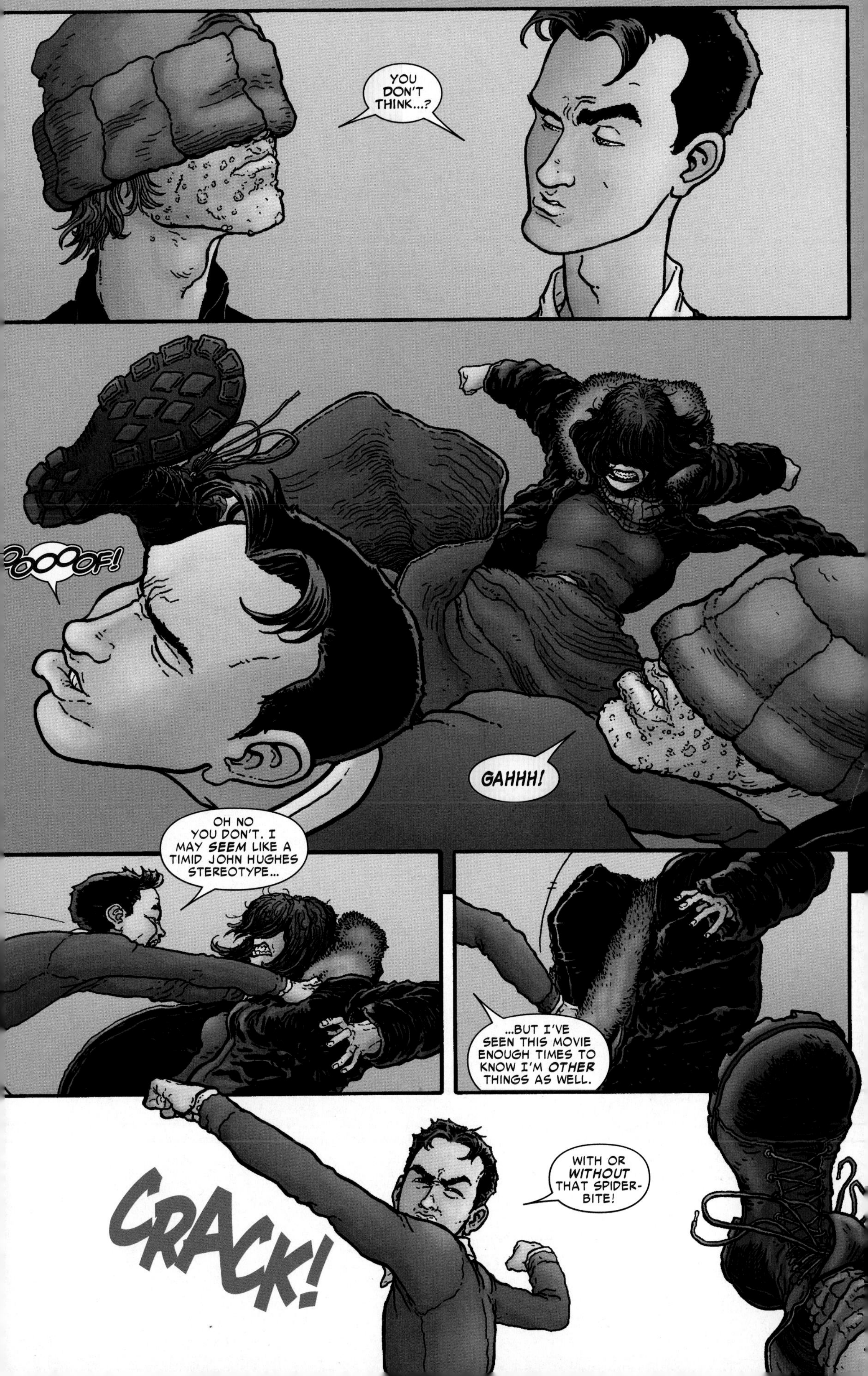
YOU DON'T THINK...?
OOOOOF!
GAHHH!
OH NO YOU DON'T. I MAY SEEM LIKE A TIMID JOHN HUGHES STEREOTYPE...
...BUT I'VE SEEN THIS MOVIE ENOUGH TIMES TO KNOW I'M OTHER THINGS AS WELL.
CRACK!
WITH OR WITHOUT THAT SPIDER-BITE!

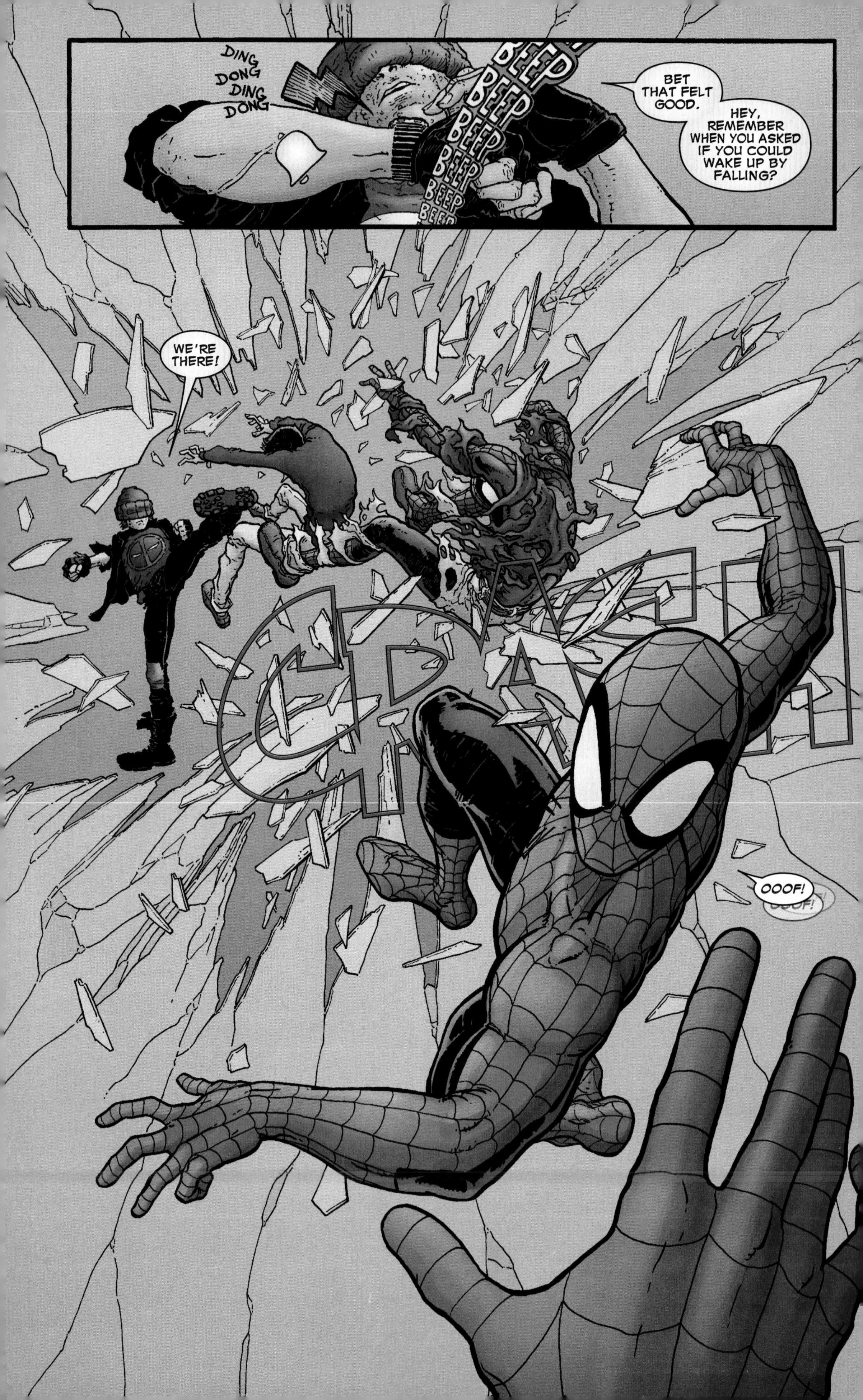
DING
DONG
DING
DONG
BEEP
BEEP
BEEP
BEEP
BEEP
BEEP
BET THAT FELT GOOD.
HEY, REMEMBER WHEN YOU ASKED IF YOU COULD WAKE UP BY FALLING?
WE'RE THERE!
CRACK
OOOF!
OOOF!

W-WHAT HAPPENED?

UH-OH. THIS FEELS "REAL". I THINK I'M--

COOL! YOU'RE AWAKE!

THE *GOOD* NEWS...

...IS THAT WHEN I SAID SOMEONE WAS TRYING TO ACCESS YOUR MIND, I WASN'T LYING.

THE *BAD* NEWS...

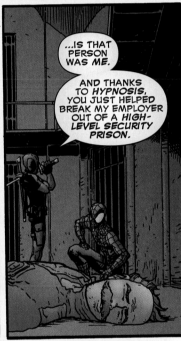

...IS THAT PERSON WAS *ME*.

AND THANKS TO *HYPNOSIS*, YOU JUST HELPED BREAK MY EMPLOYER OUT OF A *HIGH-LEVEL SECURITY PRISON*.

HOW MUCH, DEADPOOL!? HOW MUCH *MONEY* DID IT TAKE TO GET YOU TO SELL THE LITTLE BIT OF DECENCY YOU HAD IN YOU?

Twenty-nine ninety-nine! No, Wait! Go lower. LOWER! ONE DOLLAR!

BELIEVE IT OR NOT, SPIDEY, I DIDN'T DO IT FOR MONEY.

MY EMPLOYER SAID HE FOUND A WAY TO *KILL* ME.

AND AS YOU MAY HAVE HEARD, I'M HAVING A LITTLE TROUBLE WITH THAT LATELY.

GREAT. AND WHO IS THIS CON-ARTIST?

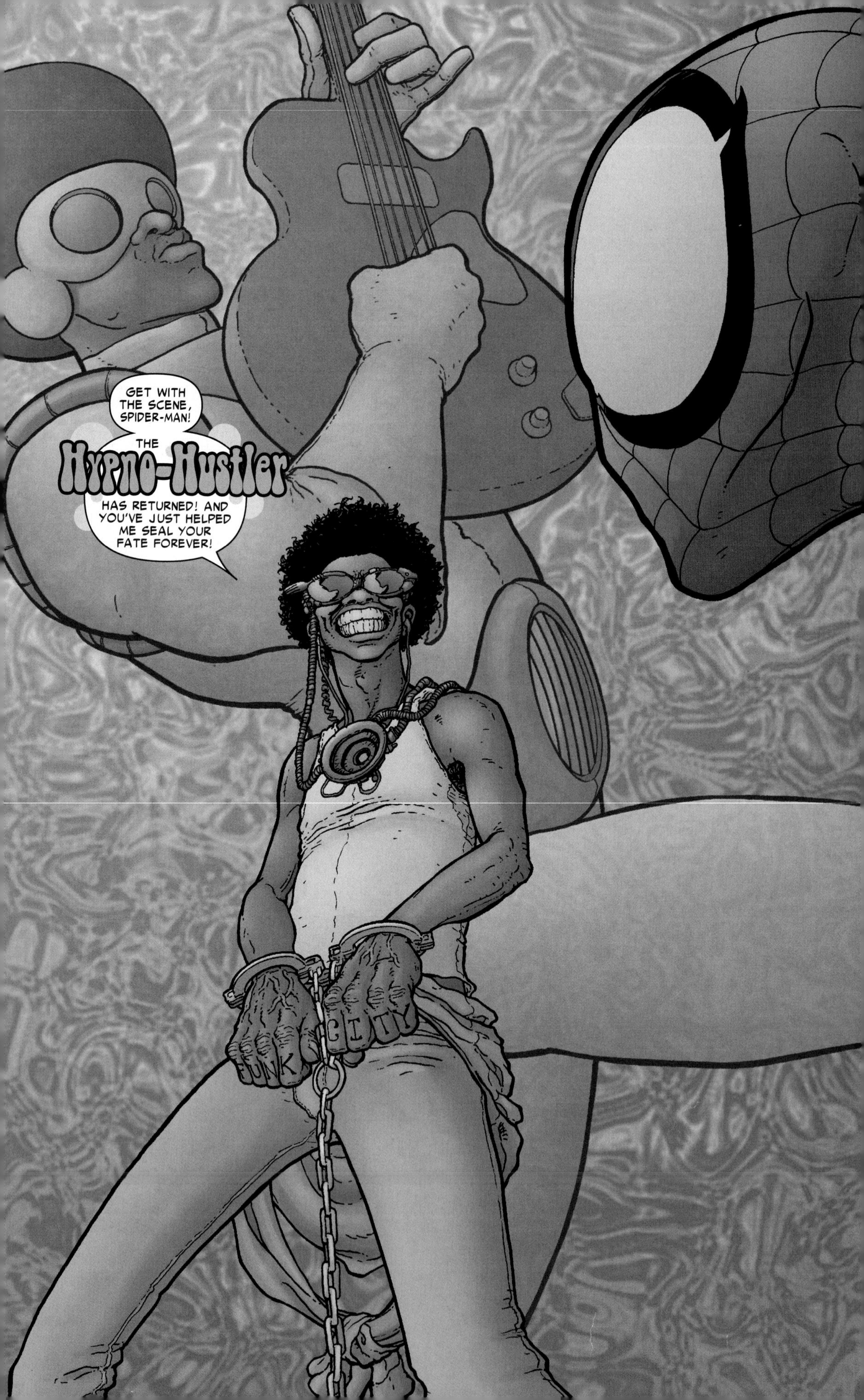
GET WITH THE SCENE, SPIDER-MAN!
THE
Hypno-Hustler
HAS RETURNED! AND YOU'VE JUST HELPED ME SEAL YOUR FATE FOREVER!
FUNK CITY

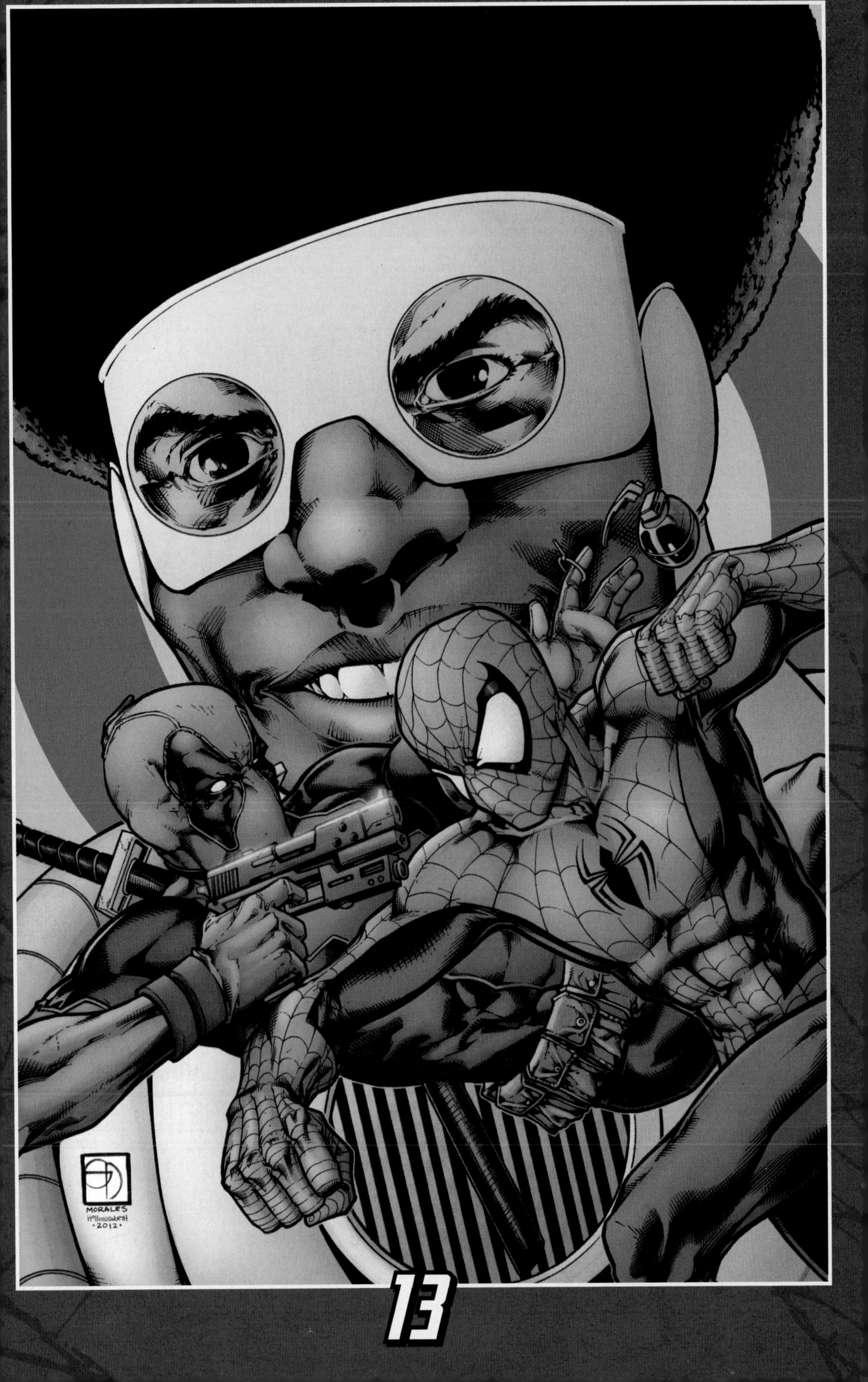
MORALES
HOLLINGSWORTH
•2012•

13

While attending a demonstration in radiology, high school student Peter Parker was bitten by a spider that had accidentally been exposed to radioactive rays. Through a miracle of science, Pet... soon found that he had gained the spider's powers…and had, in effe... ...der Later he joined the Avengers. And now he is the

ALL RIGHT, ALREADY! WE GET IT. HE HAS SPIDER-POWERS!

AVENGING
SPIDER-MAN

After being diagnosed with cancer, the deadly mercenary Wade Wilson volunteered for the Weapon X program hoping that they would be able to give him a cure. Their solution was to give him a healing factor similar t... Wolverine's. Now, he's the Merc with a Mouth, the Regeneratin' D...

CAN WE GET WAID TO WRITE THIS? I'D LOVE TO WIN AN EISNER OR HARVEY AWARD.

DEADPOOL

AVENGING
SPIDER-MAN

PREVIOUSLY...

Spider-Man and Deadpool fought their way through a high school dreamscape only to realize that the high school was actually a prison holding the Hypno-Hustler, who had hired Deadpool to trick Spidey into breaking him out.

HYPNO-HUSTLER HAS PROMISED TO HELP ME DIE IF OUR PLAN SUCCEEDS.

And this story takes place before Deadpool #50...so dying is all Deadpool really wants.

"TO DIE...TO SLEEP..." AND ALSO TO KNOW WHAT WOULD HAVE HAPPENED IF "AWAKE" HAD GOTTEN A SECOND SEASON.

Not to stop talking to yourself in captions?

NO! WHO ELSE WOULD LAUGH AT MY JOKES? I COULD GO FOR A BURRITO THOUGH.

WRITER: **KEVIN SHINICK**   ART: **AARON KUDER**

COLOR ART: **MATT HOLLINGSWORTH**   LETTERER: **VC's JOE CARAMAGNA**

COVER: **DAVIS, MORALES AND HOLLINGSWORTH**

JEEZ. YA THINK THIS BOOK'S GOT ENOUGH EDITORS?

ASSISTANT EDITOR: **ELLIE PYLE**   ASSOCIATE EDITOR: **SANA AMANAT**   EDITOR: **STEPHEN WACKER**

EXECUTIVE EDITOR: **TOM BREVOORT**   EDITOR IN CHIEF: **AXEL ALONSO**

CHIEF CREATIVE OFFICER: **JOE QUESADA**   PUBLISHER: **DAN BUCKLEY**   EXECUTIVE PRODUCER: **ALAN FINE**

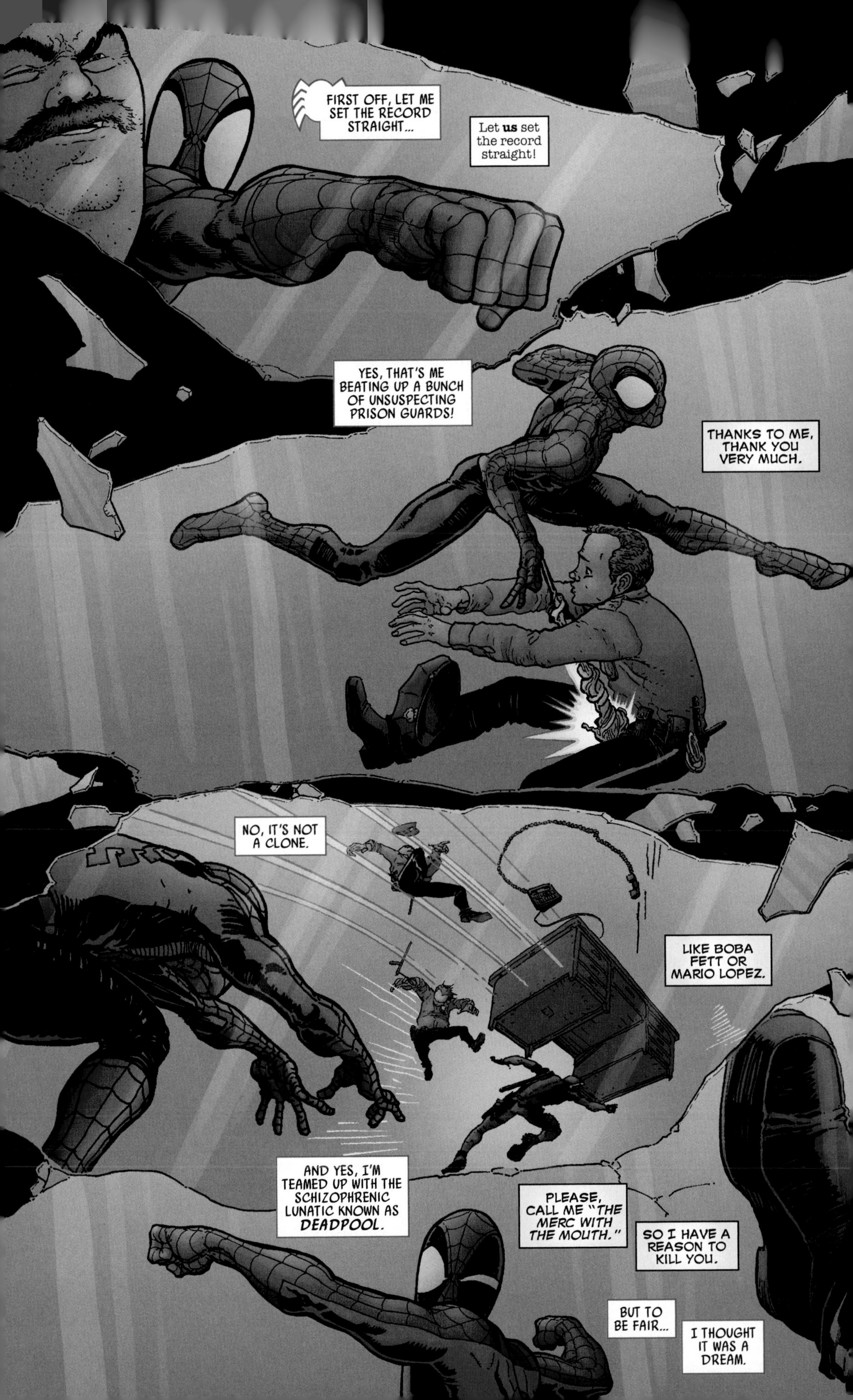
FIRST OFF, LET ME SET THE RECORD STRAIGHT...
Let **us** set the record straight!
YES, THAT'S ME BEATING UP A BUNCH OF UNSUSPECTING PRISON GUARDS!
THANKS TO ME, THANK YOU VERY MUCH.
NO, IT'S NOT A CLONE.
LIKE BOBA FETT OR MARIO LOPEZ.
AND YES, I'M TEAMED UP WITH THE SCHIZOPHRENIC LUNATIC KNOWN AS *DEADPOOL*.
PLEASE, CALL ME "*THE MERC WITH THE MOUTH.*"
SO I HAVE A REASON TO KILL YOU.
BUT TO BE FAIR...
I THOUGHT IT WAS A DREAM.

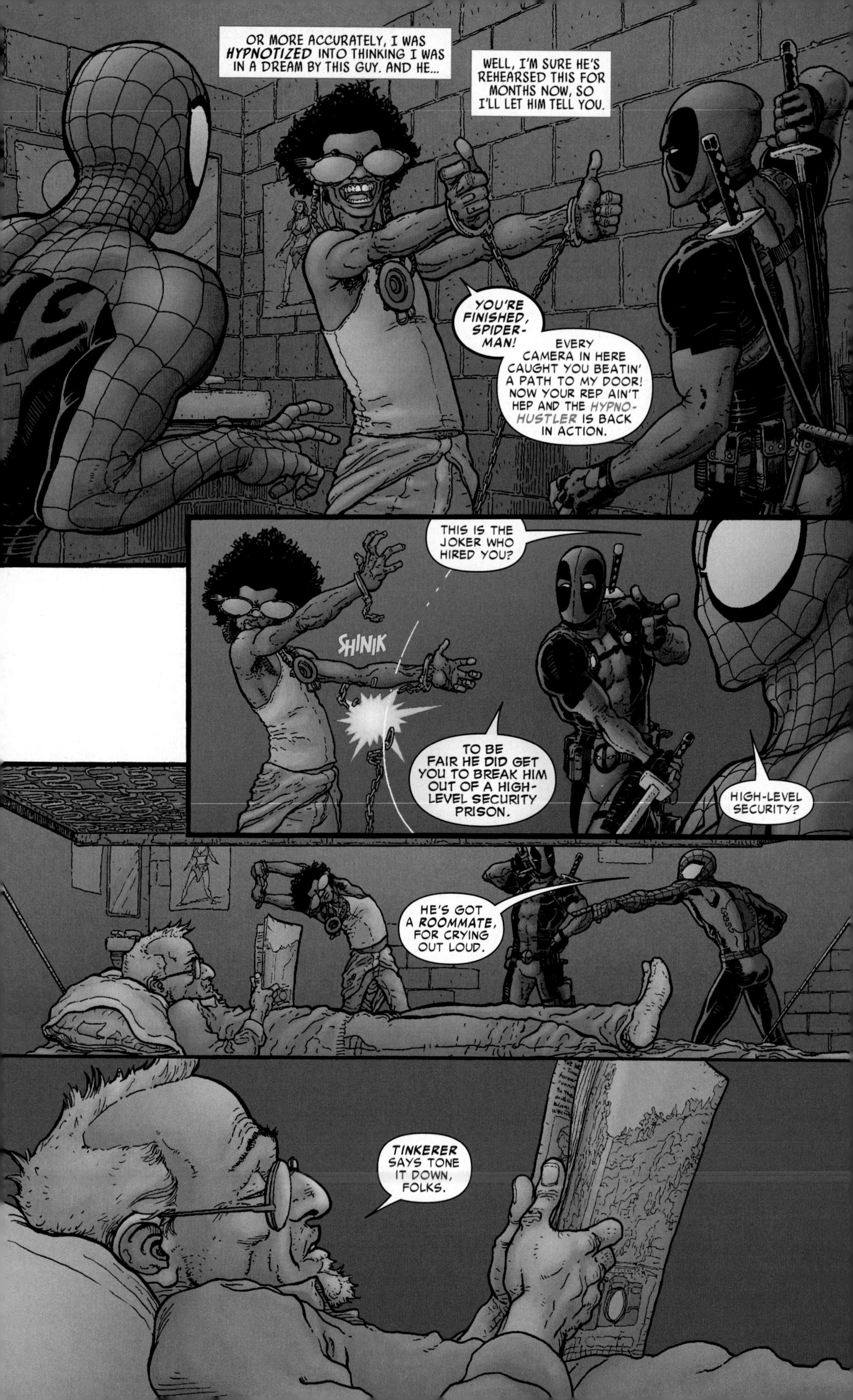
OR MORE ACCURATELY, I WAS HYPNOTIZED INTO THINKING I WAS IN A DREAM BY THIS GUY. AND HE...
WELL, I'M SURE HE'S REHEARSED THIS FOR MONTHS NOW, SO I'LL LET HIM TELL YOU.
YOU'RE FINISHED, SPIDER-MAN!
EVERY CAMERA IN HERE CAUGHT YOU BEATIN' A PATH TO MY DOOR! NOW YOUR REP AIN'T HEP AND THE HYPNO-HUSTLER IS BACK IN ACTION.
THIS IS THE JOKER WHO HIRED YOU?
SHINIK
TO BE FAIR HE DID GET YOU TO BREAK HIM OUT OF A HIGH-LEVEL SECURITY PRISON.
HIGH-LEVEL SECURITY?
HE'S GOT A ROOMMATE, FOR CRYING OUT LOUD.
TINKERER SAYS TONE IT DOWN, FOLKS.

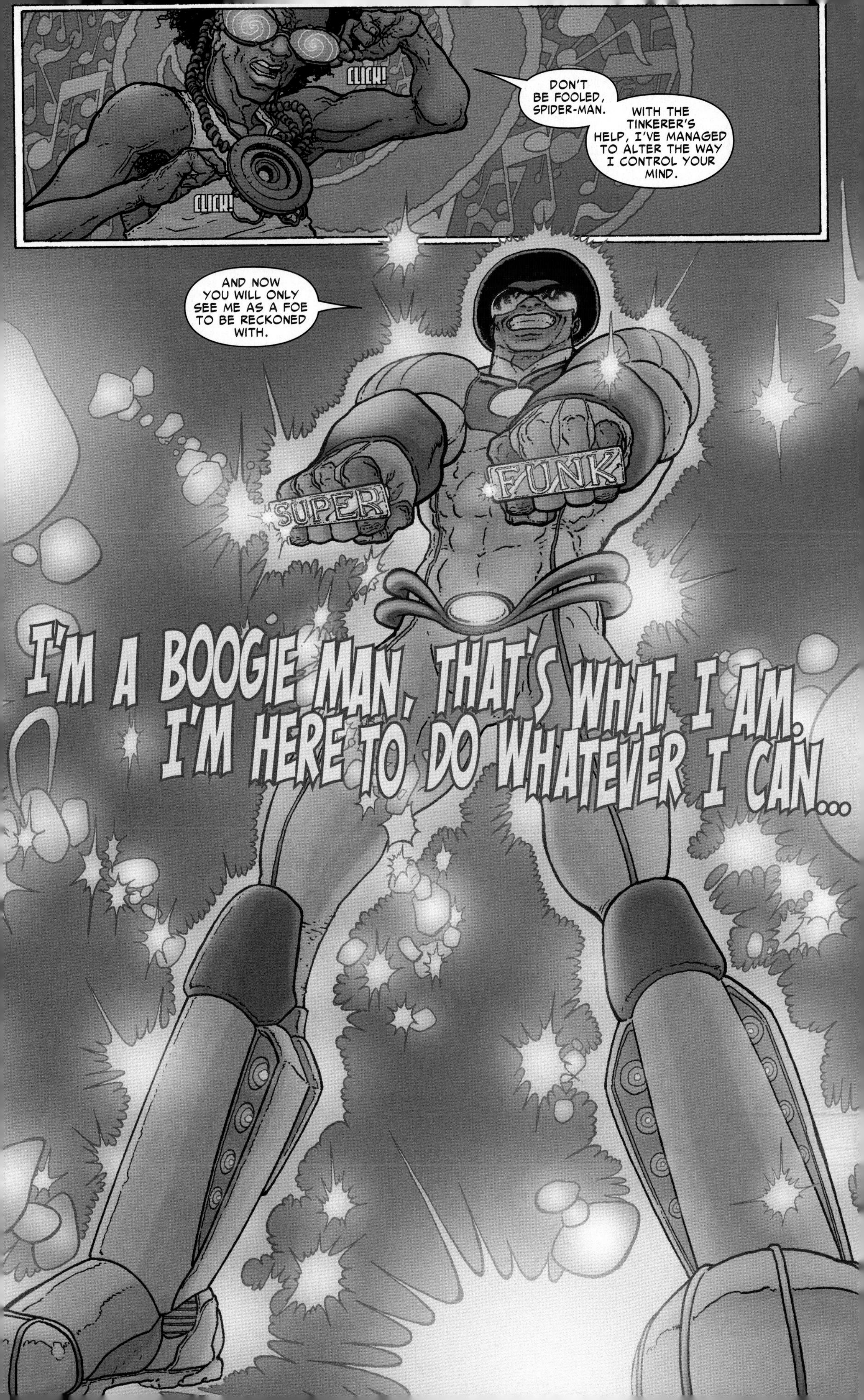
CLICK!
CLICK!
DON'T BE FOOLED, SPIDER-MAN.
WITH THE TINKERER'S HELP, I'VE MANAGED TO ALTER THE WAY I CONTROL YOUR MIND.
AND NOW YOU WILL ONLY SEE ME AS A FOE TO BE RECKONED WITH.
SUPER
FUNK
I'M A BOOGIE MAN, THAT'S WHAT I AM.
I'M HERE TO DO WHATEVER I CAN...

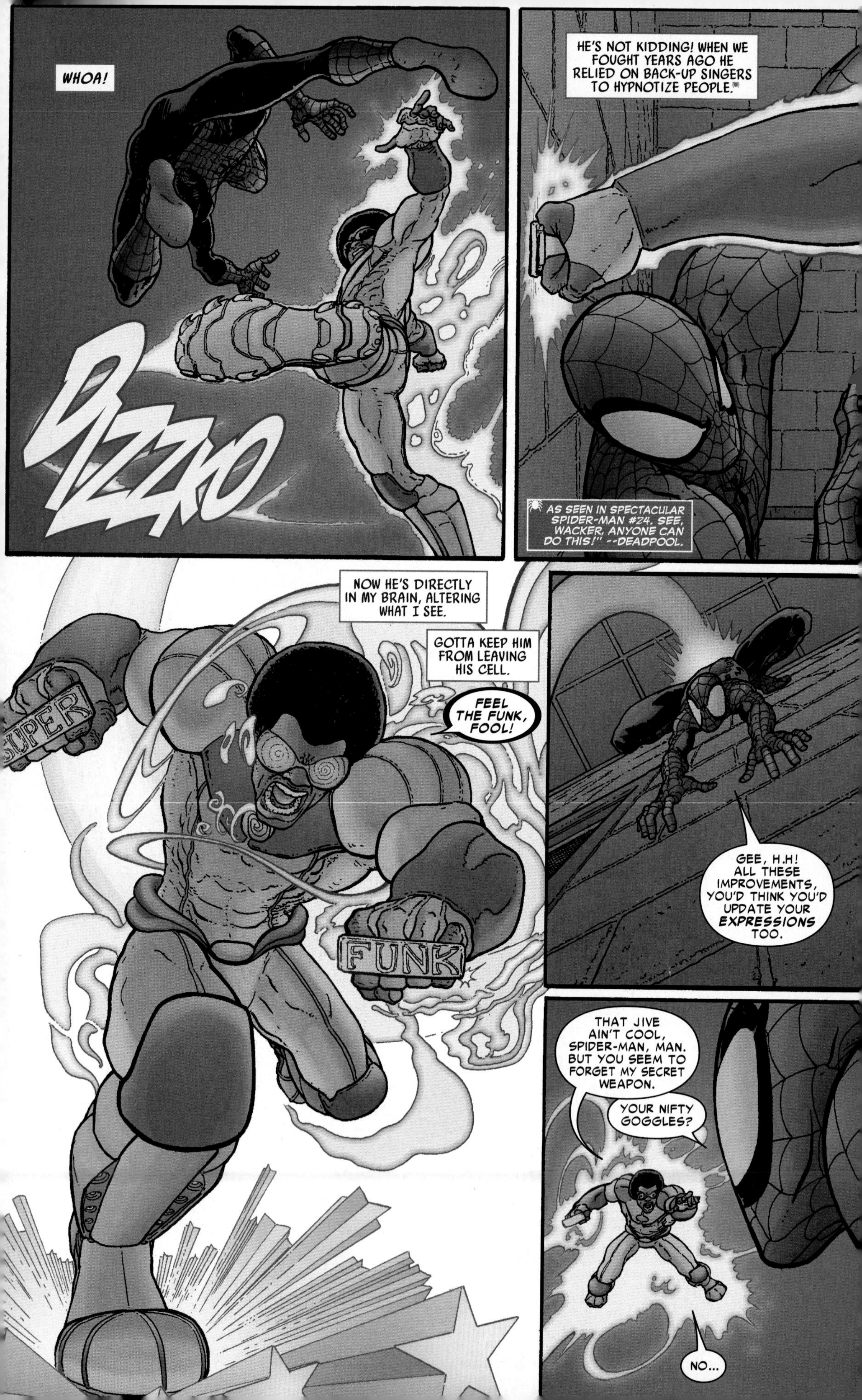
WHOA!
DIZZKO
HE'S NOT KIDDING! WHEN WE FOUGHT YEARS AGO HE RELIED ON BACK-UP SINGERS TO HYPNOTIZE PEOPLE.*
*AS SEEN IN SPECTACULAR SPIDER-MAN #24. SEE, WACKER, ANYONE CAN DO THIS!" --DEADPOOL.
NOW HE'S DIRECTLY IN MY BRAIN, ALTERING WHAT I SEE.
GOTTA KEEP HIM FROM LEAVING HIS CELL.
FEEL THE FUNK, FOOL!
SUPER
FUNK
GEE, H.H! ALL THESE IMPROVEMENTS, YOU'D THINK YOU'D UPDATE YOUR EXPRESSIONS TOO.
THAT JIVE AIN'T COOL, SPIDER-MAN, MAN. BUT YOU SEEM TO FORGET MY SECRET WEAPON.
YOUR NIFTY GOGGLES?
NO...

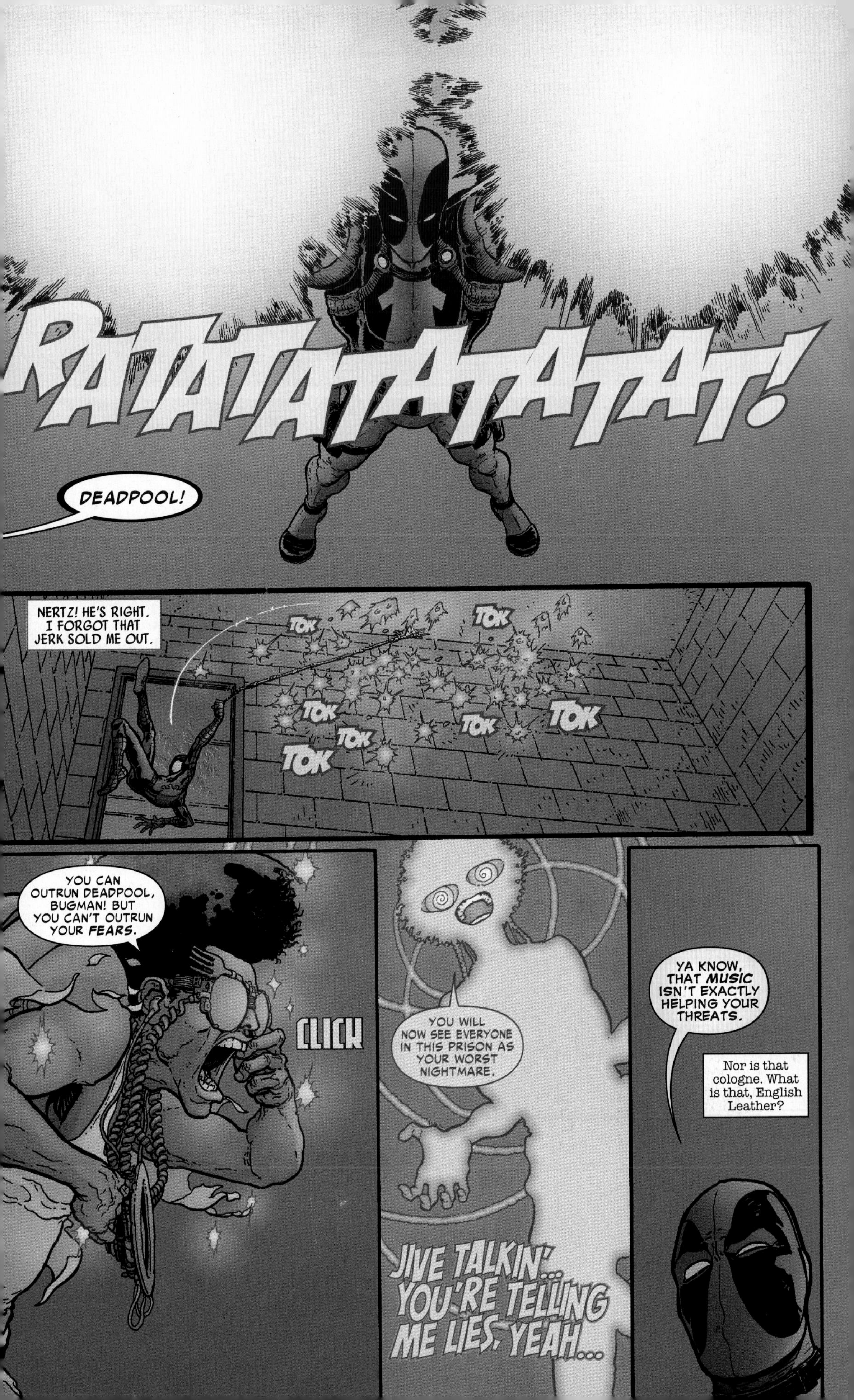
RATATATATATATAT!
DEADPOOL!
NERTZ! HE'S RIGHT. I FORGOT THAT JERK SOLD ME OUT.
TOK
TOK
TOK
TOK
TOK
TOK
TOK
YOU CAN OUTRUN DEADPOOL, BUGMAN! BUT YOU CAN'T OUTRUN YOUR FEARS.
CLICK
YOU WILL NOW SEE EVERYONE IN THIS PRISON AS YOUR WORST NIGHTMARE.
JIVE TALKIN'... YOU'RE TELLING ME LIES, YEAH...
YA KNOW, THAT MUSIC ISN'T EXACTLY HELPING YOUR THREATS.
Nor is that cologne. What is that, English Leather?

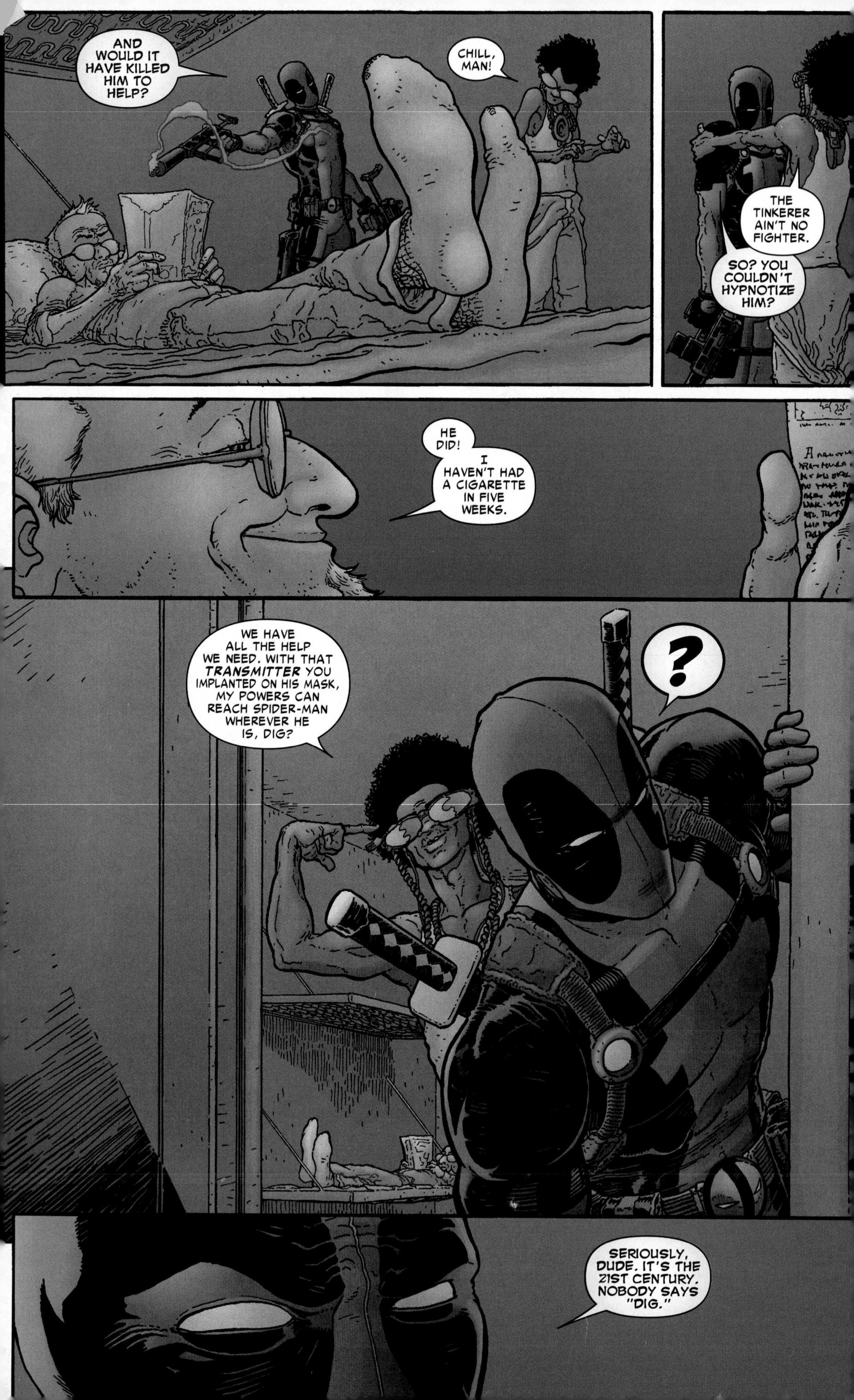
AND WOULD IT HAVE KILLED HIM TO HELP?
CHILL, MAN!
THE TINKERER AIN'T NO FIGHTER.
SO? YOU COULDN'T HYPNOTIZE HIM?
HE DID!
I HAVEN'T HAD A CIGARETTE IN FIVE WEEKS.
WE HAVE ALL THE HELP WE NEED. WITH THAT TRANSMITTER YOU IMPLANTED ON HIS MASK, MY POWERS CAN REACH SPIDER-MAN WHEREVER HE IS, DIG?
?
SERIOUSLY, DUDE. IT'S THE 21ST CENTURY. NOBODY SAYS "DIG."

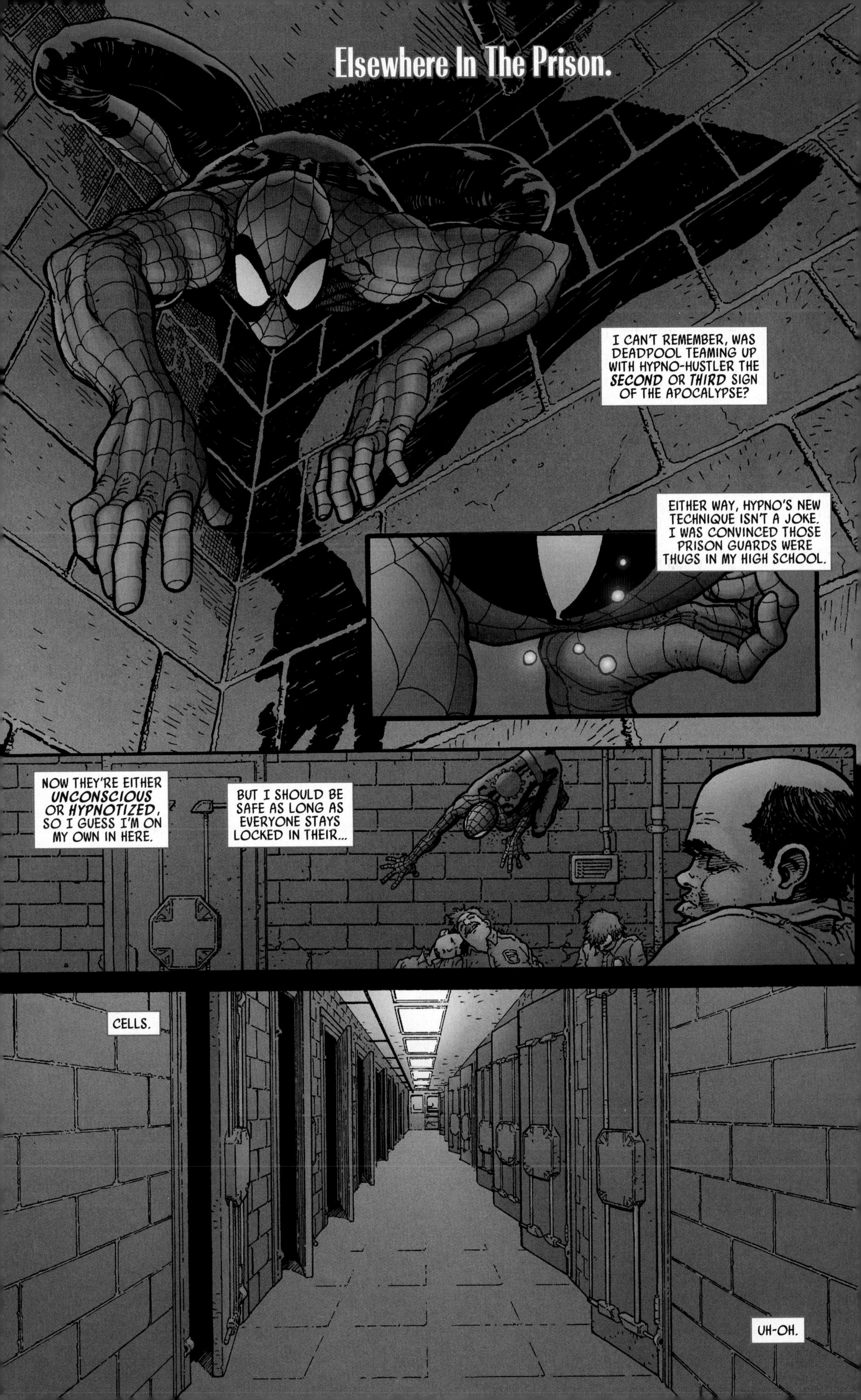
Elsewhere In The Prison.
I CAN'T REMEMBER, WAS DEADPOOL TEAMING UP WITH HYPNO-HUSTLER THE SECOND OR THIRD SIGN OF THE APOCALYPSE?
EITHER WAY, HYPNO'S NEW TECHNIQUE ISN'T A JOKE. I WAS CONVINCED THOSE PRISON GUARDS WERE THUGS IN MY HIGH SCHOOL.
NOW THEY'RE EITHER UNCONSCIOUS OR HYPNOTIZED, SO I GUESS I'M ON MY OWN IN HERE.
BUT I SHOULD BE SAFE AS LONG AS EVERYONE STAYS LOCKED IN THEIR...
CELLS.
UH-OH.

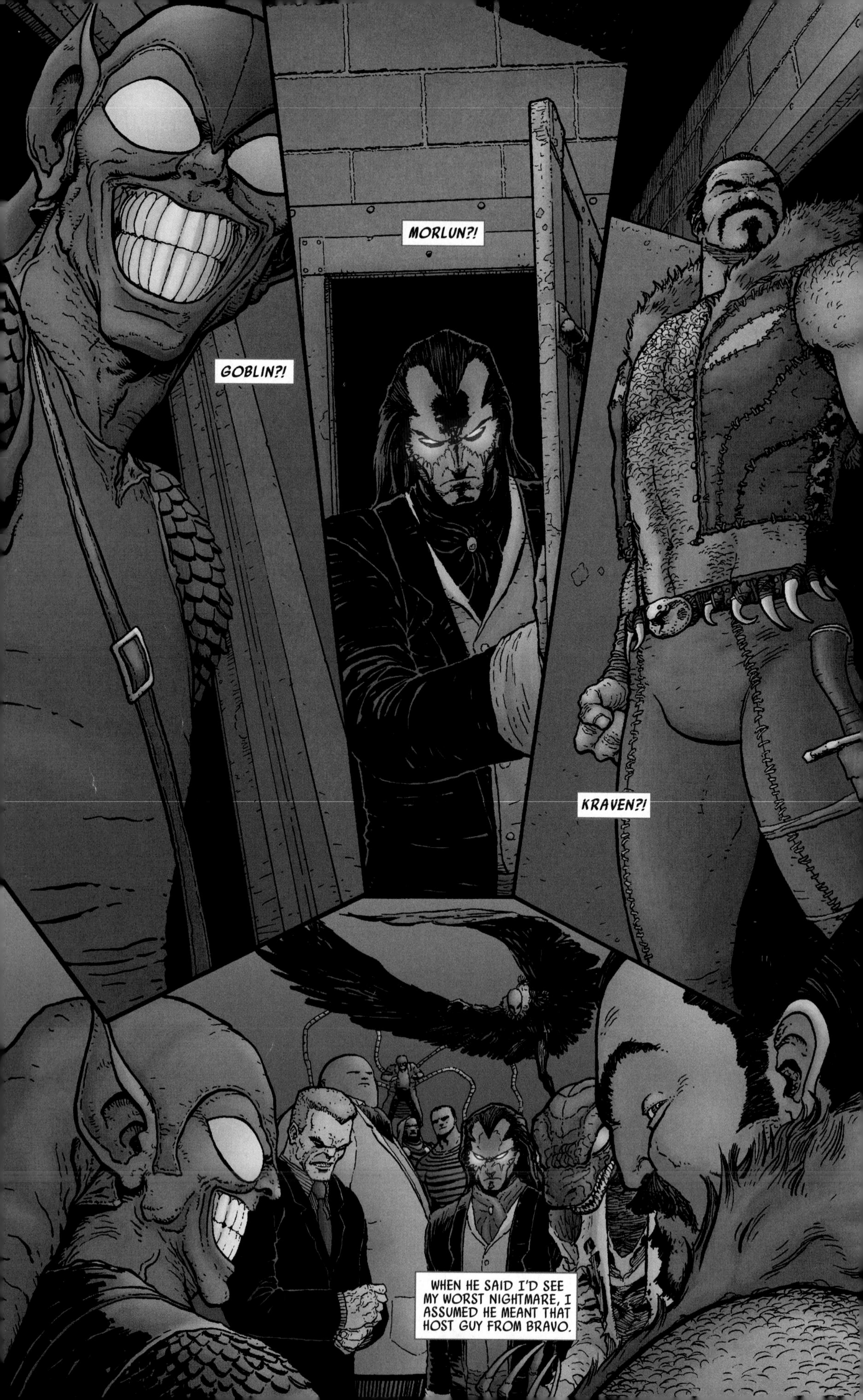
GOBLIN?!
MORLUN?!
KRAVEN?!
WHEN HE SAID I'D SEE MY WORST NIGHTMARE, I ASSUMED HE MEANT THAT HOST GUY FROM BRAVO.

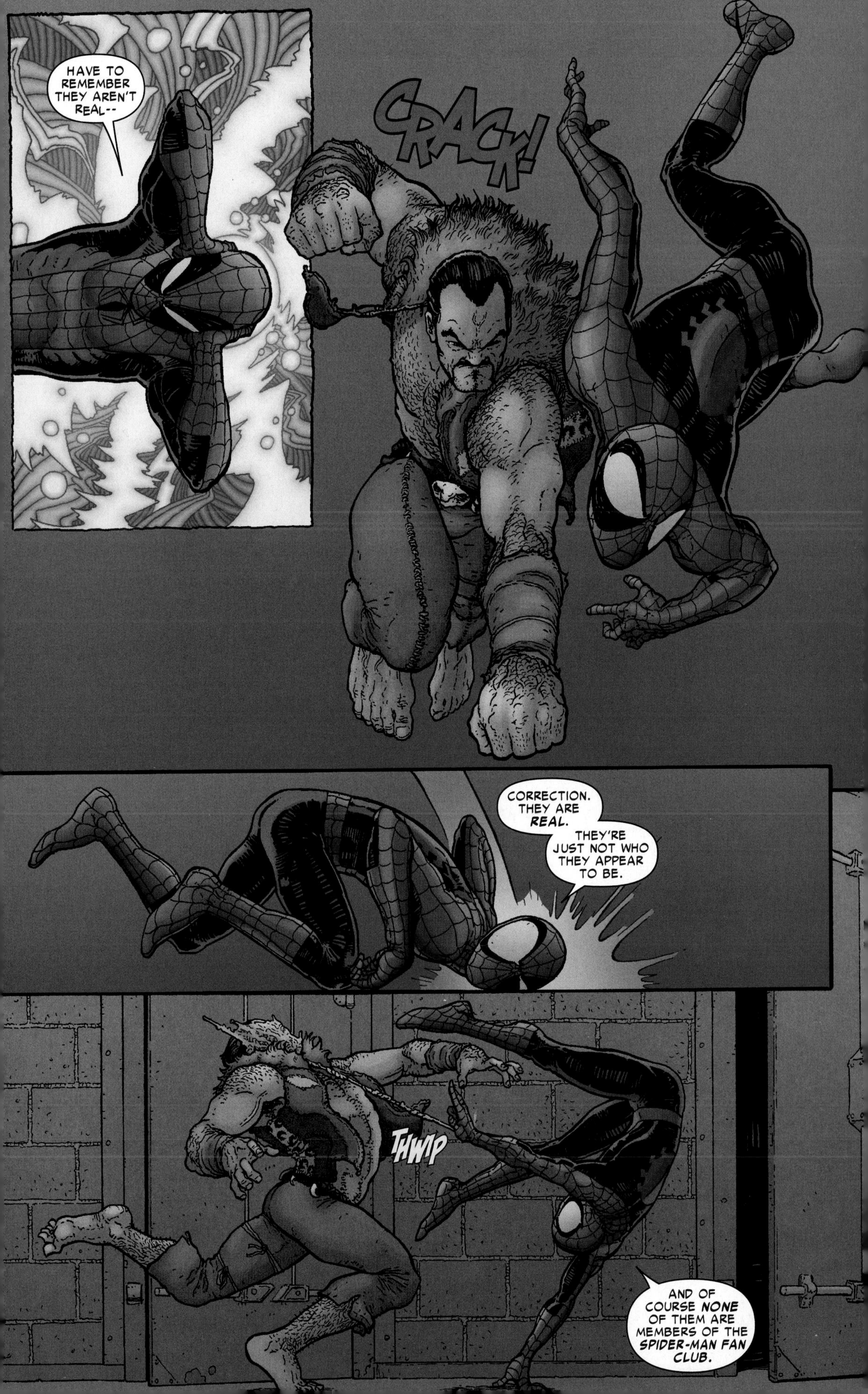
HAVE TO REMEMBER THEY AREN'T REAL--
CRACK!
CORRECTION. THEY ARE REAL.
THEY'RE JUST NOT WHO THEY APPEAR TO BE.
THWIP
AND OF COURSE NONE OF THEM ARE MEMBERS OF THE SPIDER-MAN FAN CLUB.

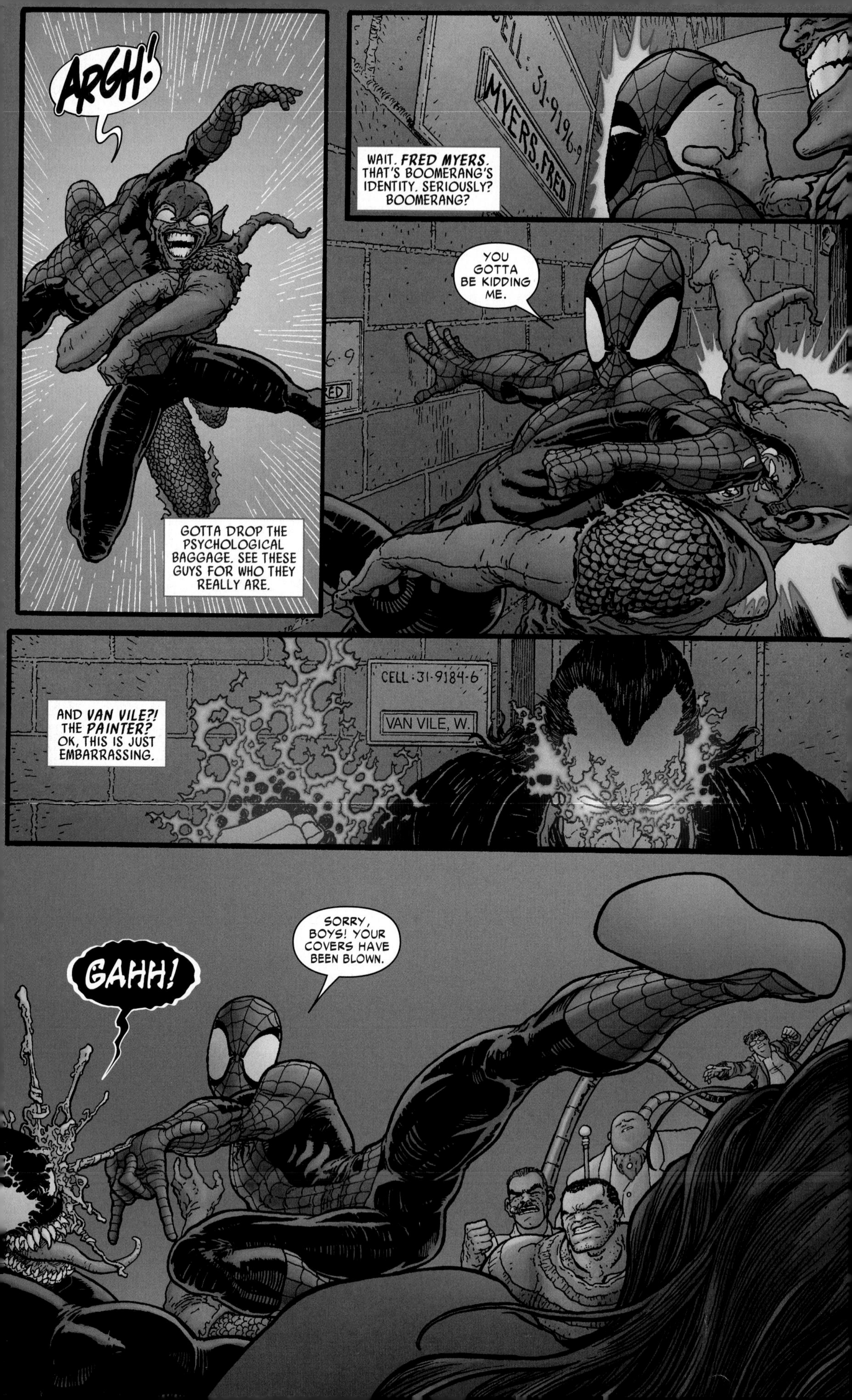
ARGH!
GOTTA DROP THE PSYCHOLOGICAL BAGGAGE. SEE THESE GUYS FOR WHO THEY REALLY ARE.
CELL: 31-9196-9
MYERS, FRED
WAIT. FRED MYERS. THAT'S BOOMERANG'S IDENTITY. SERIOUSLY? BOOMERANG?
YOU GOTTA BE KIDDING ME.
CELL-31-9184-6
VAN VILE, W.
AND VAN VILE?! THE PAINTER? OK, THIS IS JUST EMBARRASSING.
GAHH!
SORRY, BOYS! YOUR COVERS HAVE BEEN BLOWN.

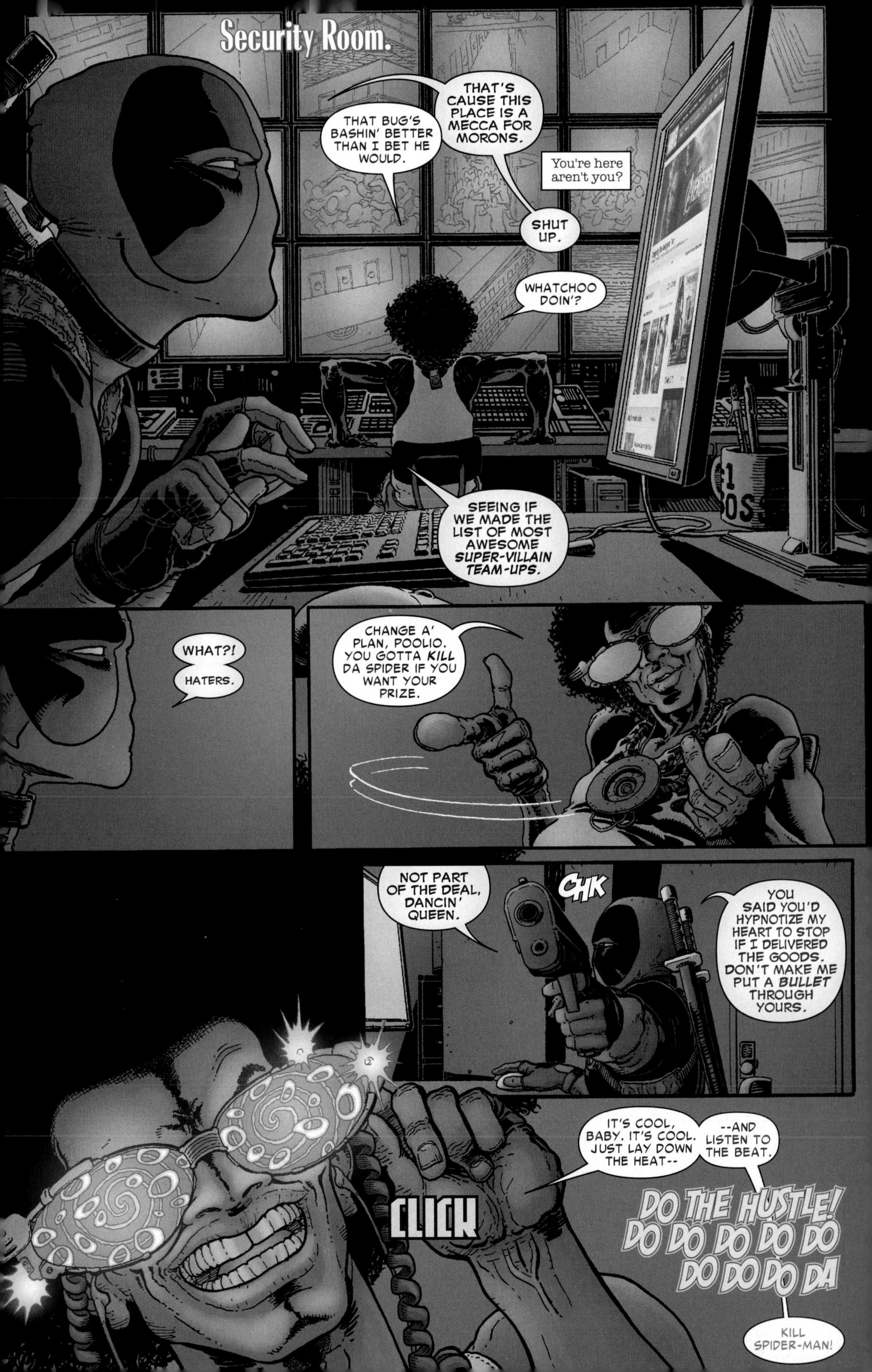

Security Room.
THAT BUG'S BASHIN' BETTER THAN I BET HE WOULD.
THAT'S CAUSE THIS PLACE IS A MECCA FOR MORONS.
You're here aren't you?
SHUT UP.
WHATCHOO DOIN'?
SEEING IF WE MADE THE LIST OF MOST AWESOME SUPER-VILLAIN TEAM-UPS.
WHAT?!
HATERS.
CHANGE A' PLAN, POOLIO. YOU GOTTA KILL DA SPIDER IF YOU WANT YOUR PRIZE.
NOT PART OF THE DEAL, DANCIN' QUEEN.
CHK
YOU SAID YOU'D HYPNOTIZE MY HEART TO STOP IF I DELIVERED THE GOODS. DON'T MAKE ME PUT A BULLET THROUGH YOURS.
IT'S COOL, BABY. IT'S COOL. JUST LAY DOWN THE HEAT--
--AND LISTEN TO THE BEAT.
CLICK
DO THE HUSTLE! DO DO DO DO DO DO DO DO DA
KILL SPIDER-MAN!

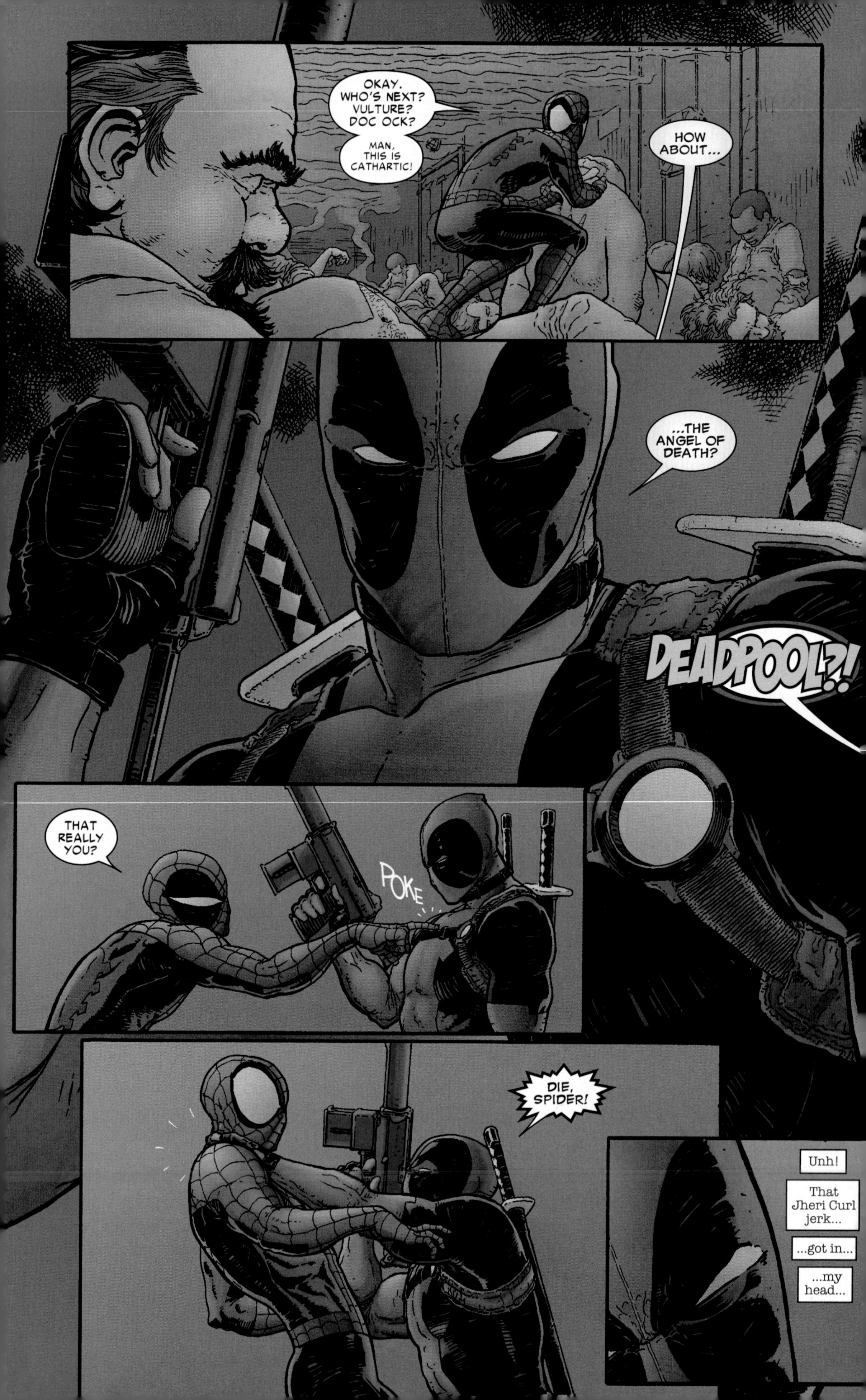
OKAY. WHO'S NEXT? VULTURE? DOC OCK?
MAN, THIS IS CATHARTIC!
HOW ABOUT...
...THE ANGEL OF DEATH?
DEADPOOL?!
THAT REALLY YOU?
POKE
DIE, SPIDER!
Unh!
That Jheri Curl jerk...
...got in...
...my head...

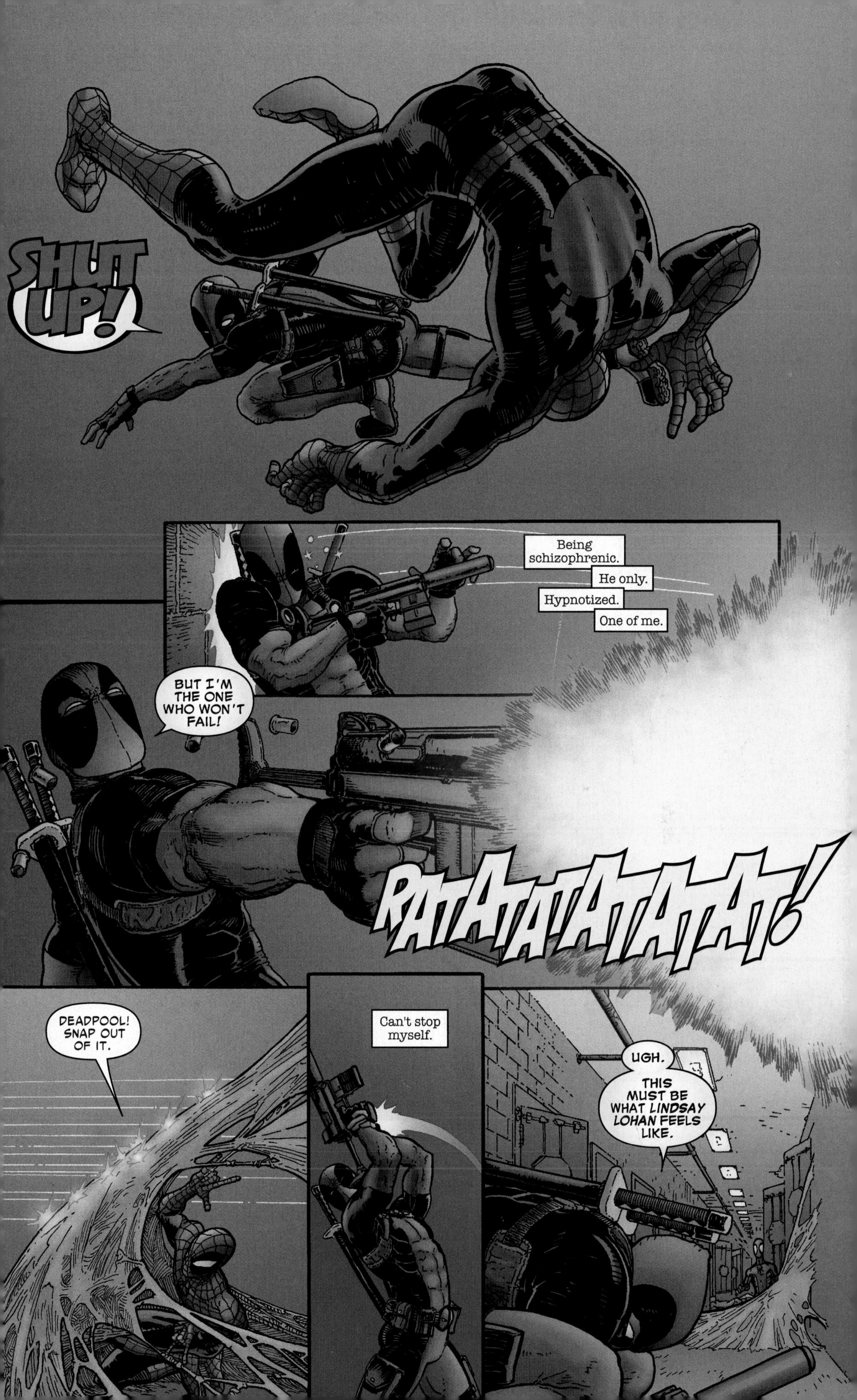
SHUT UP!
Being schizophrenic.
He only.
Hypnotized.
One of me.
BUT I'M THE ONE WHO WON'T FAIL!
RATATATATATATAT!
DEADPOOL! SNAP OUT OF IT.
Can't stop myself.
UGH.
THIS MUST BE WHAT LINDSAY LOHAN FEELS LIKE.

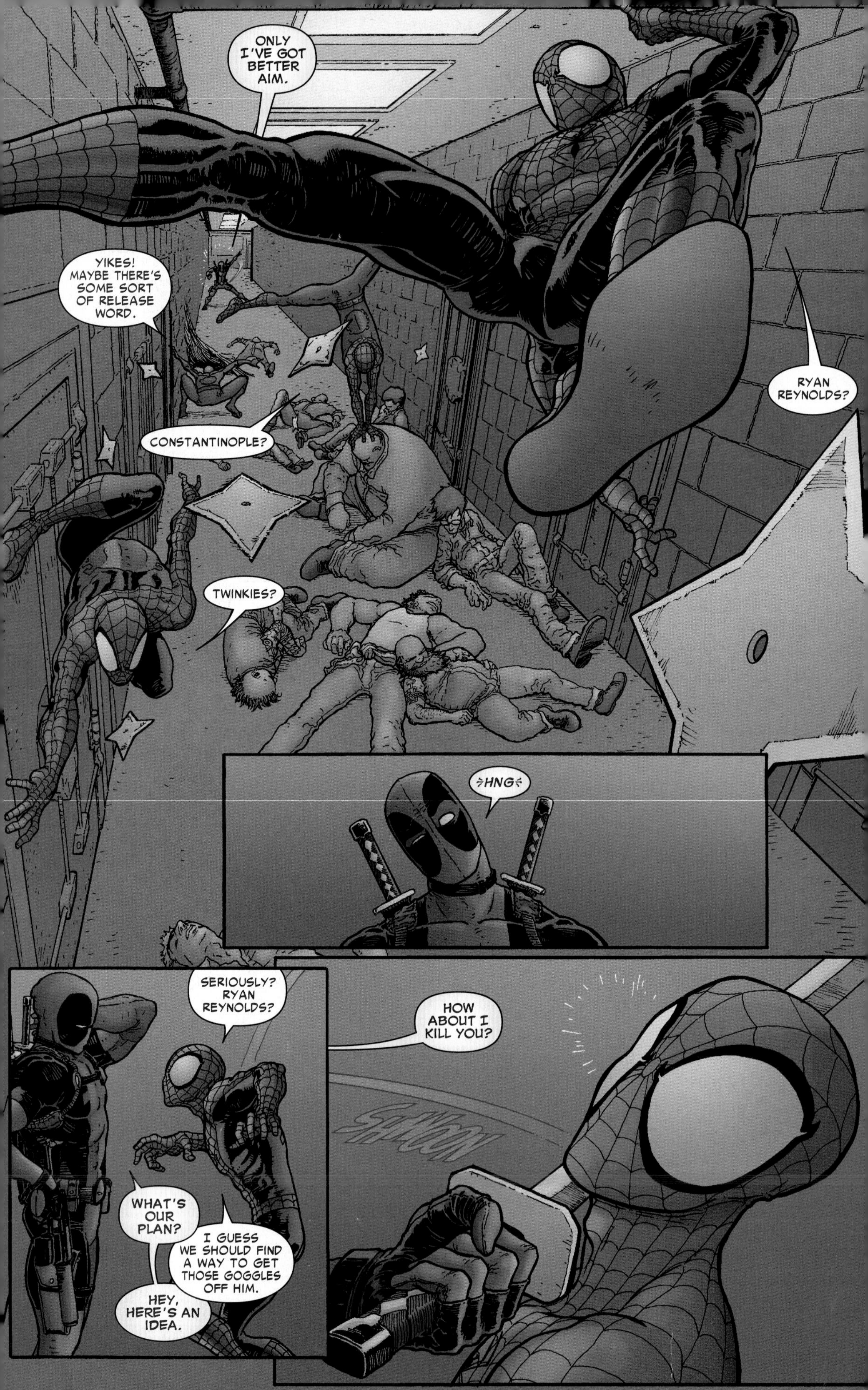
ONLY I'VE GOT BETTER AIM.
YIKES! MAYBE THERE'S SOME SORT OF RELEASE WORD.
CONSTANTINOPLE?
TWINKIES?
RYAN REYNOLDS?
HNG
SERIOUSLY? RYAN REYNOLDS?
WHAT'S OUR PLAN?
I GUESS WE SHOULD FIND A WAY TO GET THOSE GOGGLES OFF HIM.
HEY, HERE'S AN IDEA.
HOW ABOUT I KILL YOU?

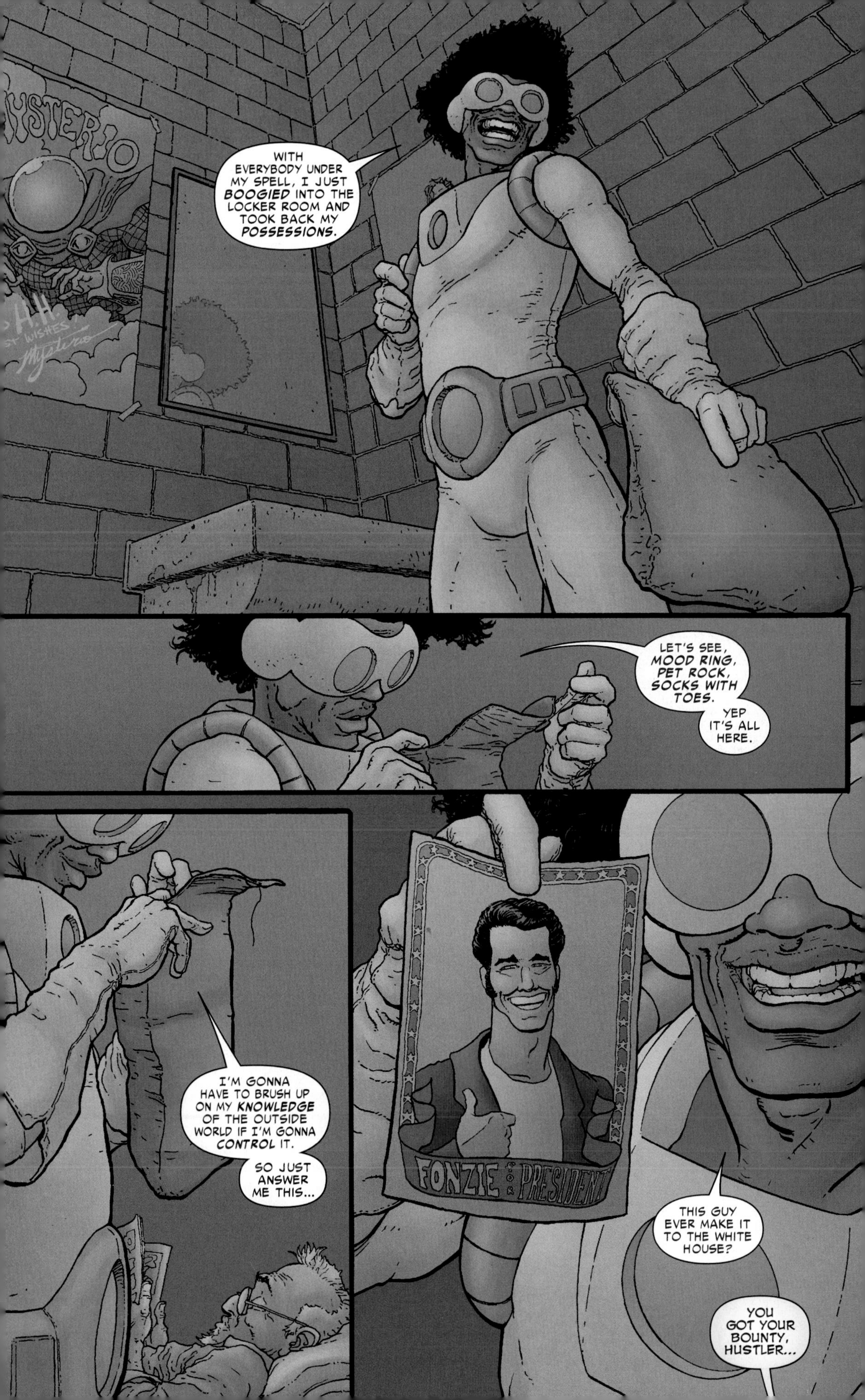
MYSTERIO
WITH EVERYBODY UNDER MY SPELL, I JUST BOOGIED INTO THE LOCKER ROOM AND TOOK BACK MY POSSESSIONS.
LET'S SEE, MOOD RING, PET ROCK, SOCKS WITH TOES.
YEP IT'S ALL HERE.
I'M GONNA HAVE TO BRUSH UP ON MY KNOWLEDGE OF THE OUTSIDE WORLD IF I'M GONNA CONTROL IT.
SO JUST ANSWER ME THIS...
FONZIE FOR PRESIDENT
THIS GUY EVER MAKE IT TO THE WHITE HOUSE?
YOU GOT YOUR BOUNTY, HUSTLER...

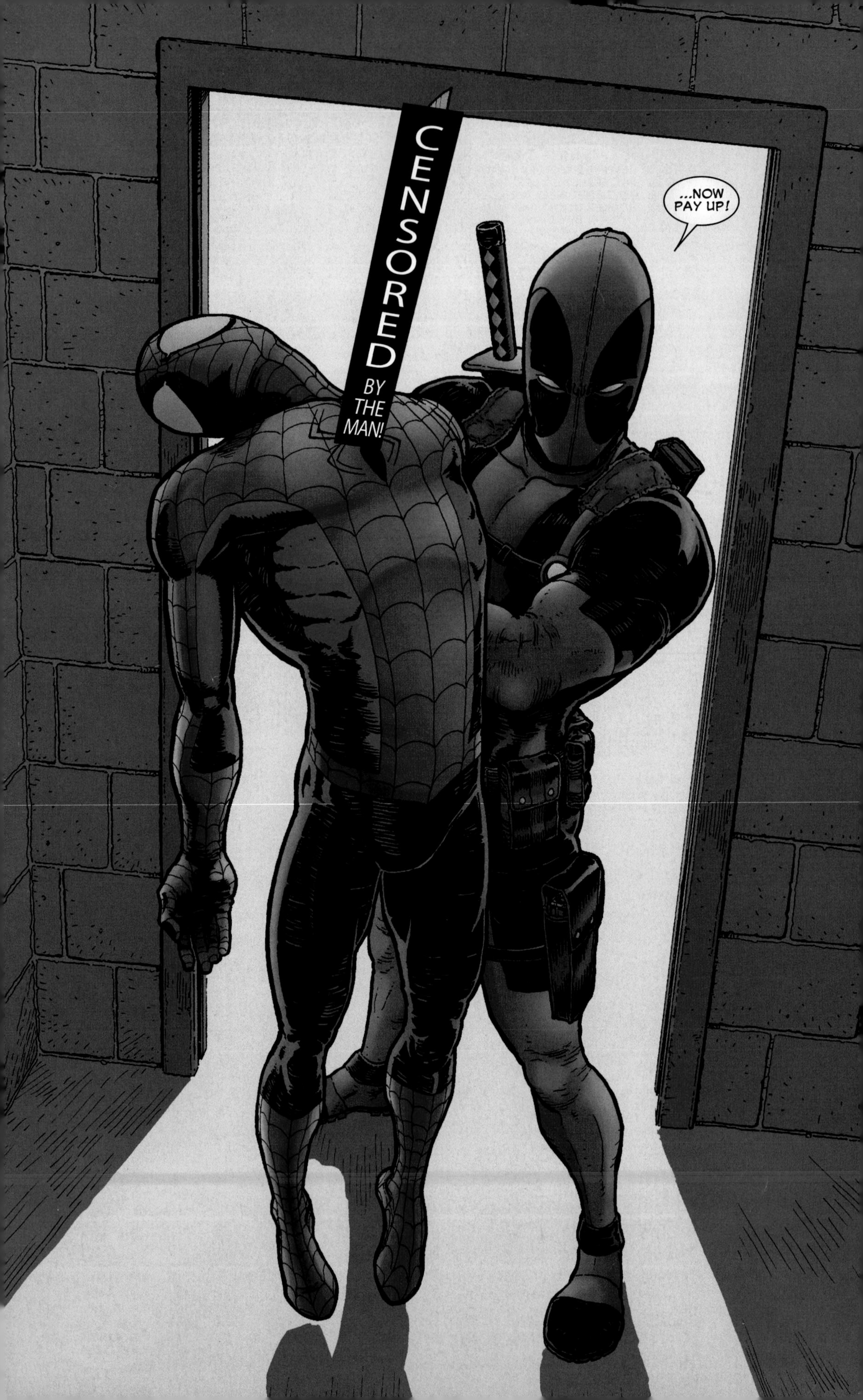
CENSORED BY THE MAN!
...NOW PAY UP!

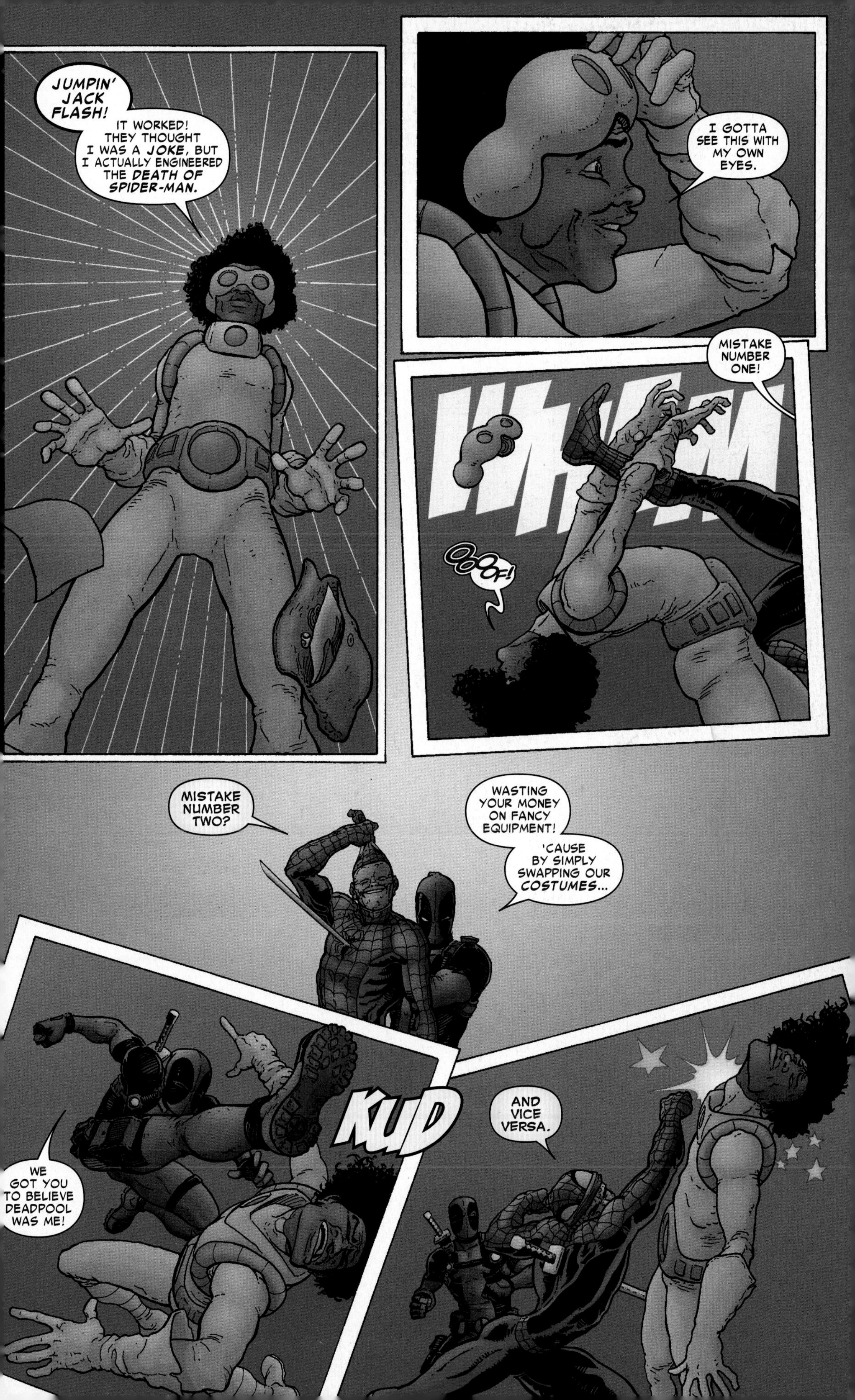
JUMPIN' JACK FLASH!
IT WORKED! THEY THOUGHT I WAS A JOKE, BUT I ACTUALLY ENGINEERED THE DEATH OF SPIDER-MAN.
I GOTTA SEE THIS WITH MY OWN EYES.
MISTAKE NUMBER ONE!
WHAM
OOOOF!
MISTAKE NUMBER TWO?
WASTING YOUR MONEY ON FANCY EQUIPMENT!
'CAUSE BY SIMPLY SWAPPING OUR COSTUMES...
WE GOT YOU TO BELIEVE DEADPOOL WAS ME!
KUD
AND VICE VERSA.

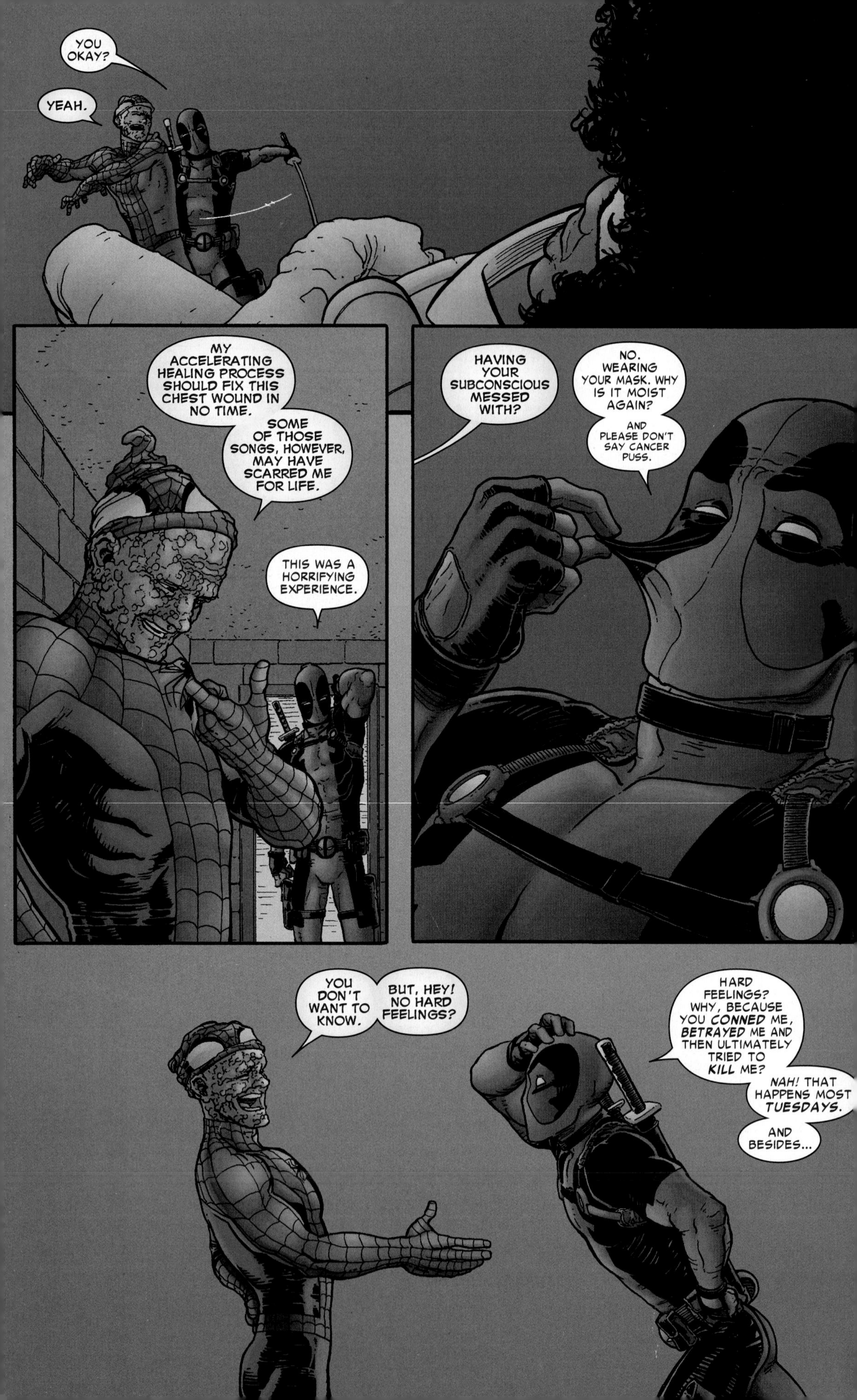

YOU OKAY?
YEAH.
MY ACCELERATING HEALING PROCESS SHOULD FIX THIS CHEST WOUND IN NO TIME.
SOME OF THOSE SONGS, HOWEVER, MAY HAVE SCARRED ME FOR LIFE.
THIS WAS A HORRIFYING EXPERIENCE.
HAVING YOUR SUBCONSCIOUS MESSED WITH?
NO. WEARING YOUR MASK. WHY IS IT MOIST AGAIN?
AND PLEASE DON'T SAY CANCER PUSS.
YOU DON'T WANT TO KNOW.
BUT, HEY! NO HARD FEELINGS?
HARD FEELINGS? WHY, BECAUSE YOU CONNED ME, BETRAYED ME AND THEN ULTIMATELY TRIED TO KILL ME?
NAH! THAT HAPPENS MOST TUESDAYS.
AND BESIDES...

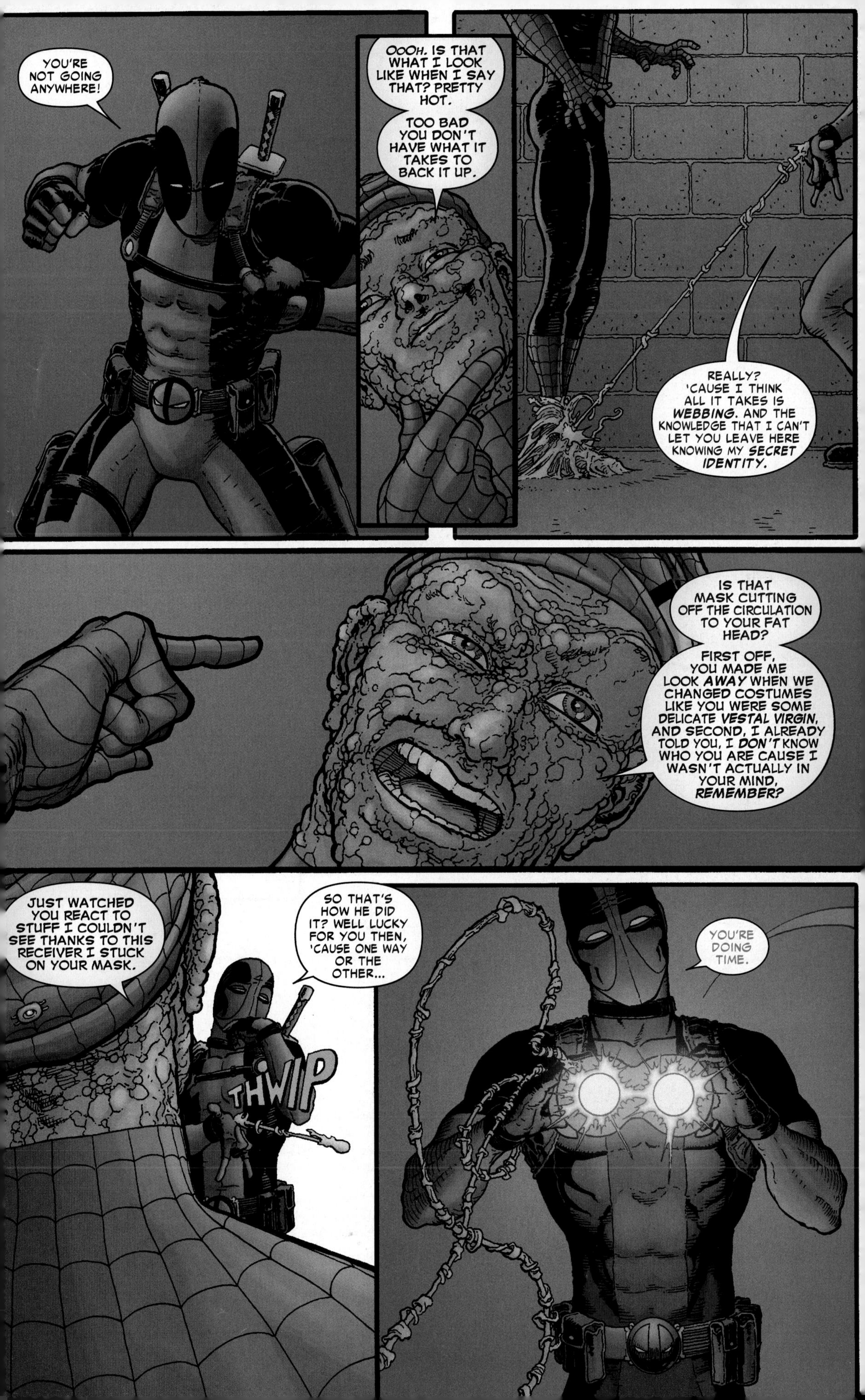
YOU'RE NOT GOING ANYWHERE!
OOOH. IS THAT WHAT I LOOK LIKE WHEN I SAY THAT? PRETTY HOT.
TOO BAD YOU DON'T HAVE WHAT IT TAKES TO BACK IT UP.
REALLY? 'CAUSE I THINK ALL IT TAKES IS WEBBING. AND THE KNOWLEDGE THAT I CAN'T LET YOU LEAVE HERE KNOWING MY SECRET IDENTITY.
IS THAT MASK CUTTING OFF THE CIRCULATION TO YOUR FAT HEAD?
FIRST OFF, YOU MADE ME LOOK AWAY WHEN WE CHANGED COSTUMES LIKE YOU WERE SOME DELICATE VESTAL VIRGIN, AND SECOND, I ALREADY TOLD YOU, I DON'T KNOW WHO YOU ARE CAUSE I WASN'T ACTUALLY IN YOUR MIND, REMEMBER?
JUST WATCHED YOU REACT TO STUFF I COULDN'T SEE THANKS TO THIS RECEIVER I STUCK ON YOUR MASK.
SO THAT'S HOW HE DID IT? WELL LUCKY FOR YOU THEN, 'CAUSE ONE WAY OR THE OTHER...
THWIP
YOU'RE DOING TIME.

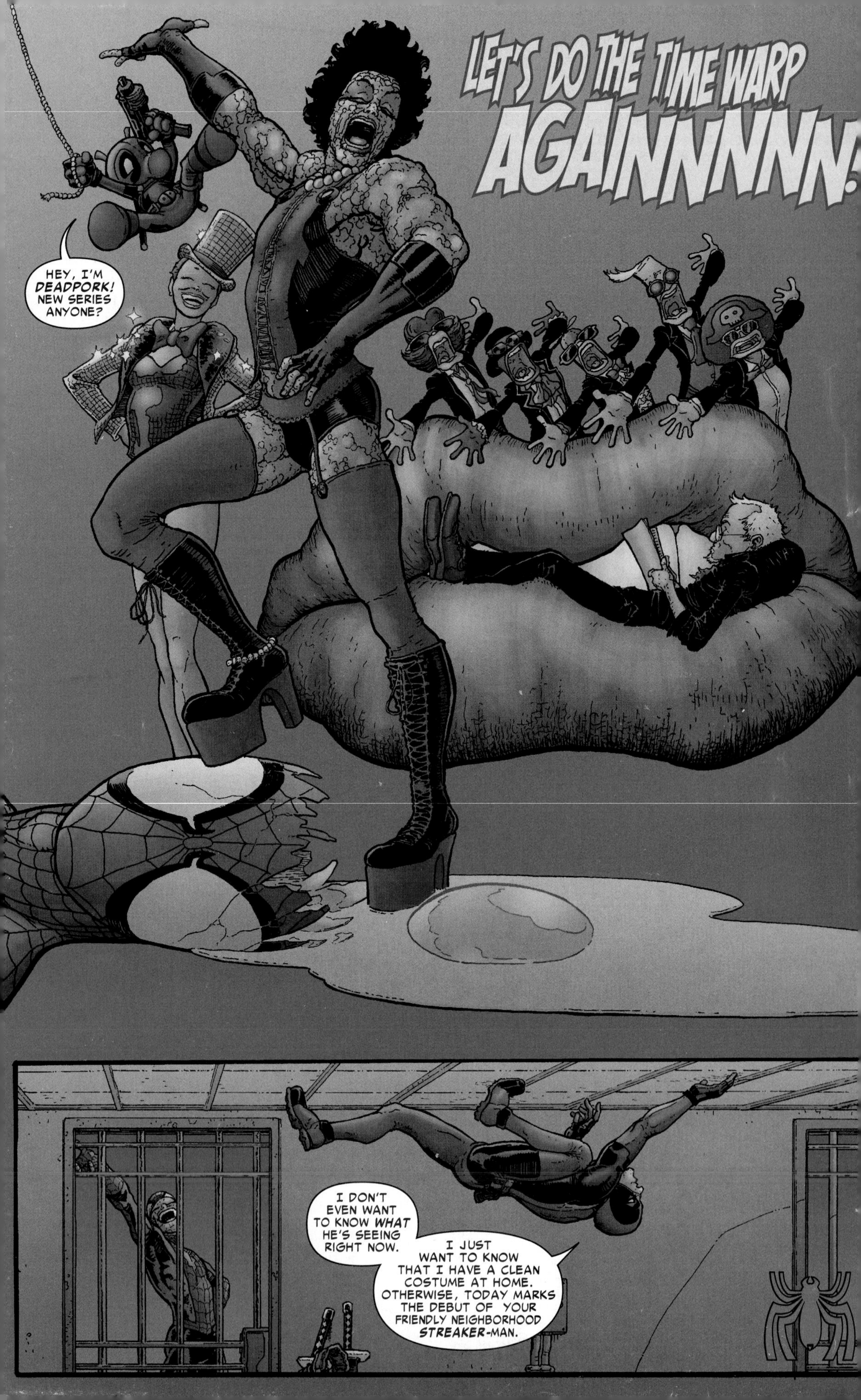
LET'S DO THE TIME WARP AGAINNNNN!
HEY, I'M DEADPORK! NEW SERIES ANYONE?
I DON'T EVEN WANT TO KNOW WHAT HE'S SEEING RIGHT NOW.
I JUST WANT TO KNOW THAT I HAVE A CLEAN COSTUME AT HOME. OTHERWISE, TODAY MARKS THE DEBUT OF YOUR FRIENDLY NEIGHBORHOOD STREAKER-MAN.